The **Princeton Review**®

Cracking the

AP®

U.S. GOVERNMENT & POLITICS EXAM

2019 Edition

The Staff of The Princeton Review

PrincetonReview.com

Penguin Random House

The Princeton Review
110 East 42nd Street, 7th Floor
New York, NY 10017
Email: editorialsupport@review.com

Published in the United States by Penguin Random House LLC, New York, and in Canada by Random House of Canada, a division of Penguin Random House Ltd., Toronto.

Terms of Service: The Princeton Review Online Companion Tools ("Student Tools") for retail books are available for only the two most recent editions of that book. Student Tools may be activated only twice per eligible book purchased for two consecutive 12-month periods, for a total of 24 months of access. Activation of Student Tools more than twice per book is in direct violation of these Terms of Service and may result in discontinuation of access to Student Tools Services.

ISBN: 978-0-525-56761-5
eBook ISBN: 978-0-525-56773-8
ISSN: 2380-4092

AP is a trademark registered and owned by the College Board, which is not affiliated with, and does not endorse, this product.

The Princeton Review is not affiliated with Princeton University.

Permission has been granted to reprint excerpts or graphics from the following sources:

"Number of viewers of the State of the Union addresses from 1993 to 2018 (in millions)," accessed May 23, 2018, https://www.statista.com/statistics/252425/state-of-the-union-address-viewer-numbers/. © Statista 2018.

Mike Keefe, InToon.com.

"Voter Identification Laws and the Suppression of Minority Votes," The Journal of Politics, volume 79, number 2. Published online January 5, 2017. http://dx.doi.org/10.1086/688343. © 2016 by the Southern Political Science Association. All rights reserved.

"Drug executives to testify before Congress about their role in U.S. opioid crisis," The Washington Post, 2018. All right reserved.

"Habeas Corpus" by Adam Zyglis, PoliticalCartoons.com, © 2018.

"The Evolution of North Carolina's 12th Congressional District," by Professor Alasdair Rae, © 2018.

"Throw the Bums Out," Rick McKee, PoliticalCartoons.com, © 2014.

"4 Ways Technology Has Impacted Presidential Elections" from Entrepreneur, July 16 © 2015 Entrepreneur Media Inc. All rights reserved. Used by permission and protected by the Copyright Laws of the United States. The printing, copying, redistribution, or retransmission of this Content without express written permission is prohibited.

Editor: Aaron Riccio
Production Editors: Lee Elder, Emily Epstein White
Production Artist: Deborah Weber
Content Contributors: Thomas Broderick, Gina Donegan, Jerry Dresner

Printed in the United States of America on partially recycled paper.

10 9 8 7 6 5 4 3 2 1

2019 Edition

Editorial
Rob Franek, Editor-in-Chief
Mary Beth Garrick, Executive Director of Production
Craig Patches, Production Design Manager
Selena Coppock, Managing Editor
Meave Shelton, Senior Editor
Colleen Day, Editor
Sarah Litt, Editor
Aaron Riccio, Editor
Orion McBean, Associate Editor

Random House Publishing Team
Tom Russell, VP, Publisher
Alison Stoltzfus, Publishing Director
Ellen Reed, Production Manager
Amanda Yee, Associate Managing Editor
Suzanne Lee, Designer

Acknowledgments

The Princeton Review would like to thank Thomas Broderick, Gina Donegan, and Jerry Dresner for their tireless efforts to stay up to date with the changes to the AP U.S. Government and Politics Exam throughout work on the 2019 edition of this book. Special appreciation as well to the Production team for their attention to detail, from the work of Deborah Weber and Craig Patches in the various illustrations to the close reads from Lee Elder and Emily Epstein White.

Contents

Get More (Free) Content

1 Go to **PrincetonReview.com/cracking.**

2 Enter the following ISBN for your book: 9780525567615.

3 Answer a few simple questions to set up an exclusive Princeton Review account. (If you already have one, you can just log in.)

4 Click the "Student Tools" button, also found under "My Account" from the top toolbar. You're all set to access your bonus content!

Need to report a potential **content** issue?

Contact **EditorialSupport@review.com**.
Include:

- full title of the book
- ISBN
- page number

Need to report a **technical** issue?

Contact **TPRStudentTech@review.com** and provide:

- your full name
- email address used to register the book
- full book title and ISBN
- computer OS (Mac/PC) and browser (Firefox, Safari, etc.)

Once you've registered, you can...

- Take a full-length practice SAT and ACT

- Get valuable advice about the college application process, including tips for writing a great essay and where to apply for financial aid

- If you're still choosing between colleges, use our searchable rankings of *The Best 384 Colleges* to find out more information about your dream school

- Access a study guide and a variety of printable resources, including bubble sheets for the practice tests in this book, and a glossary of key terms to aid in your review

- Check to see if there have been any corrections or updates to this edition

- Get our take on any recent or pending updates to the AP U.S. Government and Politics Exam

Look For These Icons Throughout The Book

 ONLINE ARTICLES

 PROVEN TECHNIQUES

 ANOTHER APPROACH

 ASK YOURSELF

 MORE GREAT BOOKS

 COLLEGE ADVISOR APP

 GOING DEEPER

 TIME SAVING TIP

 WATCH OUT

Part I
Using This
Book to Improve
Your AP Score

- Preview: Your Knowledge, Your Expectations
- Your Guide to Using This Book
- How to Begin

PREVIEW: YOUR KNOWLEDGE, YOUR EXPECTATIONS

Your route to a high score on the AP U.S. Government and Politics Exam depends a lot on how you plan to use this book. Respond to the following:

1. Rate your level of confidence about your knowledge of the content tested by the AP U.S. Government and Politics Exam.

    A. Very confident—I know it all.
    B. I'm pretty confident, but there are topics for which I could use help.
    C. Not confident—I need quite a bit of support.
    D. I'm not sure.

2. If you have a goal score in mind, circle your goal score for the AP U.S. Government and Politics Exam:

    5   4   3   2   1   I'm not sure yet

3. What do you expect to learn from this book? Circle all that apply to you.

    A. A general overview of the test and what to expect
    B. Strategies for how to approach the test
    C. The content tested by this exam
    D. I'm not sure yet

YOUR GUIDE TO USING THIS BOOK

This book is organized to provide as much—or as little—support as you need, so you can use this book in whatever way will be most helpful for improving your score on the AP U.S. Government and Politics Exam.

*   The remainder of **Part I** will provide guidance on how to use this book and help you determine your strengths and weaknesses.

*   **Part II** of this book contains Practice Test 1 and its answers and explanations. We recommend that you take this test before going any further in order to realistically determine
    o   your starting point right now
    o   which question types you're ready for and which you might need to practice
    o   which content topics you are familiar with and which you will want to carefully review
    Once you have nailed down your strengths and weaknesses with regard to this exam, you can focus your test preparation, build a study plan, and be efficient with your time.

- **Part III** of this book will
  - o provide information about the structure, scoring, and content of the AP U.S. Government and Politics Exam
  - o help you to make a study plan
  - o point you toward additional resources

- **Part IV** of this book will explore various strategies, including
  - o how to attack multiple-choice questions
  - o how to write high-scoring free-response answers
  - o how to manage your time to maximize the number of points available to you

- **Part V** of this book covers the content you need for the AP U.S. Government and Politics Exam.

- **Part VI** of this book contains **Practice Test 2**, its answers and explanations, and a scoring guide. If you skipped Practice Test 1, we recommend that you do both (with at least a day or two between them) so that you can compare your progress between the two. Additionally, this will help to identify any external issues: if you consistently get a certain type of question wrong, you probably need to review it. If you got it wrong only once, you may have run out of time or been distracted by something. In either case, this will allow you to focus on the factors that caused the discrepancy in scores and to be as prepared as possible on the day of the test.

You may choose to use some parts of this book over others, or you may work through the entire book. This will depend on your needs and how much time you have. Let's now look how to make this determination.

HOW TO BEGIN

1. **Take a Test**
   Before you can decide how to use this book, we recommend that you take a practice test. Doing so will give you an insight into your strengths and weaknesses, and the test will also help you make an effective study plan. If you're feeling test-phobic, remind yourself that a practice test is a tool for diagnosing yourself—it's not how well you do that matters but how you use the information gleaned from your performance to guide your preparation.

   So, before you read further, take Practice Test 1 starting at page 9 of this book. Be sure to do so in one sitting, following the instructions that appear before the test.

Scoring Worksheets
We've included a scoring worksheet for each of the Practice Tests. (This is the first page of each Practice Test Answers and Explanations chapter.) Remember that these worksheets are meant to serve as a rough guideline only. AP exam scores are weighted according to a statistical process that varies slightly every year based on how students perform on the exam. But you can use the worksheets to approximate your score!

2. **Check Your Answers**
Using the answer key on page 29, count how many multiple-choice questions you answered correctly and how many you missed. Don't worry about the explanations for now, and don't worry about why you missed some of the questions. We'll get to that soon.

3. **Reflect on the Test**
After you take your first test, respond to the following questions:

   - How much time did you spend on the multiple-choice questions?

   - How much time did you spend on each essay?

   - How many multiple-choice questions did you miss?

   - Do you feel you had the knowledge to address the subject matter in the free-response questions?

   - Do you feel that you wrote well-organized, thoughtful free responses?

   - Circle the content areas that were most challenging for you and draw a line through the ones in which you felt confident and/or did well.

4. **Read Part III of this Book and Complete the Self-Evaluation**
Part III will provide information on how the test is structured and scored. It will also explain the areas of content that are tested.

   As you read Part III, re-evaluate your answers to the questions above. At the end of Part III, you will revisit the questions on the previous page and refine your answers to them. Use the diagnostic answer key to identify the content chapters of this book in which you missed the most questions, as that may present you with a good place to begin your review. Make a study plan, based on your needs and available time, that will help you to use this book most effectively.

5. **Engage with Parts IV and V as Needed**
Notice the word *engage*. You'll get more out of this book if you use it intentionally than if you read it passively, hoping for an improved score through osmosis.

   Strategy chapters will help you think about your approach to the types of questions on this exam. Part IV will open with a reminder to think about how you approach questions now and then close with a reflection section asking you to think about how/whether you will change your approach in the future.

Content chapters are designed to provide a review of the content tested on the AP U.S. Government and Politics Exam, including the level of detail you need to know and how your knowledge of the content is tested. You will have the opportunity to assess your mastery of each chapter through test-appropriate questions and a reflection section at the end.

6. **Take Another Test and Assess Your Performance**
    Once you feel you have developed the strategies you need and gained the knowledge you lacked, you should take Practice Test 2, which starts on page 265 of this book. You should do so in one sitting, following the instructions at the beginning of the test.

    When you are done, check your answers to the multiple-choice section with the correct responses on page 285. Then, see if a teacher will read your essays and provide feedback for your improvement.

    Once you have taken the test, reflect on which areas you still need to work on, and revisit the chapters in this book that address those deficiencies.

7. **Keep Working**
    As discussed in Part III, there are other resources available to you, including a wealth of information on the official AP Students website. There you can continue to explore areas that you can improve upon and engage in those areas right up until the day of the test. You should use a mix of web resources and book review to solidify your understanding of any questions or subjects that you keep getting wrong.

You can find a course description and overview on the AP Students website, located here: https://apstudent.college board.org/apcourse/ap-united-states-government-and-politics

This site also includes course details straight from the horse's mouth, so to speak, as well as links to .gov resources that provide primary source information on the Constitution, Declaration of Independence, and the various branches of government.

Part II
Practice Test 1

Practice Test 1

Completely darken bubbles with a No. 2 pencil. If you make a mistake, be sure to erase mark completely. Erase all stray marks.

1. YOUR NAME:
(Print)   Last   First   M.I.

SIGNATURE: _____ DATE: _____ / _____ / _____

HOME ADDRESS: _____
(Print)   Number and Street

_____
City   State   Zip Code

PHONE NO. : _____
(Print)

IMPORTANT: Please fill in these boxes exactly as shown on the back cover of your test book.

2. TEST FORM

5. YOUR NAME

First 4 letters of last name				FIRST INIT	MID INIT
Ⓐ	Ⓐ	Ⓐ	Ⓐ	Ⓐ	Ⓐ
Ⓑ	Ⓑ	Ⓑ	Ⓑ	Ⓑ	Ⓑ
Ⓒ	Ⓒ	Ⓒ	Ⓒ	Ⓒ	Ⓒ
Ⓓ	Ⓓ	Ⓓ	Ⓓ	Ⓓ	Ⓓ
Ⓔ	Ⓔ	Ⓔ	Ⓔ	Ⓔ	Ⓔ
Ⓕ	Ⓕ	Ⓕ	Ⓕ	Ⓕ	Ⓕ
Ⓖ	Ⓖ	Ⓖ	Ⓖ	Ⓖ	Ⓖ
Ⓗ	Ⓗ	Ⓗ	Ⓗ	Ⓗ	Ⓗ
Ⓘ	Ⓘ	Ⓘ	Ⓘ	Ⓘ	Ⓘ
Ⓙ	Ⓙ	Ⓙ	Ⓙ	Ⓙ	Ⓙ
Ⓚ	Ⓚ	Ⓚ	Ⓚ	Ⓚ	Ⓚ
Ⓛ	Ⓛ	Ⓛ	Ⓛ	Ⓛ	Ⓛ
Ⓜ	Ⓜ	Ⓜ	Ⓜ	Ⓜ	Ⓜ
Ⓝ	Ⓝ	Ⓝ	Ⓝ	Ⓝ	Ⓝ
Ⓞ	Ⓞ	Ⓞ	Ⓞ	Ⓞ	Ⓞ
Ⓟ	Ⓟ	Ⓟ	Ⓟ	Ⓟ	Ⓟ
Ⓠ	Ⓠ	Ⓠ	Ⓠ	Ⓠ	Ⓠ
Ⓡ	Ⓡ	Ⓡ	Ⓡ	Ⓡ	Ⓡ
Ⓢ	Ⓢ	Ⓢ	Ⓢ	Ⓢ	Ⓢ
Ⓣ	Ⓣ	Ⓣ	Ⓣ	Ⓣ	Ⓣ
Ⓤ	Ⓤ	Ⓤ	Ⓤ	Ⓤ	Ⓤ
Ⓥ	Ⓥ	Ⓥ	Ⓥ	Ⓥ	Ⓥ
Ⓦ	Ⓦ	Ⓦ	Ⓦ	Ⓦ	Ⓦ
Ⓧ	Ⓧ	Ⓧ	Ⓧ	Ⓧ	Ⓧ
Ⓨ	Ⓨ	Ⓨ	Ⓨ	Ⓨ	Ⓨ
Ⓩ	Ⓩ	Ⓩ	Ⓩ	Ⓩ	Ⓩ

3. TEST CODE   **4. REGISTRATION NUMBER**

⓪	Ⓐ	⓪	⓪	⓪	⓪	⓪	⓪	⓪	⓪	⓪
①	Ⓑ	①	①	①	①	①	①	①	①	①
②	Ⓒ	②	②	②	②	②	②	②	②	②
③	Ⓓ	③	③	③	③	③	③	③	③	③
④	Ⓔ	④	④	④	④	④	④	④	④	④
⑤	Ⓕ	⑤	⑤	⑤	⑤	⑤	⑤	⑤	⑤	⑤
⑥	⑥	⑥	⑥	⑥	⑥	⑥	⑥	⑥	⑥	⑥
⑦	⑦	⑦	⑦	⑦	⑦	⑦	⑦	⑦	⑦	⑦
⑧	⑧	⑧	⑧	⑧	⑧	⑧	⑧	⑧	⑧	⑧
⑨	⑨	⑨	⑨	⑨	⑨	⑨	⑨	⑨	⑨	⑨

6. DATE OF BIRTH

Month	Day		Year	
◯ JAN				
◯ FEB				
◯ MAR	⓪	⓪	⓪	⓪
◯ APR	①	①	①	①
◯ MAY	②	②	②	②
◯ JUN	③	③	③	③
◯ JUL		④	④	④
◯ AUG		⑤	⑤	⑤
◯ SEP		⑥	⑥	⑥
◯ OCT		⑦	⑦	⑦
◯ NOV		⑧	⑧	⑧
◯ DEC		⑨	⑨	⑨

7. SEX
◯ MALE
◯ FEMALE

The Princeton Review®

© The Princeton Review, Inc.
FORM NO. 00001-PR

Section ① Start with number 1 for each new section.
If a section has fewer questions than answer spaces, leave the extra answer spaces blank.

1. Ⓐ Ⓑ Ⓒ Ⓓ
2. Ⓐ Ⓑ Ⓒ Ⓓ
3. Ⓐ Ⓑ Ⓒ Ⓓ
4. Ⓐ Ⓑ Ⓒ Ⓓ
5. Ⓐ Ⓑ Ⓒ Ⓓ
6. Ⓐ Ⓑ Ⓒ Ⓓ
7. Ⓐ Ⓑ Ⓒ Ⓓ
8. Ⓐ Ⓑ Ⓒ Ⓓ
9. Ⓐ Ⓑ Ⓒ Ⓓ
10. Ⓐ Ⓑ Ⓒ Ⓓ
11. Ⓐ Ⓑ Ⓒ Ⓓ
12. Ⓐ Ⓑ Ⓒ Ⓓ
13. Ⓐ Ⓑ Ⓒ Ⓓ
14. Ⓐ Ⓑ Ⓒ Ⓓ
15. Ⓐ Ⓑ Ⓒ Ⓓ

16. Ⓐ Ⓑ Ⓒ Ⓓ
17. Ⓐ Ⓑ Ⓒ Ⓓ
18. Ⓐ Ⓑ Ⓒ Ⓓ
19. Ⓐ Ⓑ Ⓒ Ⓓ
20. Ⓐ Ⓑ Ⓒ Ⓓ
21. Ⓐ Ⓑ Ⓒ Ⓓ
22. Ⓐ Ⓑ Ⓒ Ⓓ
23. Ⓐ Ⓑ Ⓒ Ⓓ
24. Ⓐ Ⓑ Ⓒ Ⓓ
25. Ⓐ Ⓑ Ⓒ Ⓓ
26. Ⓐ Ⓑ Ⓒ Ⓓ
27. Ⓐ Ⓑ Ⓒ Ⓓ
28. Ⓐ Ⓑ Ⓒ Ⓓ
29. Ⓐ Ⓑ Ⓒ Ⓓ
30. Ⓐ Ⓑ Ⓒ Ⓓ

31. Ⓐ Ⓑ Ⓒ Ⓓ
32. Ⓐ Ⓑ Ⓒ Ⓓ
33. Ⓐ Ⓑ Ⓒ Ⓓ
34. Ⓐ Ⓑ Ⓒ Ⓓ
35. Ⓐ Ⓑ Ⓒ Ⓓ
36. Ⓐ Ⓑ Ⓒ Ⓓ
37. Ⓐ Ⓑ Ⓒ Ⓓ
38. Ⓐ Ⓑ Ⓒ Ⓓ
39. Ⓐ Ⓑ Ⓒ Ⓓ
40. Ⓐ Ⓑ Ⓒ Ⓓ
41. Ⓐ Ⓑ Ⓒ Ⓓ
42. Ⓐ Ⓑ Ⓒ Ⓓ
43. Ⓐ Ⓑ Ⓒ Ⓓ
44. Ⓐ Ⓑ Ⓒ Ⓓ
45. Ⓐ Ⓑ Ⓒ Ⓓ

46. Ⓐ Ⓑ Ⓒ Ⓓ
47. Ⓐ Ⓑ Ⓒ Ⓓ
48. Ⓐ Ⓑ Ⓒ Ⓓ
49. Ⓐ Ⓑ Ⓒ Ⓓ
50. Ⓐ Ⓑ Ⓒ Ⓓ
51. Ⓐ Ⓑ Ⓒ Ⓓ
52. Ⓐ Ⓑ Ⓒ Ⓓ
53. Ⓐ Ⓑ Ⓒ Ⓓ
54. Ⓐ Ⓑ Ⓒ Ⓓ
55. Ⓐ Ⓑ Ⓒ Ⓓ

AP® U.S. Government and Politics Exam

SECTION I: Multiple-Choice Questions

DO NOT OPEN THIS BOOKLET UNTIL YOU ARE TOLD TO DO SO.

At a Glance

Total Time
80 minutes
Number of Questions
55
Percent of Total Grade
50%
Writing Instrument
Pencil required

Instructions

Section I of this examination contains 55 multiple-choice questions. Fill in only the ovals for numbers 1 through 55 on your answer sheet.

Indicate all of your answers to the multiple-choice questions on the answer sheet. No credit will be given for anything written in this exam booklet, but you may use the booklet for notes or scratch work. After you have decided which of the suggested answers is best, completely fill in the corresponding oval on the answer sheet. Give only one answer to each question. If you change an answer, be sure that the previous mark is erased completely. Here is a sample question and answer.

Sample Question   Sample Answer

Chicago is a   Ⓐ ● Ⓒ Ⓓ
(A) state
(B) city
(C) country
(D) continent

Use your time effectively, working as quickly as you can without losing accuracy. Do not spend too much time on any one question. Go on to other questions and come back to the ones you have not answered if you have time. It is not expected that everyone will know the answers to all the multiple-choice questions.

About Guessing

Many candidates wonder whether or not to guess the answers to questions about which they are not certain. Multiple-choice scores are based on the number of questions answered correctly. Points are not deducted for incorrect answers, and no points are awarded for unanswered questions. Because points are not deducted for incorrect answers, you are encouraged to answer all multiple-choice questions. On any questions you do not know the answer to, you should eliminate as many choices as you can, and then select the best answer among the remaining choices.

GO ON TO THE NEXT PAGE.

UNITED STATES GOVERNMENT AND POLITICS

Section I

Time—80 minutes

55 Questions

<u>Directions</u>: Each of the questions or incomplete statements below is followed by four suggested answers or completions. Select the one that is best in each case and then fill in the corresponding oval on the answer sheet.

Questions 1 and 2 refer to the graph below.

Number of viewers of the State of the Union addresses from 1993 to 2018 (in millions)

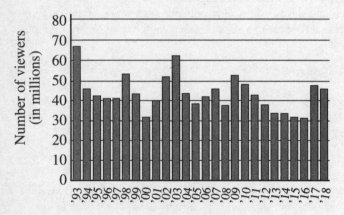

Source: Statista, © 2018.

1. Which of the following statements best reflects a trend in the graph above?

(A) Republican presidents receive fewer viewers during their State of the Union addresses.

(B) Since 1993, the State of the Union has fallen in importance in American political life.

(C) Viewership generally wanes in the later years of a president's term.

(D) Americans watch the State of the Union in higher numbers during an economic recession.

2. Based on the information in the bar graph, which of the following is true about the State of the Union?

(A) A president's first State of the Union is his or her best chance to connect with the nation.

(B) The State of the Union is no longer an effective method for presidents to communicate with the American people.

(C) A president should announce broad policy goals during his or her final two State of the Union addresses.

(D) Broadcasting the State of the Union has little to no effect on a president's policy proposals.

Questions 3 and 4 refer to the graph below.

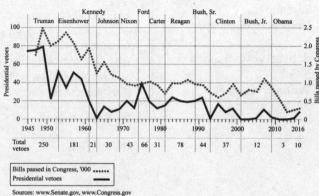

Sources: www.Senate.gov, www.Congress.gov

3. Which of the following best describes a trend in the graph above?

(A) The number of presidential vetoes rose dramatically in the 1990s.

(B) The number of vetoes matched the number of passed bills in 1975.

(C) Presidents are more likely to veto bills in years when Congress passes fewer bills.

(D) Presidents issued the largest number of vetoes between 1945 and 1961.

4. Which of the following can be inferred from the high number of vetoes issued by Republican presidents between 1953 and 1993?

(A) Republican presidents use the veto to enact their policies.

(B) Congress was very unproductive during this time period.

(C) Republican presidents were highly unpopular.

(D) Congress was controlled by the Democratic Party.

GO ON TO THE NEXT PAGE.

Questions 5 and 6 refer to the cartoon below.

Source: Mike Keefe, InToon.com

5. Which of the following statements describes the message in the political cartoon?

   (A) The National Security Agency is an American intelligence agency.
   (B) American citizens do not know that the government is spying on them.
   (C) Government actions violate protections enshrined in the Constitution.
   (D) Stopping government surveillance would not repair civil liberties.

6. A lawyer arguing against the government actions as depicted by the political cartoon would invoke which constitutional amendment?

   (A) Third Amendment
   (B) Fourth Amendment
   (C) Fifth Amendment
   (D) Eighth Amendment

Questions 7 and 8 refer to the graph below.

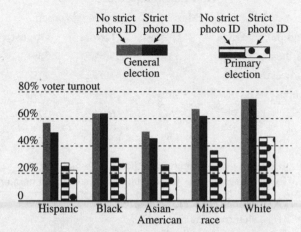

Source: "Voter Identification Laws and the Suppression of Minority Votes," *The Journal of Politics.*

7. Which of the following statements is best supported by the information in the bar graph?

   (A) White voters turn out in fewer numbers in states that require approved ID.
   (B) Mixed race Americans vote in higher numbers than white Americans.
   (C) Members of minority groups are more likely not to have approved ID.
   (D) Black Americans are the least likely group to vote in primary elections.

8. Based on the information in the graph, why would opponents of voter ID laws argue that these laws violate the Voting Rights Act of 1965?

   (A) Voter ID laws affect the voting patterns of all races.
   (B) Voter ID laws do not protect elections against fraudulent votes.
   (C) Voter ID laws result in a decrease in minority turnout during elections.
   (D) Voter ID laws are just another form of literacy tests or poll taxes.

GO ON TO THE NEXT PAGE.

Questions 9 and 10 refer to the table below.

**Opinions on Support for Congressional
Gun Control Measures**

	Men		Women	
Region	Favor	Oppose	Favor	Oppose
Northeast	56%	33%	58%	33%
Midwest	41%	48%	39%	49%
South	31%	56%	31%	57%
West	65%	26%	64%	27%

9. Based on the information in the table, which of the following categories has the largest difference in opinion?

   (A) Women from the Midwest
   (B) Men from the South
   (C) Women from the Northeast
   (D) Men from the West

10. Which of the following is an accurate conclusion about the information in the table?

    (A) There are more guns in the West than in other parts of the country.
    (B) Women grow up with identical beliefs about gun control.
    (C) The region where one lives affects one's political socialization.
    (D) Gun ownership is a topic that Congress should address with legislation.

Questions 11 to 13 refer to the passage below.

In San Francisco a few weeks ago, I saw demonstrators carrying signs reading: "Lose in Vietnam, bring the boys home."

Well, one of the strengths of our free society is that any American has a right to reach that conclusion and to advocate that point of view. But as President of the United States, I would be untrue to my oath of office if I allowed the policy of this Nation to be dictated by the minority who hold that point of view and who try to impose it on the Nation by mounting demonstrations in the street.

For almost 200 years, the policy of this Nation has been made under our Constitution by those leaders in the Congress and the White House elected by all of the people. If a vocal minority, however fervent its cause, prevails over reason and the will of the majority, this Nation has no future as a free society.

—President Richard Nixon, "Silent Majority" Speech, 1969

11. Which of the following statements best summarizes President Nixon's message in the passage above?

    (A) People protesting the Vietnam war should not have the right to do so.
    (B) A political minority is always incorrect.
    (C) A single-interest group does not represent the will of the people.
    (D) Protesting undermines the military effort in Vietnam.

12. Which statement best describes why President Nixon is giving this speech?

    (A) To connect with the Americans who are not protesting the Vietnam War
    (B) To appeal to the Americans who are protesting the Vietnam War
    (C) To campaign for the presidency
    (D) To beg the American people to keep supporting the war effort

13. Which of the following is a reasonable assumption to make about the demonstrators?

    (A) They wish to overthrow the government.
    (B) They wish for the government to change its policies.
    (C) They wish that President Nixon would not pander to them.
    (D) They wish to create a tyranny of the minority.

GO ON TO THE NEXT PAGE.

Questions 14 to 17 refer to the passage below.

When the legislative and executive powers are united in the same person, or in the same body of magistrates, there can be no liberty; because apprehensions may arise, lest the same monarch or senate should enact tyrannical laws, to execute them in a tyrannical manner.

Again, there is no liberty, if the judiciary power be not separated from the legislative and executive. Were it joined with the legislative, the life and liberty of the subject would be exposed to arbitrary control; for the judge would be then the legislator. Were it joined to the executive power, the judge might behave with violence and oppression. There would be an end of everything, were the same man, or the same body, whether of the nobles or of the people, to exercise those three powers, that of enacting laws, that of executing the public resolutions, and of trying the causes of individuals.

—Baron de Montesquieu, *The Spirit of the Laws*, 1748

14. Which of the following statements best summarizes the passage?

    (A) The separation of powers helps ensure liberty.
    (B) The separation of powers ensures domestic tranquility and international peace.
    (C) People, after experiencing a dictator's oppression, will rise up in protest.
    (D) Governments where one person wields legislative, executive, and judicial power are always corrupt.

15. How did James Madison expand on Montesquieu's ideas when he wrote Federalist No. 51?

    (A) He argued that three branches of government would best serve the United States.
    (B) He wrote a draft of the Constitution that incorporated Montesquieu's ideas.
    (C) He proposed clear dividing lines between the branches of government.
    (D) He studied the fates of different governments that had attempted to separate government power.

16. Which of the following events best reflects Montesquieu's ideas in action?

    (A) The passage of the Affordable Healthcare Act in 2010
    (B) Vice President Lyndon Johnson becoming president after the assassination of President John Kennedy in 1963
    (C) Supreme Court justices attending the annual State of the Union address
    (D) The impeachment of President Clinton in 1998

17. Based on the text, which of the following statements would the author most likely agree with?

    (A) Conflict between the branches of government is a sign of a healthy democracy.
    (B) Conflict between the branches of government slows down the government's functions.
    (C) The different branches of government should not know what the others are doing.
    (D) The different branches of government should always cooperate with one another.

GO ON TO THE NEXT PAGE.

Questions 18 and 19 refer to the table below.

**Party Affiliation in the United States Based
on Educational Attainment**

Highest Level of Educational Attainment	Males		Females	
	Republicans	Democrats	Republicans	Democrats
Grade School	12%	85%	13%	87%
High School Diploma	13%	80%	21%	72%
Vocational Degree	24%	72%	28%	58%
College Degree	36%	64%	36%	52%
Master's Degree	49%	51%	30%	61%
Doctoral Degree	56%	34%	19%	70%

18. Which of the following statements does the above table support?

(A) Women whose highest educational level is a master's degree are more likely to identify as Republicans as compared to all other groups.

(B) Men who have attained a doctoral degree are more likely to identify as Democrats than are those with only a college degree.

(C) Women whose highest level of education is grade school and men whose highest level of education is high school are equally likely to identify as Republicans.

(D) Women who have attained a doctoral degree are the most reliable group of Democratic women voters.

19. One can infer that a man with a college degree would likely agree with which of the following proposals?

(A) The United States should project its military power abroad.

(B) Congress should spend more money on social welfare programs.

(C) The Supreme Court should overturn *Roe v. Wade*.

(D) The Justice Department should more harshly prosecute drug users.

GO ON TO THE NEXT PAGE.

Question 20 and 21 refer to the table below.

INDEPENDENT VOTERS AND PRESIDENTIAL ELECTIONS (1980–2012)									
Percent of Independents Voting for Candidates, by Party									
	1980	**1984**	**1988**	**1992**	**1996**	**2000**	**2004**	**2008**	**2012**
Democratic	29.8	33.0	42.6	39.2	48.7	44.3	52.4	51.1	42.3
Republican	55.2	66.5	57.1	30.4	33.4	48.6	47.5	48.5	50.1
Percent of Popular Vote Won, by Party (Incumbents' results in *italics*)									
Democratic	*41.0*	40.6	45.7	40.3	*49.2*	48.4	48.3	52.9	*51.1*
Republican	50.8	*58.8*	53.4	*37.5*	40.7	47.9	*50.7*	45.7	47.2
Other	6.6	*	*	18.9	8.4	*	*	*	*

*No third-party candidate won more than 5% of the popular vote in these elections.

20. The table above supports which of the following statements about independent voters during presidential elections?

    (A) Independent voters often prefer the challenger when a president runs for reelection.
    (B) The independent vote generally aligns with the popular vote.
    (C) The unpredictability of the independent voters is why politicians do not try to attract independent voters.
    (D) Republicans have won a plurality of independent votes whenever there was a viable third-party candidate.

21. Which of the following statements best explains the voting decisions made by independent voters from 2000 to 2012?

    (A) The majority of independent voters did not have an alternative to the traditional two-party system.
    (B) The Republican and Democratic parties fielded the strongest candidates in these elections.
    (C) The other party candidates were extremely charismatic.
    (D) Changes in election law gave independent voters more options at the ballot box.

GO ON TO THE NEXT PAGE.

Questions 22 and 23 refer to the table below.

Reported Voting and Registration, by Race, Hispanic Origin, Sex and Age, for the United States: November 2016 (in thousands)									
All races		Total Population	US Citizens						
			Total Citizen Population	Reported registered		Reported not registered		No response to registration[1]	
				Number	Percent	Number	Percent	Number	Percent
Both Sexes	Total 18 years and over	245,502	224,059	157,596	70.3	32,622	14.6	33,841	15.1
	18 to 24 years	29,320	26,913	14,905	55.4	6,650	24.7	5,358	19.9
	25 to 44 years	83,698	72,610	48,629	67.0	12,467	17.2	11,514	15.9
	45 to 64years	83,799	77,544	57,394	74.0	9,063	11.7	11,087	14.3
	65 to 74 years	28,832	27,839	21,908	78.7	2,502	9.0	3,429	12.3
	75 years and over	19,852	19,154	14,759	77.1	1,941	10.1	2,454	12.8
Male	Total 18 years and over	118,488	107,554	73,761	68.6	17,068	15.9	16,724	15.5
	18 to 24 years	14,822	13,530	7,200	53.2	3,579	26.5	2,752	20.3
	25 to 44 years	41,264	35,431	22,718	64.1	6,733	19.0	5,980	16.9
	45 to 64years	40,642	37,516	27,229	72.6	4,853	12.9	5,434	14.5
	65 to 74 years	13,428	13,018	10,245	78.7	1,211	9.3	1,561	12.0
	75 years and over	8,333	8,059	6,369	79.0	692	8.6	997	12.4
Female	Total 18 years and over	127,013	116,505	83,835	72.0	15,553	13.3	17,117	14.7
	18 to 24 years	14,498	13,382	7,706	57.6	3,070	22.9	2,606	19.5
	25 to 44 years	42,435	37,178	25,911	69.7	5,734	15.4	5,533	14.9
	45 to 64years	43,157	40,028	30,165	75.4	4,210	10.5	5,653	14.1
	65 to 74 years	15,404	14,821	11,663	78.7	1,291	8.7	1,868	12.6
	75 years and over	11,519	11,095	8,390	75.6	1,249	11.3	1,456	13.1

[1]'No response to registration' includes those who were not asked if they were registered as well as those who responded 'Don't know,' and 'Refused.'

22. Which of the following is an accurate statement about the information in the table?

(A) Women are more likely to be registered voters than men.

(B) There are approximately 20,000 adults living in the U.S. that are not citizens.

(C) As men and women age, they are less likely to be registered voters.

(D) Men tend to live longer lives than women.

23. Which of the following statements is an accurate conclusion based on the comparison between citizens who are registered, not registered, and had no response to registration?

(A) Age plays little role in whether men or women are politically active.

(B) Male registered voters between the ages of 18 and 24 are the most valuable voting block for presidential candidates.

(C) A large percentage of the population is apathetic to voting presidential elections.

(D) Millions of Americans cannot vote for various reasons.

GO ON TO THE NEXT PAGE.

24. Which of the following was a belief of the Federalists during the Constitutional Convention of 1787?

(A) The Legislative Branch should have a Senate.
(B) The federal government should be stronger than state governments.
(C) The slave trade was a necessary institution.
(D) A small republic was the best form the United States could take.

25. Which of the following businesses could Congress affect through legislation based upon the commerce clause?

(A) A French bakery that plans to import croissants to New Jersey.
(B) A workshop in rural Tennessee that repairs tractors for local farmers.
(C) A service center in Oakland, California, that repairs 18-wheeler trucks registered in the state.
(D) A restaurant in Kansas that plans to build three more restaurants throughout the state.

26. Federalism is a principle of government in which

(A) power is shared between the national government and the state governments
(B) states have equal representation in the national government
(C) individual liberties are guaranteed by a Bill of Rights
(D) legislative, executive, and judicial powers are separated

27. According to the Constitution, who determines voter eligibility requirements?

(A) The president
(B) Congress
(C) State legislatures
(D) The Supreme Court

28. Which of the following best describes the balance the Supreme Court has struck between the establishment clause and the free-exercise clause?

(A) Freedom of speech is protected except in certain situations, such as yelling "fire" in a crowded theater.
(B) Once a church has been recognized by the federal government, its tax-exempt status can never be revoked.
(C) Once Congress has created an administrative agency, that agency can be dissolved only by a constitutional amendment.
(D) State-sponsored prayer during school hours is prohibited, but voluntary prayer by student groups before school is allowed.

29. In which of the following cases did the Supreme Court decision establish the "separate but equal" doctrine of state-sponsored racial segregation?

(A) *Plessy v. Ferguson*
(B) *McCulloch v. Maryland*
(C) *Gibbons v. Ogden*
(D) *Brown v. Board of Education*

30. Which of the following scenarios reflects a conservative political belief?

(A) A state passes a law to protect an endangered species.
(B) A city hall makes its restrooms gender neutral.
(C) A person waits five days before receiving a gun they purchased.
(D) A new military base opens in a rural community, providing jobs to residents.

31. Which of the following would have the least effect on changing the vote of someone who strongly identifies with a political party?

(A) The voter has a child.
(B) The voter loses their job during a recession.
(C) The voter changes their religion.
(D) The voter watches a new television channel to get their news.

32. Which of the following statements about political action committees (PACs) is most accurate?

(A) They funnel donations directly to political candidates.
(B) Their activities are not regulated by the Federal Election Commission (FEC).
(C) Their activities are limited to national presidential elections.
(D) They raise money to influence federal, state, and local elections.

33. The opposition of the American Civil Liberties Union (ACLU), the National Association of Women Lawyers (NAWL), and the American Federation of Labor and Congress of Industrial Organization (AFL-CIO) to Samuel Alito's 2006 nomination to the Supreme Court is an example of

(A) Realignment
(B) Coalition building
(C) Logrolling
(D) Non-commitment

GO ON TO THE NEXT PAGE.

34. Which of the following statements about the House of Representatives is true?

    (A) All revenue bills must originate in the Senate before moving to the House.
    (B) Representation in the House is allocated equally among the states, while representation in the Senate is allocated proportional to population.
    (C) The Speaker of the House wields less power than the president *pro tempore* of the Senate.
    (D) The House has a Committee on Ways and Means, while the Senate does not.

35. Which of the following statements best characterizes cooperative federalism?

    (A) The executive and legislative branches working on legislation together
    (B) The federal government granting power over a policy area to the states
    (C) Governments working with businesses to address an issue
    (D) State and federal governments working on the same issue

36. The attorney general is the head of which of the following entities?

    (A) The Senate Judiciary Committee
    (B) The Department of Justice
    (C) The Department of State
    (D) The Judge Advocate General's Corps

37. Which of the following situations is an example of logrolling?

    (A) Giving up one's political position to win a short-term victory
    (B) Changing the shape of congressional district to favor one party
    (C) Gaining federal funding for one's home district
    (D) Two congresspersons agreeing to vote on each other's bills

38. The Voting Rights Act of 1965 has had which of the following effects?

    (A) States have been prohibited from establishing voter identification requirements.
    (B) Voters must now pass literacy tests before voting.
    (C) Voting participation for racial minority voters has increased.
    (D) The voting age was lowered from 21 to 18.

39. In *Brown v. Board of Education* (1954), the Supreme Court based its decision on which provision of the Fourteenth Amendment?

    (A) Automatic citizenship for persons born in the United States
    (B) Equal protection under the law
    (C) Overturning the three-fifths compromise
    (D) Refusal of compensation for freed slaves

40. How did *New York Times Co. v. United States* (1971) affect the interpretation of the First Amendment?

    (A) It shielded newspapers from government lawsuits.
    (B) It limited the government's power to interfere with the press.
    (C) It codified the process of gaining a restraining order against a newspaper.
    (D) It changed what the government could and could not classify as Top Secret.

41. Senator Smith ran on a platform of political efficacy. After winning the election, which of the following actions would fulfill his platform?

    (A) Going after special interest groups
    (B) Raising voters' trust in the democratic process
    (C) Investigating how checks and balances can be strengthened
    (D) Holding town halls to persuade voters to support a piece of legislation

42. Which of the following is most likely to lead to a decrease in political knowledge among Americans?

    (A) A media outlet that reports only one point of view
    (B) A media outlet that routinely interviews candidates
    (C) A media outlet that protects its sources
    (D) A media outlet that summarizes the day's news events

GO ON TO THE NEXT PAGE.

43. Which of the following is an accurate comparison of the Articles of Confederation and the Constitution?

	The Articles of Confederation	Constitution
(A)	Bicameral legislative branch	Unicameral legislative branch
(B)	Term limits for legislative branch	No term limits for legislative branch
(C)	Forbids *ex post facto* laws	Does not forbid *ex post facto* laws
(D)	The Supreme Court settles disputes between states	Congress settles disputes between states

44. Which of the following accurately compares the roles of the Federal Elections Commission (FEC) and Securities and Exchange Commission (SEC)?

	FEC	SEC
(A)	Enforce campaign finance law	Promote an orderly and fair stock market
(B)	Oversee the nation's infrastructure	Enforce environmental regulations
(C)	Enforce civil rights legislation regarding elections	Protect the nation from external threats
(D)	Regulate the banking industry	Set education policy at the federal level

45. Which of the following is an accurate comparison of the two court cases?

	Gideon v. Wainwright (1963)	*Miranda v. Arizona* (1965)
(A)	Police officers have to inform people under arrest of their constitutional rights	Overturned state laws concerning literacy tests
(B)	Guaranteed right to an attorney for all criminal cases	Police officers have to inform people under arrest of their constitutional rights
(C)	Guaranteed a woman's access to contraception	Overturned state laws prohibiting interracial marriage
(D)	Incorporated the Sixth Amendment to the states	Guaranteed a woman's access to contraception

46. Which of the following is an accurate comparison between voters and the Electoral College in a presidential election?

	Voters	The Electoral College
(A)	Have to register in their state of residence	Like the president, must be over the age of 35
(B)	A candidate must win the popular vote to win the presidency	Chosen by a state legislature or other organization
(C)	Candidates campaign to them	Have the final say of who becomes president
(D)	Must follow rules regarding whom to vote for	A candidate must win a majority of Electoral College votes to win the presidency

47. Which of the following is an accurate comparison between conservative and liberal beliefs?

	Conservative	Liberal
(A)	Favor restricting access to abortion	Favor longer sentences for criminals
(B)	Promote reduced military spending	Oppose separation of church and state
(C)	Favor expansion of immigration	Favor legalized access to abortion
(D)	Believe in limited regulation of business	Support gay marriage

48. Which of the following statements best expresses the prevailing belief concerning the government's role in Americans' daily lives?

(A) The government should ensure equality of opportunity.
(B) The government should ensure equality of outcome.
(C) The government should ensure both equality of outcome and equality of opportunity.
(D) The government should ensure neither equality of outcome nor equality of opportunity.

GO ON TO THE NEXT PAGE.

49. Which of the following activities are interest groups barred from taking part in?

    (A) Sending lawmakers to educational seminars
    (B) Giving tangible gifts to lawmakers
    (C) Providing research to government officials
    (D) Staging protest and boycotts

50. Which of the following defines an open primary election?

    (A) Voters select the winner by caucus instead of by individual ballots.
    (B) The election results are not binding.
    (C) Any registered voter may participate, regardless of party affiliation.
    (D) Voters may registers to vote on the day of the election.

51. Which of the following statements accurately describes the legal impact of *United States v. Lopez* (1996)?

    (A) Congress gained expanded power over the states.
    (B) The Supreme Court completely redefined federalism as a concept.
    (C) There are limitations to Congress using the commerce clause to justify legislation.
    (D) For the first time, states could pass gun control legislation.

52. Which of the following is an example of an implied power of Congress?

    (A) Passing laws regulating interstate trade
    (B) Raising the debt limit every year
    (C) Overseeing executive branch agencies
    (D) Declaring war on Japan in 1941

53. Which of the following would occur if Congress were to pass legislation and declare a recess, and the president took no action on the bill within ten days of its passage?

    (A) A line-item veto
    (B) A pocket veto
    (C) An adjournment
    (D) A writ of *certiorari*

54. Which of the following statements best describes the purpose of gerrymandering?

    (A) To increase the control voters have over their elected officials
    (B) To divide like-minded voters into several districts to reduce their influence
    (C) To put all racial minorities into a single district
    (D) To equally divide a state's congressional districts by size.

55. Which of the following statements outlines a key weakness of the Articles of Confederation?

    (A) Free residents of each state given "all the privileges and immunities of free citizens in the several states."
    (B) Individual states had to negotiate with one another concerning interstate commerce.
    (C) Governmental departments oversaw foreign affairs, armed conflict, shipping, and government spending.
    (D) Canada was given the right to become part of the United States at any time.

STOP
END OF SECTION I
IF YOU FINISH BEFORE TIME IS CALLED, YOU MAY CHECK YOUR WORK ON THIS SECTION.
DO NOT GO ON TO SECTION II UNTIL YOU ARE TOLD TO DO SO.

UNITED STATES GOVERNMENT AND POLITICS

Section II

Time—1 hour and 40 minutes

<u>Directions:</u> It is suggested that you take a few minutes to plan and outline each answer. It is suggested that you spend approximately 20 minutes each on questions 1, 2, and 3 and 40 minutes on question 4. Unless directions indicate otherwise, respond to all parts of all four questions. In your response use substantive examples where appropriate.

1. "Current and former executives with the pharmaceutical distributors that are accused of flooding communities with powerful prescription painkillers have been summoned to testify before Congress about their role in the U.S. opioid epidemic….The pharmaceutical executives are expected to face tough questions under oath about why their companies pumped so many highly addictive pain pills into West Virginia and other states, fueling what has become the deadliest drug crisis in U.S. history."

"Drug executives to testify before Congress about their role in U.S. opioid crisis," *The Washington Post,* 2018

After reading the scenario, respond to A, B, and C below:

(a) Describe a power Congress could use to address the comments outlined in the scenario.

(b) In the context of the scenario, explain how the use of congressional power described in Part A can be affected by its interaction with the Supreme Court.

(c) In the context of the scenario, explain the responsibilities of states like West Virginia as described under the Tenth Amendment.

GO ON TO THE NEXT PAGE.

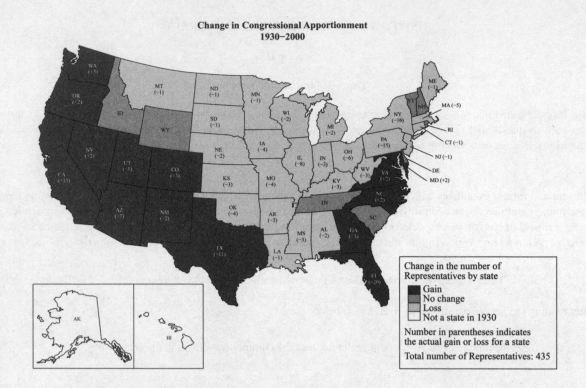

Change in Congressional Apportionment
1930–2000

Change in the number of
Representatives by state

■ Gain
■ No change
■ Loss
□ Not a state in 1930

Number in parentheses indicates
the actual gain or loss for a state

Total number of Representatives: 435

2. Use the following graphic to answer the questions.

(a) Identify the two states that have gained the most seats through congressional apportionment between 1930 and 2000.

(b) Describe a trend based on how congressional apportionment has shifted between 1930 and 2000.

(c) Explain how the changes in congressional apportionment over time as shown in the information graphic reflects one principle set forth in Article I of the Constitution.

GO ON TO THE NEXT PAGE.

3. In the summer of 1964, Clarence Brandenburg, an Ohio resident and KKK leader, organized a Klan rally where he and other Klan members espoused hate speech against African Americans, Jewish Americans, and the U.S. government's efforts to enact civil rights legislation. Brandenburg was arrested after making calls for a KKK march on Washington, D.C. Ohio charged him with advocating violence, although he had made no specific threats.

In the ensuing case, *Brandenburg v. Ohio* (1969), the Supreme Court unanimously ruled that Brandenburg's comment during the KKK rallies did not suggest that Brandenburg or fellow KKK members were about to commit any "imminent lawless action." Since then, *Brandenburg* has been the litmus test used by law enforcement and the courts to determine whether or not to arrest individuals speaking or writing inflammatory speech.

(a) Identify the constitutional clause that is common to both *Brandenburg v. Ohio* (1969) and *Schenck v. United States* (1919).

(b) Based on the constitutional clause in Part A, explain why the court found differently in *Brandenburg v. Ohio* than it did in *Schenck v. United States*.

(c) Describe an action that local governments who disagree with the holding in *Brandenburg v. Ohio* could take to limit its impact in their communities.

GO ON TO THE NEXT PAGE.

4. Develop an argument that explains which of the three forms of action taken by the federal government—constitutional amendments, Supreme Court rulings, or legislation—has best ensured the civil rights of minorities and historically repressed groups.

   In your essay, you must:

   - Articulate a defensible claim or thesis that responds to the prompt and establishes a line of reasoning

   - Support your claim with at least TWO pieces of accurate and relevant information:
     - At least ONE piece of evidence must be from one of the following foundational documents:
       - Federalist No. 10
       - The Declaration of Independence
       - "Letter from a Birmingham Jail" (MLK)
     - Use a second piece of evidence from another foundational document from the list or from your study of civil rights

   - Use reasoning to explain why your evidence supports your claim/thesis

   - Respond to an opposing or alternative perspective using refutation, concession, or rebuttal

END OF EXAMINATION

Practice Test 1: Answers and Explanations

PRACTICE TEST 1 SCORING WORKSHEET

Section I: Multiple-Choice

_____ × 1.0000 = _____
Number of Correct   Weighted
(out of 55)   Section I Score
                       (Do not round)

Section II: Free Response

Question 1   _____ × 3.000 = _____
               (out of 3)   (Do not round)

Question 2   _____ × 4.000 = _____
               (out of 3)   (Do not round)

Question 3   _____ × 4.000 = _____
               (out of 3)   (Do not round)

Question 4   _____ × 5.500 = _____
               (out of 4)   (Do not round)

Sum   = _____
               Weighted Section II
               Score (Do not round)

The following conversion chart provides only a rough estimate, as the new 2019 Exam has not yet been scored and may have a different range.

AP Score Conversion Chart U.S. Government and Politics

Composite Score Range	AP Score
83–110	5
72–82	4
56–71	3
38–55	2
0–37	1

Composite Score

_____ + _____ = _____
Weighted   Weighted   Composite Score
Section I Score   Section II Score   (Round to nearest
                                          whole number)

PRACTICE TEST 1 ANSWER KEY

1.	C	21.	A	41.	B
2.	A	22.	A	42.	A
3.	D	23.	C	43.	B
4.	D	24.	B	44.	A
5.	C	25.	A	45.	B
6.	B	26.	A	46.	C
7.	C	27.	C	47.	D
8.	C	28.	D	48.	A
9.	D	29.	A	49.	B
10.	C	30.	D	50.	C
11.	C	31.	D	51.	C
12.	A	32.	D	52.	C
13.	B	33.	B	53.	B
14.	A	34.	D	54.	B
15.	A	35.	D	55.	B
16.	D	36.	B		
17.	A	37.	D		
18.	C	38.	C		
19.	B	39.	B		
20.	A	40.	B		

MULTIPLE-CHOICE SECTION: ANSWERS AND EXPLANATIONS

Section I

1. **C** The graph shows how many Americans watched the president's State of the Union address between 1993 and 2018. Choice (A) can be eliminated as some addresses given by Republican presidents were watched by more Americans than some addresses given by Democratic presidents. Choice (B) can be eliminated as viewership has gone up and down since 1993. Choice (D) can be eliminated as viewership peaks occurred during the economic recession of the early 1990s and late 2000s. The correct answer is (C) because Americans are more likely to tune in to the State of the Union in the early years of a presidency, as happened in 1993, 2001–2002, and 2009–2010.

2. **A** Choice (B) can be eliminated as millions of Americans still watch the State of the Union address. Choice (C) can be eliminated as the fewest number of viewers tune into a president's final two State of the Union addresses. Choice (D) is incorrect as the president can use the State of the Union as a way to measure the public's reaction to policy goals. Accordingly, (A) is the correct answer: because the highest number of viewers tune in to a president's first State of the Union, that moment represents the president's best chance to connect with Americans.

3. **D** The graph compares the number of bills passed by Congress between 1945 and 2016 with the number of presidential vetoes issued during that same timeframe. Choice (A) can be eliminated as the number of vetoes fell throughout the first half of the 1990s before making a slight rebound. Choice (B) can be eliminated as although the two lines in the graph touch, they do not represent the same number. Choice (C) can be eliminated as it describes a relationship that is the opposite of what the graph portrays. Therefore, (D) is correct as the graph supports this statement.

4. **D** Choice (A) is incorrect as the graph gives no information concerning Republican presidents' policies. Choice (B) is incorrect as although the number of bills passed by Congress lessened over time, Congress still passed tens of thousands of bills into law. Choice (C) is incorrect as the graph does not provide information on the popularity of Republican presidents. Therefore, (D) is correct as Congress issued more vetoes during the tenure of Republican presidents that it did during the tenure of Democratic ones.

5. **C** The cartoon portrays the National Security Agency spying on American citizens. Choice (A) can be eliminated as the cartoon portrays the committing of an act beyond the NSA's scope of responsibilities. Choice (B) can be eliminated as the citizens in the cartoon are aware of the NSA's actions. Choice (D) can be eliminated as the cartoon does not portray the surveillance stopping. Therefore, (C) is correct as spying on American citizens damages the "civil liberties" enshrined in the Constitution.

6. **B** Choice (A) is incorrect as the cartoon does not depict American soldiers. Choice (C) is incorrect as neither of the American citizens depicted in the cartoon are on trial. Choice (D) is incorrect as the American citizens depicted in the cartoon are not being punished for a crime. Therefore, (B) is

correct as the government's actions, recording Americans' conversations without a warrant, violates the Fourth Amendment's protections against unreasonable search and seizure.

7. **C** The table depicts voter turnout of different races in states with and without voter ID laws. Choice (A) is incorrect as white voter turnout does not decrease in states with voter ID laws. Choice (B) is incorrect as mixed race voters turn out in lower numbers compared to white Americans. Choice (D) is incorrect as Asian Americans vote in fewer numbers than black Americans. Therefore, (C) is correct as minority voter turnout is less in states with voter ID laws.

8. **C** Choice (A) is incorrect as voting ID laws do not affect the voting patterns of white Americans. Choice (B) is incorrect as the graph does not provide information regarding fraudulent voting. Choice (D) is incorrect as the graph does not make that argument. The only valid argument an opponent could make is (C), that voter ID laws negatively affect groups that the Voting Rights Act of 1965 was passed to protect.

9. **D** The table depicts Americans' opinions on gun control based on sex and region of the country. Choice (A) is incorrect as the difference in opinion is only 10%. Choice (B) is incorrect as the difference in opinion is 25%. Choice (C) is incorrect as the difference in opinion is 25%. Choice (D) is correct as the difference in opinion is 39%.

10. **C** Choice (A) is incorrect as the graph does not provide information about the number of guns throughout the United States. Choice (B) is incorrect as the opinions of women on gun control are not identical throughout the country. Choice (D) is incorrect as the survey did not ask Americans about the steps Congress should take. As a result, (C) is correct as each region has a unique opinion about gun control.

11. **C** The quote conveys President Nixon's opinion of Americans protesting the Vietnam War. Choice (A) is incorrect as Nixon praises the First Amendment. Choice (B) is incorrect as Nixon does not directly or indirectly make this assertion. Choice (D) is incorrect as Nixon does not make the connection between the protestors and America's military effort in Vietnam. Choice (C) is correct as Nixon makes the point that a small but loud interest group will not influence American policy concerning the war.

12. **A** Choice (B) can be eliminated as Nixon talks about the protesters in the third person. Choice (C) can be eliminated as Nixon does not address his reelection campaign for president. Choice (D) can be eliminated as Nixon does not directly address the war effort. As a result, (A) is correct as Nixon is addressing the "silent majority," the group of Americans who still support the war effort.

13. **B** Choice (A) can be eliminated as Nixon describes the protesters' beliefs in the first sentence. Choice (C) can be eliminated as Nixon does not pander to the protesters in his speech. Choice (D) is incorrect as that is not the protesters' intention despite Nixon's claim. As a result, (B) is correct as the protesters want the government to end the war and bring the troops home.

14. **A** In *The Spirit of the Laws*, Baron de Montesquieu laid out his ideas for a just government. In this passage, he addresses the dangers of combining legislative and executive power in the same person

or group. Choice (B) is incorrect as Montesquieu does not speak of international relations. Choice (C) is incorrect as the passage does not address people's reaction to tyranny. Choice (D) is incorrect as Montesquieu does not make this broad assumption; he states that tyranny *can* happen in the situation he describes. Accordingly, the correct answer is (A) as "there can be no liberty" in a nation where the executive and legislative branches are the same person or group.

15. **A** Choice (B) is incorrect as a proposed draft of the Constitution had already been written when Madison wrote Federalist No. 51. Choice (C) is incorrect as Madison does not propose a way to separate government power different from that in the then-proposed Constitution. Choice (D) is incorrect as Madison did not compare different governments from history in Federalist No. 51. As a result, (A) is correct as Madison argues the benefits of how the separation of powers will prevent the tyranny Montesquieu describes in *The Spirit of the Laws*.

16. **D** Choice (A) is incorrect as the legislative and executive branches cooperated on the passage of the Affordable Care Act. Choice (B) is incorrect as the scenario deals exclusively with the Executive Branch. Choice (C) is incorrect as the scenario does not describe conflict or cooperation between two branches of government. Therefore, (D) is correct as the impeachment of President Clinton in 1998 is an example of the Legislative Branch checking the power of the Executive Branch.

17. **A** Choice (B) is incorrect as Montesquieu does not discuss how the separation of powers affects the speed at which a government operates. Choice (C) is incorrect as Montesquieu does not bring up this idea in his text. Choice (D) is incorrect as it contradicts Montesquieu's main point. Therefore, (A) is correct as conflict between branches of government shows that no one faction or groups has complete control of the government.

18. **C** The table reports on political party affiliation classified by respondents' level of education and gender. Choice (A) is incorrect as the opposite is true. Choice (B) is incorrect as the opposite is true. Choice (D) is incorrect as women with only a grade school education are the most reliable Democratic voters. As a result, (C) is correct as 13% of women who have completed grade school and 13% of men who completed high school identify as Republicans.

19. **B** Choice (A) is incorrect as Democrats support less military intervention abroad. Choice (C) is incorrect as Democrats support abortion rights. Choice (D) is incorrect as Democrats support lighter sentences for drug users. Therefore, (B) is correct as Democrats support expanding social welfare programs.

20. **A** The charts display the preferences of independents alongside the popular vote for the presidential elections between 2000 and 2012. Choice (B) is incorrect as the preferences of independents often do not align with the popular vote. Choice (C) is incorrect as the chart does not report on the campaign practices of politicians running for president. Choice (D) is incorrect as from 2000 to 2012, no viable third party candidate attracted more than 5% of popular vote. Therefore, (A) is correct as in 2004 and 2012, independents did not favor the incumbent president running for reelection.

21. **A** Choice (B) is incorrect as the chart does not describe the candidates' strengths during these presidential elections. Choice (C) is incorrect as no "other party candidate" gained more than 5% of

the vote. Choice (D) is incorrect as the chart does not provide information about changes in election law. As a result, (A) best explains why independents voted the way the did; they had no other option besides the Democratic or Republican candidate.

22. **A**   The table presents data on registered voters in the United States broken down by sex and age. Choice (B) is incorrect: because the data is presented (in thousands), the actual number is closer to 20,000,000. Choice (C) is incorrect as the number of registered voters rises and falls as men and women age. Choice (D) is incorrect as the chart does not provide data regarding the lifespans of men and women. Therefore, (A) is correct as approximately 9,000,000 more American women are registered to vote than American men.

23. **C**   Choice (A) is incorrect as people age, their likelihood of voting changes. Choice (B) is incorrect as male registered voters between the ages of 18 and 24 are not the largest voting block. Choice (D) is incorrect as the graph does not display information regarding legal barriers to voting. As a result, (C) is correct as the data shows that a large number of Americans eligible to vote in presidential elections have not registered, implying disinterest.

24. **B**   After the drafting of the Constitution in 1787, Federalists and Anti-Federalists argued about the role of the federal government in a series of writings known as the Federalist and Anti-Federalist Papers. Choice (A) is incorrect as the failures of the Articles of Confederation had already shown the limitations of a unitary legislative branch. Choice (C) is incorrect as slavery was widely supported by Anti-Federalists from agricultural areas. Choice (D) is incorrect as Anti-Federalists favored a small republic. Therefore, (B) is correct as the primary tenant of Federalist beliefs is that the power of the federal government should supersede that of the state governments.

25. **A**   The interstate commerce clause gives Congress the power to regulate interstate and foreign trade. Choices (B), (C), and (D) all deal with businesses that work exclusively in one state, making them intrastate commerce. As a result, (A) is correct as if a French bakery wants to export its croissants to the United States, Congress can regulate their import through the commerce clause.

26. **A**   In addition to the Bill of Rights, the Constitution laid the framework for Federalism in the United States. Choice (B) is incorrect as states do not have equal representation in the House of Representatives. Choice (C) is incorrect as Federalism does not deal with individual liberty. Choice (D) is incorrect as the separation of powers deals with the relationship between the three branches of the federal government, not the relationship between the states and the federal government. Therefore, (A) is correct as it accurately describes the principle of federalism.

27. **C**   Voter eligibility requirements concern the regulations surrounding who is eligible to vote in an election. Choice (A) is incorrect as the president has no role in this process. Although Congress has passed constitutional amendments expanding voting rights, Choice (B) is incorrect as determining voter eligibility is not one of Congress's powers. Choice (D) is incorrect as the Supreme Court can only interpret the constitutionality of laws regarding voter eligibility, not create them. As a result, (C) is correct as the Constitution allows states to set their voter eligibility requirements as long as these requirements do not violate the Constitution.

28. **D** The establishment clause does not allow the federal government to recognize a state religion, and the free-exercise clause allows Americans to observe (or not) the religion of their choice. Choice (A) is incorrect as the scenario does not involve either clause. Choice (B) is incorrect as religious institutions can lose their tax-exempt status. Choice (C) is incorrect as the scenario does not involve either clause. Therefore, (D) is correct as a public school cannot force students to pray, but students still have the right to do so on their own.

29. **A** "Separate but equal" refers to a Supreme Court ruling that held up state-sponsored segregation, mainly in the American South in the century after the Civil War. Choice (B) is incorrect as *McCulloch v. Maryland* dealt with Congress' implied powers. Choice (C) is incorrect as *Gibbons v. Odgen* upheld the federal government's right to regulate interstate commerce. Choice (D) is incorrect as *Brown v. Board of Education* overturned the legal concept of "separate but equal." Choice (A) is correct because in *Plessy vs. Ferguson*, the Supreme Court ruled that racial segregation was constitutional as long as "separate but equal" resources (such as segregated schools) were allocated to African Americans.

30. **D** The majority of conservative political beliefs center on the concepts of small government, a strong military, and minimal government interference in citizens' lives. Choice (A) can be eliminated as this law would interfere with private property and business. Choice (B) can be eliminated as conservatives might see it as an attempt to redefine gender. Choice (C) is incorrect as it would be viewed as an infringement on citizens' Second Amendment rights. Therefore, (D) is correct as conservatives support a strong military.

31. **D** Political socialization mainly occurs when someone is young, but dramatic life events can change people's political views. Choices (A), (B), and (C) all classify as life-changing events. As a result, (D) would have the least effect on someone's political preferences, even if that new television channel espoused a different political viewpoint.

32. **D** In recent years, PACs have raised billions of dollars to influence elections throughout the United States. Choice (A) is incorrect as PACs cannot donate directly to political candidates. Choice (B) is incorrect as the FEC does regulate PACs. Choice (C) is incorrect as PACs raise money to support state and local candidates, as well. Therefore, (D) is correct as PACs attempt to influence elections at every level of government.

33. **B** In 2006, many liberal groups attempted to block the nomination of Samuel Alito to the Supreme Court. Choice (A) is incorrect as realignment refers to a group changing its beliefs over time. Choice (C) is incorrect as these groups did not exchange favors. Choice (D) is incorrect as these groups were committed to the cause of blocking Alito. As a result, (B) is correct as the groups built a united coalition of resistance against Congress confirming Alito to the Supreme Court.

34. **D** As laid out in the Constitution, the House of Representatives and Senate have different responsibilities and powers. Choice (A) is incorrect as all revenue bills must originate in the House. Choice (B) is incorrect as the opposite is true. Choice (C) is incorrect as the president *pro tempore* of the Senate has very little power compared to the Speaker of the House. Therefore, (D) is correct as the

House Committee on Ways and Means creates revenue bills, a task the Constitution delegated to the House of Representatives.

35. **D** Cooperative federalism refers to cooperation between the federal government and one or more state governments. Choice (A) can be eliminated as the scenario takes place within the federal government. Choice (B) can be eliminated as the scenario involves only the actions of the federal government. Choice (C) can be eliminated as private businesses do not represent their states. As a result, (D) is correct as the scenario includes both the state and federal governments working together.

36. **B** The attorney general is the federal government's most powerful lawyer. Choice (A) can be eliminated as the attorney general is not a member of Congress. Choice (C) can be eliminated as the secretary of state leads the State Department. Choice (D) can be eliminated as the JAG Corps are a branch of the military and not the civilian government. Therefore, (B) is correct as the attorney general leads the Department of Justice.

37. **D** Logrolling refers to two or more politicians exchanging political favors. Choice (A) is incorrect as it involves only one politician. Choice (B) is incorrect as the scenario refers to gerrymandering. Choice (C) is incorrect as the scenario refers to pork-barrel spending. Therefore, (D) is correct as the scenario accurately describes logrolling.

38. **C** The Voting Rights Act of 1965 was a landmark piece of legislation that strengthened voting rights in the United States. Choice (A) is incorrect as states still have the power to establish their voter identification requirements, as long as these requirements do not violate the Constitution. Choice (B) is incorrect as the law banned literacy tests. Choice (D) is incorrect as the Twenty-sixth Amendment lowered the nationwide voting age from 21 to 18. As a result, (C) is correct as since the law's passage, millions of minority voters have been able to vote without hindrance.

39. **B** The Fourteenth Amendment played a crucial role when the Supreme Court decided *Brown v. Board of Education* in 1954. Choice (A) is incorrect as the court case did not hinge on the issue of African Americans' citizenship. Choice (C) is incorrect as the case did not deal with states' representation in Congress. Choice (D) is incorrect as the case was about school access, not compensation for slavery. Therefore, (B) is correct as the Supreme Court ruled that segregation violated the Fourteenth Amendment's guarantee of equal protection under the law.

40. **B** *New York Times Co. v. United States* was a landmark case that involved the New York Times' publication of the Pentagon Papers, government documents that detailed the history of the U.S.'s post-WWII involvement in Vietnam. Choice (A) is incorrect as the ruling did not interfere with the government's right to sue. Choice (C) is incorrect as the ruling did not change the legal process of obtaining a restraining order. Choice (D) is incorrect as the Supreme Court cannot interfere with what the Executive or Legislative Branches classify as Top Secret. As a result, (B) is correct as the Supreme Court struck down the concept of "prior restraint," the government suppressing news stories.

41. **B** "Political efficacy" refers to the concept of the public's trust in their government and a belief that their voices are heard by those in power. Choice (A) can be eliminated as special interest groups are not political institutions. Choice (C) can be eliminated as this scenario does not involve the public. Choice (D) can be eliminated as Senator Smith is persuading voters on an issue; the voters themselves have little to no say. Therefore, (B) is correct as it is the definition of political efficacy.

42. **A** Americans get their news from many different media outlets. Choice (B) can be eliminated as interviews reveal the beliefs of political candidates. Choice (C) can be eliminated as journalists protecting sources has been a long-established journalistic practice. Choice (D) can be eliminated as all media sources summarize the day's news events in some way or form. As a result, (A) is correct as reporting only one point of view can have the effect of decreasing political knowledge and politically radicalizing consumers.

43. **B** The Articles of Confederation was the first attempt by America's founders to bind the states together into a single country. Its failures and limitations led to the writing of the Constitution in 1787. Choices (A), (C), and (D) can be eliminated as the statements for each choice would need to be switched for them to be correct. Therefore, (B) is correct as the Articles of Confederation set terms limits for members of Congress. The Constitution sets no such limits.

44. **A** The Federal Election Commission (FEC) and Securities & Exchange Commission (SEC) are two critical regulatory agencies within the Executive Branch. Choice (B) is incorrect as the EPA oversees environmental protections. Choice (C) is incorrect as the Justice Department enforces civil rights legislation. The Department of Homeland Security helps protect the nation against external threats. Choice (D) is incorrect as the Department of Education sets educational policy at the federal level. As a result, (A) is correct as the FEC enforces campaign finance law and the SEC promotes an orderly and fair stock market.

45. **B** *Gideon v. Wainwright* and *Miranda v. Arizona* were two landmark cases that expanded rights for people accused of crimes. Choice (A) is incorrect as the Civil Rights Act of 1965 forbade literacy tests to vote. Choice (C) is incorrect as *Griswold v. Connecticut* (1965) guaranteed women's access to contraception. *Loving v. Virginia* (1967) overturned state laws banning interracial marriage. Choice (D) is incorrect as although *Gideon* is described accurately, the text for *Miranda* refers to the *Griswold* ruling. Therefore, (B) is correct: the statements accurately describe *Gideon* and *Miranda*.

46. **C** Voters and the Electoral College both cast votes in a presidential election. Choice (A) is incorrect as there is no rule on how old an elector must be. Choice (B) is incorrect as the popular vote does not always coincide with the winner of a presidential election. Choice (D) is incorrect as voters do not have to follow rules regarding who to vote for; electors have rules regarding voting and can face fines or other consequences in their home states if their vote does not reflect the popular vote. As a result, (C) is correct as presidential candidates appeal directly to voters and the electoral college makes the final determination of who becomes president.

47. **D** In the United States, there is often a large gap between conservative and liberal political beliefs. Choice (A) can be eliminated as liberals do not favor longer sentences for criminals. Choice (B) can be eliminated as the statement would need to be switched to be correct. Choice (C) is incorrect as conservatives do not favor expansion of immigration. Therefore, (D) is correct as conservatives believe in limited regulation of business and liberals support gay marriage.

48. **A** The prevailing belief concerning the government's role in Americans' daily lives is influenced by both the actions of citizens and the government. Choices (B) and (C) are incorrect as "equality of outcome" suggests a Communist form of a government. Choice (D) is incorrect as the civil rights movement suggests that Americans are deeply invested in the concept of "equality of opportunity." As a result, (A) is correct as Americans' civil liberties and the government's respect for civil rights suggests that the government should ensure equality of opportunity.

49. **B** Interest groups such as PACs play a significant role in electing candidates to office. Choices (A), (C), and (D) can be eliminated as these scenarios are all legal activities interest groups perform. As a result, (B) is correct as tangible gifts constitute bribery.

50. **C** Primaries are a valuable tool political parties use to select their best candidate for the general election. Like in the general election, voters select the candidate through voting at the ballot box. Choice (A) is incorrect as a caucus is a separate method of selecting a candidate. Choice (B) is incorrect as the results of an open primary are binding. Choice (D) is incorrect as open primaries do not necessitate that voters be allowed to register on the day of the primary. Therefore, (C) is correct as any registered voter may participate in an open primary; during closed primaries, only voters registered with a specific political party may participate.

51. **C** *United States v. Lopez* (1996) was a landmark case regarding the federal government's ability to make public schools gun-free zones. Choice (A) can be eliminated as Congress lost power due to the Court's ruling. Choice (B) is incorrect as the Court's ruling did not redefine federalism between the federal government and states. Choice (D) is incorrect as states had always had the right to pass gun control legislation that did not infringe on the Second Amendment. As a result, (C) is correct as the Court ruled that Congress could not use the commerce clause to justify gun control legislation on a national level.

52. **C** The "necessary and proper" clause in the Constitution gives Congress implied powers—powers that Congress uses to accomplish its expressed powers. Choices (A), (B), and (D) are incorrect as regulating trade, borrowing money, and declaring war are all expressed powers. Therefore, (C) is correct as overseeing executive branch agencies is not an expressed power mentioned in the Constitution.

53. **B** There are specific rules regarding how a president may or may not approve of a bill passed by Congress. Choice (A) is incorrect as line-item vetoes refer to a president vetoing only part of a bill; the Supreme Court ruled this practice unconstitutional in the mid-1990s. Choice (C) is incorrect as "adjournment" is a term used in a jury trial. Choice (D) is incorrect as a writ of *certiorari* is an appeal to the Supreme Court to take up a case. As a result, (B) is correct as a pocket veto refers to how a president's inaction on a passed bill can have the same effect as a regular veto; in recent

years, Congress never takes a recess within ten days of passing a bill to make it impossible for a president to use the pocket veto.

54. **B** Gerrymandering is an attempt by one political party to redraw a state's congressional districts to their advantage. Choice (A) is incorrect as gerrymandering reduces voters' influence in elections. Choice (C) is incorrect as although gerrymandering has been used as a tool to reduce the importance of the minority vote, that is not its explicit intent. Choice (D) is incorrect as gerrymandered districts are not all the same size. Therefore, (B) is correct as the purpose of gerrymandering is to isolate members of the opposition party into a single district as to reduce their influence in elections.

55. **B** The Articles of Confederation was the nation's first attempt to bind the states together. It had many flaws, which led to the creation of the Constitution in 1787. Choices (A) and (C) can be eliminated as these ideas were later incorporated into the Constitution. Choice (D) can be eliminated as pre-approving Canada for statehood did not negatively affect how the federal government and states interacted. As a result, (B) is correct as since states had to negotiate with one another regarding commerce, multiple sets of laws slowed down commerce between the states, weakening the nation as a whole.

FREE-RESPONSE SECTION: ANSWERS AND EXPLANATIONS

Remember that you need to answer all four free-response questions in 1 hour and 40 minutes, so you do not have time to waste, nor can you skip any questions. Nevertheless, you should take time to brainstorm some ideas and to organize what you come up with before you start to write each response. Otherwise, your responses will probably be incomplete, disorganized, or both.

You should average about 25 minutes per question. Make sure you read each question carefully and respond directly to each of its components in your response. The questions are about broad issues, but they ask for specific information. A general free response that fails to address specific concerns raised by the question will not earn a high score.

Question 1

(a) Describe a power Congress could use to address the comments outlined in the scenario.

Some of the powers that Congress could use include:
- Interstate commerce clause: Congress could invoke this to regulate the interstate transport of legal narcotics through appropriate legislation, thus reducing the number of pain pills that enter West Virginia.
- Subpoenas: Congress could use these to force pharmaceutical executives to testify and provide evidence of how they are addressing the problem.

(b)   In the context of the scenario, explain how the use of congressional power described in Part A can be affected by its interaction with the Supreme Court.
- Interstate commerce clause: The pharmaceutical distributors could sue the federal government, taking the case to the Supreme Court. Such as with *Gonzales v. Raich,* the Supreme Court can reinterpret Congress' power concerning the commerce clause.
- Subpoenas: An executive could refuse to testify or provide evidence, at which point the Supreme Court would need to become involved.

(c)   In the context of the scenario, explain the responsibilities of states like West Virginia as described under the Tenth Amendment.

The Tenth Amendment gives states like West Virginia the power to regulate its healthcare industry. From interpreting the amendment, it is the state's ultimate responsibility to address the issue of painkiller abuse. A way West Virginia could do this is regulating opioid prescriptions once the pills have entered the state. This action would not violate the interstate commerce clause, as the state would not attempt to interfere with the number of pills that cross state lines.

Question 2

(a)   Identify the two states that have gained the most seats through congressional apportionment between 1930 and 2000.
- California and Florida have gained the most seats through congressional apportionment.

(b)   Describe a trend based on how congressional apportionment has shifted between 1930 and 2000.
- Large numbers of Americans moved to the western United States between 1930 and 2000.
- Large numbers of Americans left the Midwest and Northeast during this time.

(c)   Explain how the changes in congressional apportionment over time as shown in the information graphic reflect one principle set forth in Article I of the Constitution.
- One principle from Article I the changes reflect is the requirement to modify congressional apportionment every ten years based on the results of the national census.

Question 3

(a)   Identify the constitutional clause that is common to both *Brandenburg v. Ohio* (1969) and *Schenck v. United States* (1919).
- The First Amendment is relevant to both cases as both defendants were charged with making anti-government speech.

(b)   Based on the constitutional clause in Part A, explain why the court found differently in *Brandenburg v. Ohio* than it did in *Schenck v. United States.*
- *Schenck* was prompted by the first Red Scare—an attempt to suppress Communists in the United States. The court did not apply this or any other political agenda against inflammatory speech during *Brandenburg*.

(c)   Describe an action that local governments who disagree with the holding in *Brandenburg v. Ohio* could take to limit its impact in their communities.

- A local government could deny the KKK or similar group a permit to march or have a large gathering. Also, a local government could also put on its own events that encourage racial equality and integration.

Question 4

Develop an argument that explains which of the three forms of action taken by the federal government—constitutional amendments, Supreme Court rulings, or legislation—has best ensured the civil rights of minorities and historically repressed groups.

Articulate a defensible claim.

Constitutional amendments have best ensured the rights of minorities and historically repressed groups.

Support your claim.

- In his <u>Letter from a Birmingham Jail</u>, MLK spoke out against legislation at the state level suppressing African Americans. This reasoning implies that at the time of the letter's writing, legislation was more of a hindrance than a help in ensuring civil rights.
- The group of white Americans suppressing the civil rights of minorities constitute a political faction as defined by Madison's <u>Federalist No. 10</u>. A strong central government, backed by a Constitution, can suppress factions that infringe on citizens' rights.
- The 13th-15th Amendments to the <u>Constitution</u> were the first steps to ensure civil rights for minorities. In the 20th century, the 19th, 24th, and 26th Amendments expanded these rights for African Americans and did the same for women and young Americans.
- Madison's <u>Federalist No. 51</u> argues that a strong federal government can protect against a "tyranny of the majority" that existed within states that passed laws King and other civil rights leaders were fighting against.
- Some Supreme Court rulings, such as *Plessy v. Ferguson*, *Korematsu v. U.S.*, and *Buck v. Bell*, have restricted the civil rights of minority groups.

Use reasoning.

- Constitutional amendments make the most significant impact on how the state and federal governments interact with citizens.
- Since the writing of the Constitution, the U.S. has repealed only one constitutional amendment. This fact implies that constitutional amendments have a greater lasting power than legislation or Supreme Court decisions.
- Both federal and state governments base their legislation on what the Constitution and its amendments allow. The Supreme Court bases its decisions on constitutional provisions.

Respond to an opposing perspective.

- Opposing Perspective: Historically oppressed groups and other minorities needed immediate change to improve their lives; Congress and the states sometimes require years to draft and adopt constitutional amendments.
- Response (Refutation): Constitutional amendments give the federal government broad powers to carry them out. The legislation and Supreme Court decisions associated with the civil rights movements in the 20th century stem from the constitutional amendments strengthening civil rights.
- Opposing Perspective: From the passage of the 13th-15th Amendments until the mid 20th century, many states subverted the constitutional protections for minorities and other historically repressed groups.
- Response (Concession): At the time, the amendments did not take into account how states might subvert them. Only in later amendments, such as the 24th Amendment banning poll taxes, were these oversights remedied.

Part III
About the AP U.S. Government and Politics Exam

- The Structure of the AP U.S. Government and Politics Exam
- How the AP U.S. Government and Politics Exam Is Scored
- Overview of Content Topics
- How AP Exams Are Used
- Other Resources
- Designing Your Study Plan

THE STRUCTURE OF THE AP U.S. GOVERNMENT AND POLITICS EXAM

The AP U.S. Government and Politics Exam is a two-part test. The chart below illustrates the test's structure.

Section	Question Type	Number of Questions	Time Allowed	Percent of Final Grade
I	Multiple Choice	55	80 minutes	50
II	Free Response	4	100 minutes	50

There are several types of multiple-choice questions, which we'll get into in Chapter 1, but they all pull from the five major topics of the AP U.S. Government and Politics course. Not all subjects are tested equally; the following list is a breakdown of how they appear in the newly released 2018–2019 sample test:

Subject	Percent of Questions	Covered in Chapter #
Foundations of American Democracy	12 to 20	Chapter 4: The Constitutional Underpinnings
Interaction Among Branches of Government	20 to 30	Chapter 8: Institutions of Government Chapter 9: Public Policy
Civil Liberties and Civil Rights	15 to 20	Chapter 10: Civil Rights and Civil Liberties
American Political Ideologies and Beliefs	10 to 18	Chapter 5: Public Opinion and the Media
Political Participation	20 to 30	Chapter 6: Linkage Institutions Chapter 7: Elections

There are a wide variety of new questions on the exam that expect you to be able to analyze data, get to the heart of short reading passages and quotes, and to compare two distinct thoughts. Don't be thrown; these questions tend to boil down to the dynamics of how government operates within a political environment. For example, you may be asked how interest groups attempt to influence policy making in Congress and the bureaucracy or how the president attempts to influence Congress through public opinion. The test writers want to know whether you understand the general principles that guide U.S. government and the making of public policy.

In addition to the multiple-choice questions, there are four mandatory free-response questions. You'll have a total of 100 minutes to answer all of them. You should spend approximately 25 minutes per question, but be aware that you must manage your own time. Additional time spent on one question will reduce the

This breakdown represents the latest information to come from the College Board about their new test, which will debut in May 2019. All of the information here is in alignment with what has been announced thus far, but because it's possible that there may be some last-minute adaptations after we've gone to print, please check your online student tools for any late-breaking news!

We also strongly recommend checking the College Board's official AP Students website for any other free resources they may have released as the test approaches.

https://apstudent.college-board.org/apcourse/ap-united-states-government-and-politics

time that you have left to answer the others. Writing more than is necessary to answer the question will not earn you extra points.

HOW THE AP U.S. GOVERNMENT AND POLITICS EXAM IS SCORED

The graders assign each of your free-response answers a numerical score. Weighing the average on the free responses and the score on the multiple-choice questions each as 50%, the graders create a final score from a low of 1 to a high of 5. The chart below tells you what that final score means.

Score (Meaning)	Percentage of test takers receiving this score	Equivalent grade in a first-year college course	Credit granted for this score?
5 (extremely qualified)	11.1%	A	Most schools
4 (well qualified)	12.4%	A–, B+, B	Most schools
3 (qualified)	25.7%	B–, C+, C	Some do, but some don't
2 (possibly qualified)	24.6%	C–	Very few do
1 (no recommendation)	26.1%	D	No

The data above is from the College Board website and based on the May 2017 test administration.

To score your multiple-choice questions, award yourself one point for every correct answer, regardless of whether you guessed the answer or not. (You shouldn't have left any blanks, but if you did, they are worth nothing.)

The first administration of the AP U.S. Government and Politics's new exam is in May 2019, so the following conversion chart is an estimate based on previous years, and also based on you doing similarly well on the Section II free-response questions.

Multiple-Choice Raw Score	AP Score
0 to 19	1
20 to 26	2
27 to 33	3
34 to 39	4
40 to 45	5

How Will I Know?
Your dream college's website may list such information or you can contact the school's admission's department to verify AP exam score acceptance information.

Of course, if you follow our advice for how to write a good free-response essay, you could score higher on the free-response section than on the multiple-choice section and thus potentially increase your final score by one point.

OVERVIEW OF CONTENT TOPICS

As mentioned earlier, questions on the exam fall into five main units:

- Foundations of American Democracy
- Interaction Among Branches of Government
- Civil Liberties and Civil Rights
- American Political Ideologies and Beliefs
- Political Participation

Here are some key topics that fall into each of these categories:

Foundations of American Democracy	• the political and economic circumstances at the time of the framing of the Constitution • the motivations of the framers • the weaknesses of the Articles of Confederation • the strengths of the Constitution • separation of powers • the nature and political impact of federalism • principles of democratic government • system of checks and balances
Interaction Among Branches of Government	• the structure and function of the legislature, executive branch, judiciary, and bureaucracy • the structural and political interrelationships of the institutions of government • the connections between the national government, citizens, political parties, public opinion, elections, interest groups, and the states • the process of making public policy • citizen participation in policy making • the interactions between Congress, the courts, and the bureaucracy on policy making • the impact of elections in policy making • the participants in domestic and economic policy making • the limitations of domestic and economic policy making

Civil Liberties and Civil Rights	• substantive and procedural rights and liberties • the impact of the Fourteenth Amendment on rights and liberties • the consequences of judicial interpretation on rights and liberties
American Political Ideologies and Beliefs	• the ideological beliefs people maintain regarding their government • political socialization • public opinion and its impact on policy • how and why citizens vote as they do • the methods of political participation • the reasons citizens disagree over political beliefs and behavior
Political Participation	• what parties do and how they operate • how parties are organized • how parties link citizens to government • how parties help make and use the rules of elections • how electoral laws affect the outcome of elections • what interest groups do and what makes them effective • the role of PACs and their impact on the political process • the types of mass media • the purpose of the media • the impact of the media on the political agenda

As you can see, the primary focus of the test is the nuts and bolts of the federal government. The test also emphasizes political activity—the factors that influence individual political beliefs, the conditions that determine how and why people vote, and the process by which groups form and attempt to influence the government. Be aware that the test is always changing—especially for the 2019 iteration, so keep an eye on every area, such as constitutional issues and civil rights, which are very important for providing context to the new scenario-based questions.

PRIMARY SOURCES

One thing the course now expects from students is that they've learned the major details of fifteen different Supreme Court cases and that they are familiar with the ideas behind nine foundational documents. We touch on and reference these in the Part V content review, but you'll definitely want to go above-and-beyond in familiarizing yourself with the following:

Marbury v. Madison
McCulloch v. Maryland
Schenck v. United States
Brown v. Board of Education
Baker v. Carr
Engel v. Vitale
Gideon v. Wainwright
Tinker v. Des Moines Independent Community School District
New York Times Co. v. United States
Wisconsin v. Yoder
Roe v. Wade
Shaw v. Reno
United States v. Lopez
McDonald v. Chicago
Citizens United v. Federal Election Commission

The Declaration of Independence
The Articles of Confederation
The Constitution of the United States
The Federalist Papers Nos. 10, 51, 70, and 78
Brutus No. 1
"Letter from a Birmingham Jail"

Other Sources

While the primary sources listed above are the only ones that you'll be required to know for the exam, you should take the opportunity to widen your familiarity with other documents.

Reading political articles in newspapers and magazines, particularly those that present accompanying information in visual formats, can be helpful when preparing for the Quantitative Analysis questions. The Argument Essay in Section II allows you to cite from other sources, and the SCOTUS Comparison question will refer to lesser-known cases (although it will provide you with all the necessary facts).

If you do your own reading—and we highly recommend it!—make sure that you take into account the credibility of your sources. If you intend to reference anything on the test, make sure these other texts are both credible and reliable. That is, make sure they've been fact-checked and that they are both well-sourced and up-to-date.

Where Trust Is a Must
Just because something is on the Internet does not mean that it is a source you should use in a Free Response section. As a rule of thumb, think at least as critically about web content as you would a Qualitative Analysis question and trace it back to a source.

HOW AP EXAMS ARE USED

Different colleges use AP exams in different ways, so it is important that you visit a particular college's website in order to determine how it accepts AP exam scores. The three items below represent the main ways in which AP exam scores can be used.

- **College Credit.** Some colleges will give you college credit if you receive a high score on an AP exam. These credits count toward your graduation requirements, meaning that you can take fewer courses while in college. Given the cost of college, this could be quite a benefit, indeed.

- **Satisfy Requirements.** Some colleges will allow you to "place out" of certain requirements if you do well on an AP exam, even if they do not give you actual college credits. For example, you might not need to take an introductory-level course, or perhaps you might not need to take a class in a certain discipline at all.

- **Admissions Plus.** Even if your AP exam will not result in college credit or even allow you to place out of certain courses, most colleges will respect your decision to push yourself by taking an AP course or, even, an AP exam outside of a course. A high score on an AP exam shows mastery of more difficult content than is typically taught in many high school courses, and colleges may take that into account during the admissions process.

Want to know which colleges are best for you? Check out The Princeton Review's College Advisor app to build your ideal college list and find your perfect college fit! Available for free in the iOS App Store and Google Play Store.

OTHER RESOURCES

There are many resources available to help you improve your score on the AP U.S. Government and Politics Exam, not the least of which are your **teachers**. If you are taking an AP course, you may be able to get extra attention from your teacher, such as feedback on your essays. If you are not in an AP course, you can reach out to a teacher who teaches AP U.S. Government and Politics to ask if he or she will review your essays or otherwise help you master the content.

Another wonderful resource is **AP Students**, the official website of the AP exams. The scope of the information available on this site is quite broad and includes the following:

- a course description, which include further details on what content is covered by the exam
- sample questions from the AP U.S. Government and Politics Exam
- free-response question prompts and multiple-choice questions from previous years

More AP Info Online!
We have put together even more goodies for a handful of AP Exam subjects. For short quizzes, high level AP course and test information, and expert advice, head over to www.princetonreview. com/college-advice/ advanced-placement- resources.

Another Course? Of Course!

If you can't get enough AP U.S. Government and Politics and want to review this material with an expert, we also offer an online Cram Course that you can sign up for here: https://www.princetonreview.com/college/ap-test-prep.

The AP Students home page address is: https://apstudent.collegeboard.org/home.

Finally, **The Princeton Review** offers tutoring, small group instruction, and admissions counseling. Our expert instructors can help you refine your strategic approach and enhance your content knowledge. For more information, call 1-800-2REVIEW.

DESIGNING YOUR STUDY PLAN

In Part I, you identified some areas of potential improvement. Let's now delve further into your performance on Practice Test 1, with the goal of developing a study plan appropriate to your needs and time commitment.

Read the answers and explanations associated with the multiple-choice questions (starting at page 31). After you have done so, respond to the following questions:

- Review the topic chart on page 46. Next to each topic, indicate your rank of the topic as follows: "1" means "I need a lot of work on this," "2" means "I need to beef up my knowledge," and "3" means "I know this topic well."

- How many days/weeks/months away is your exam?

- What time of day is your best, most focused study time?

- How much time per day/week/month will you devote to preparing for your exam?

- When will you do this preparation? (Be as specific as possible: Mondays and Wednesdays from 3:00 P.M. to 4:00 P.M., for example)

- Based on the answers above, will you focus on strategy (Part IV) or content (Part V) or both?

- What are your overall goals for using this book?

Part IV
Test-Taking Strategies for the AP U.S. Government and Politics Exam

PREVIEW

Review your Practice Test 1 results and then respond to the following questions:

- How many multiple-choice questions did you miss even though you knew the answer?

- On how many multiple-choice questions did you guess blindly?

- How many multiple-choice questions did you miss after eliminating some answers and guessing based on the remaining answers?

- Did you find any of the free-response questions easier or harder than the others—and, if so, why?

HOW TO USE THE CHAPTERS IN THIS PART

Before reading the following strategy chapters, think about what you are doing now. As you read and engage in the directed practice, be sure to think critically about the ways you can change your approach.

Chapter 1
How to
Approach
Multiple-Choice
Questions

THE BASICS

Section I of the AP U.S. Government and Politics Exam consists of 55 multiple-choice questions, and you will be given 80 minutes to complete it. The types of question are as follows:

Knowledge Questions: Nearly half of the AP Exam is made up of multiple-choice questions that test your recall of terms, principles, processes, institutions, policies, and behaviors, and how well you can apply those to a variety of political scenarios.

Quantitative Analysis: Roughly 30% of the test is given over to the analysis of charts, tables, infographics, maps, diagrams, and political cartoons.

Qualitative Analysis: About 13% of the test is passage-based. You'll be presented with two short excerpts of between 100–150 words, each of which will then be followed by 3–4 questions.

Comparison Questions: About 9% of the questions ask you to select the choice that best identifies a similarity or difference for two political concepts.

Each of these questions has four choices: (A), (B), (C), and (D). Only one of these is correct for each question. There is, however, no penalty for getting a question wrong; your total score is assessed entirely by the number of questions you get correct, so make sure you don't leave any questions blank!

In short, you're being asked to do what you've done on many other multiple-choice exams: pick the best answer and then fill in the corresponding bubble on a separate sheet of paper. You will *not* be given credit for answers you record in your test booklet (by circling them, for example) but do not fill in on your answer sheet.

Knowledge Questions

The majority of questions in the multiple-choice section of the test are testing the various AP Government topics that you would have learned in class. Here's an example.

1. In which of the following situations can a president use a pocket veto?

    (A) Congress amends a bill.
    (B) The president is out of the country.
    (C) A bill passes Congress with a greater than two-thirds majority in each house.
    (D) A bill reaches the president's desk within 10 days of the end of a congressional session.

Here's How to Crack It

1.   **D**   Quickly brainstorm the key term, "pocket veto." The answer choices mostly deal with *when* a veto can be applied, so focus your recall on that aspect. In general, a veto is applied to something that has already been passed, so (A) can be eliminated. Choice (B) can also be eliminated, as a veto is an action—it has nothing to do with a president's physical location. Choice (C) is tricky, because it refers to the fact that a veto can be overridden by a two-thirds majority vote in each house, but has nothing to do with when the veto can be used. The remaining choice correctly identifies the "pocket" part of the veto, indicating that it is a special kind of veto in which the president simply runs out the clock on Congress, an act the president can only do when there are fewer than 10 days left in a congressional session (as the bill would otherwise become law after 10 days). Choice (D) is correct.

Quantitative Analysis

There will be several questions at the beginning of the section asking you to interpret a graph or chart. These questions come in paired sets: first you'll see the image, and then answer two separate questions pertaining to it.

Charts and Tables

For statistics-based questions, the first is often very direct, simply asking you to interpret the data, while the second may ask about causes, effects, or require you to make knowledge-based judgments. You will *not* have to answer one of the two questions correctly in order to answer the other, so even if you can't figure out the first, you should still read the second.

Be sure that you don't over-interpret the data. The correct answers will be indisputably supported by the information in the chart.

Here's an example.

Average, highest, and lowest approval ratings, by percentage of all eligible voters, for U.S. presidents, 1953 to 1974			
	Average	**Highest**	**Lowest**
Eisenhower	65	79	48
Kennedy	70	83	56
Johnson	55	79	35
Nixon	49	67	24

2. Which of the following conclusions can be drawn from the information presented in the chart above?

   (A) Eisenhower was the most consistently popular president in the nation's history.

   (B) Kennedy received greater congressional support for his programs than did any other president during the period in question.

   (C) Nixon's lowest approval rating was the result of the Watergate scandal.

   (D) The difference between Johnson's highest and lowest approval ratings was the greatest for any president during the period in question.

3. Which of the following explains why, despite shifts in public approval, incumbent presidents usually win reelection?

   (A) The approval ratings of incumbent presidents typically rise in the months immediately before an election.

   (B) Incumbents generally have better name recognition and campaign finance advantages than their opponents.

   (C) Incumbent presidents since 1974 have experienced generally higher approval ratings than their predecessors.

   (D) National polls do not accurately capture the true sentiments of voters in presidential elections.

Here's How to Crack It

2. **D** Charts and tables require you to find a needle in a haystack. As with all questions paired with charts/tables/passages, read the question first to find out what the question wants you to discover. The first question after the chart/table/passage will always ask a simple knowledge question. For #2, you need to draw a conclusion about the data as a whole. Now take a look at the answer choices. Immediately notice that (A), (B), and (C) all refer to information not present in the table. Even before looking at (D), we know it is the correct answer.

3. **B** The second question after a chart/table/passage will typically ask you to make an inference about the information or make a connection between the information and what you learned throughout the AP U.S. Government and Politics course. Quickly skim the question to see whether you'll need to refer to any data and, if you don't, save time by ignoring the image entirely. Choice (C) seems odd, as some of America's most beloved presidents served before 1974. So does (D), as most polls, if done correctly, are accurate. Left with (A) and (B), choose the one that makes the most sense. During an election, the incumbent president's opponent is likely to put out attack ads, which means that the president's approval ratings are likelier to drop than to rise; eliminate (A). However, the incumbent president, having likely served for a full term at this point, will have the advantage of being already established as a presidential candidate, and will generally be more recognized and better funded, which makes (B) the correct answer.

Maps, Diagrams, and Cartoons

A few questions will ask you to interpret an illustration, often a map or a political cartoon. The key is not to try to read too much between the lines. Here's an example.

Source: Adam Zyglis, PoliticalCartoons.com

4. Which of the following principles of government is most relevant to the cartoon?

    (A) judicial restraint
    (B) checks and balances
    (C) federalism
    (D) executive privilege

4. **B**   When analyzing a political cartoon, you need to first understand what the cartoon portrays. On the left, a man (President George G. Bush) stands in front of GITMO, the prison camp in Guantanamo Bay, Cuba. On the right of a line marked "Constitution" a judge holds up a document imprinted with the words "Habeas Corpus –S.C." *Habeas corpus* refers to American's right to appear in front of a judge and not be held indefinitely without trial. Now that we know the basics, we can determine which principal of government is relevant to the cartoon. Choice (A) can be eliminated as judicial restraint refers to the actions of the Supreme Court; the cartoon appears to be criticizing the president's actions. The president is standing outside the "U.S. Constitution" line. Choice (C) can be eliminated as the cartoon does not depict the relationship between the federal government and the states. Choice (D) can be eliminated as the president's actions or words do not suggest Executive Privilege, the president withholding information from the public in the name of national security. As a result, (B) is correct; the conflict between the president and Supreme Court as depicted in the cartoon is an example of checks and balances. At GITMO, President Bush attempted to keep prisoners indefinitely, but the Supreme Court invoked habeas corpus.

Qualitative Analysis

As with the Quantitative Analysis format, Qualitative Analysis questions come in sets. The difference is that instead of being about images or data, these are based on short text passages. One or two of these questions will simply test your comprehension of the meaning of the passage, which means you can solve these based entirely on the provided context, while the remaining questions will require you to apply outside knowledge. Here is an example:

THERE is an idea, which is not without its advocates, that a vigorous Executive is inconsistent with the genius of republican government…Energy in the Executive is a leading character in the definition of good government. It is essential to the protection of the community against foreign attacks; it is not less essential to the steady administration of the laws; to the protection of property against those irregular and high-handed combinations which sometimes interrupt the ordinary course of justice; to the security of liberty against the enterprises and assaults of ambition, of faction, and of anarchy. Every man the least conversant in Roman story, knows how often that republic was obliged to take refuge in the absolute power of a single man, under the formidable title of Dictator, as well against the intrigues of ambitious individuals who aspired to the tyranny, and the seditions of whole classes of the community whose conduct threatened the existence of all government, as against the invasions of external enemies who menaced the conquest and destruction of Rome.

—Alexander Hamilton, Federalist No. 70 (1788)

5. Which of the following statements best summarizes Hamilton's reasoning for why the new nation requires an executive?

(A) The United States must model itself on the Roman Republic.
(B) The Executive can act decisively to protect the United States.
(C) Giving the Legislative Branch all the power would lead to ruin.
(D) The Legislative Branch lacks Energy.

6. Which of the following events from the 20th century would support Hamilton's argument?

(A) President Wilson creating the League of Nations
(B) President Nixon breaking the law during the Watergate Scandal
(C) President Roosevelt's leadership during World War II
(D) President Regan signing tax cuts

Here's How to Crack It

5. **B** With a passage-based Qualitative Analysis question, you'll want to start by skimming the questions so that when you back and read the text, you know what you're looking for. Begin by seeking out "Executive." You can also cross out any choices that aren't directly claimed in the passage, since you're being asked to summarize it: this means (C) and (D) can be eliminated. Choice (A) is tricky, as Hamilton does talk about the Roman Republic, but as you dig deeper, the text reveals that Hamilton mentions this model as a warning, which means you can eliminate (A). The correct answer is (B): like the leaders of the Roman Republic, the Executive defends the United States from external and internal threats.

6. **C** While you may choose to skip around through the test, it's a good idea to do paired questions like this one in order, because you can take some of the work you've already done—summarizing the passage—in order to now find a historical event to link it with. Choices (A) and (D) deal with topics that Hamilton does not address in his defense of the Executive, and so both can be eliminated. Choice (B) can also be ruled out, as President Nixon's crimes would be an argument against Hamilton's opinions of the Executive. Only the correct answer, (C), calls back to Hamilton: "It is essential to the protection of the community against foreign attacks."

Comparison Questions

These questions will present you with two columns containing two similar or opposing ideas or Supreme Court cases. Your job is to choose the answer which matches the right characteristics to both columns. Here is an example:

7. Which of the following is an accurate comparison of the themes and views expressed in *Federalist #10* and *Brutus #1*?

	Federalist #10	*Brutus #1*
(A)	Was written by James Madison	Warned against the "mischiefs of faction"
(B)	Advocated for the delegation of authority to elected representatives	Advocated for a strong federal government
(C)	Warned of the dangers of a large, centralized government	Warned of the inefficiency of power diffused to individual states
(D)	Supported the notion of a large republic in order to control factionalism	Was written by an Anti-Federalist

Here's How to Crack It

7. **D** In comparison questions, if one part of the comparison is wrong, that whole answer is wrong. Before diving into the options, remind yourself that Federalists were in favor of a powerful government and a large republic. The Anti-Federalists, which included Brutus, were for the

opposite. Remembering these few bits of information help you eliminate (B) and (C). If you're stuck between the remaining two choices, pick the one that you're most confident about; would an Anti-Federalist have warned against "the mischief of faction"? Would a Federalist have supported a large republic? The correct answer is (D).

--------------------○--------------------

HOW TO CRACK THE MULTIPLE-CHOICE SECTION

The AP U.S. Government and Politics Exam is, by Educational Testing Service (ETS) standards, a straightforward test. Unlike the SAT, for example, the questions and answer choices on the AP U.S. Government and Politics Exam are not designed to trick you. These questions are not subjective, but are based on the content you've learned in this course, and which you can review in this book. You should, however, not be lulled into believing the test is easy because it covers material that can be readily obtained from reading the newspaper and watching television. This secondhand information is not enough to ensure a passing grade on the exam. While being able to recall specific examples may help to flesh out your free-response questions, the majority of knowledge you'll need is academic, so be sure that you review your textbook, especially for the topics that you feel least comfortable with.

In short, if you've paid attention in class, you should do well on this test. That said, if you haven't paid close attention, it's not too late, especially since you have this book! You may still be able to master the material if you review intensively. You can use the subject review in this book as your guide, helping you to remember what you may have forgotten. (This is what Donald Rumsfeld may have called a "known unknown.") Ultimately, you will do better if you know what to expect of the test. On the next few pages, we'll discuss some things that all AP U.S. Government and Politics Exam multiple-choice sections have in common.

The Question Types Are Varied

As you can see from the breakdown of question types, the new AP U.S. Government and Politics Exam has a lot of complicated ways in which to ask what might otherwise be familiar questions. You may find some questions easier than others, or you may prefer to work with the context provided by data analysis and passage questions than with the more formal knowledge questions. You are allowed to answer questions in any order that you wish, so don't feel as if you have to start with the material that slows you down.

There Are No Trivial Pursuit Questions on This Exam

Here's some more good news. The AP U.S. Government and Politics Exam doesn't ask about trivial matters. You will probably never see a question on the exam such as this one.

8. The American equivalent of the British Exchequer is the

(A) House Finance Committee
(B) Internal Revenue Service
(C) United States Mint
(D) Office of Management and Budget

To answer this question correctly, you would have to be fairly familiar with the British government. The AP U.S. Government and Politics Exam does not require such knowledge. This question is atypical in another way as well: it does not have a varied selection of possible answers. Even if you had known that the British Exchequer has something to do with money and government, you could not have eliminated any of the incorrect answers on this question. On an actual AP test, at least one of these answers would have been completely unrelated to finance, and you could have eliminated them to guess from among the remaining answers.

Process of Elimination

For questions that you do not confidently know the correct answer to, it is important to utilize the Process of Elimination (POE). This highly effective method for solving a multiple-choice exam relies on the fact that incorrect answers are much easier to identify than correct ones. Try it! Chances are that when you look for the correct answer, you'll try to justify why an answer might be correct. That's nice and forgiving, but what you need is brutal honesty. Look for the wrong answers, and then eliminate them with extreme prejudice. If you've done your job well, only the correct answer will be left standing at the end; at the very least, if you have to guess from only two or three choices as opposed to four, you'll be increasing your odds of answering difficult questions correctly.

Common Sense Can Help

Sometimes answers on the multiple-choice section contradict common sense. Eliminate those answers because common sense works on the AP U.S. Government and Politics Exam.

Be a Shark
Good test takers take multiple-choice tests aggressively. They sift through the answer choices, discard incorrect answers without remorse, guess with impunity, and prowl the test searching for questions they can answer, all with the tenacity and ruthlessness of a shark. All right, maybe that's a bit overdramatic, but you get the point.

Think about which of the answer choices to the question below go against common sense.

———————————◯———————————

9. Which of the following best explains the way in which federal legislation is implemented?

(A) Most laws outline general goals and restrictions, which the federal bureaucracy interprets and translates into specific guidelines.
(B) The manner of implementing federal legislation is negotiated between a joint congressional committee and a presidential advisory committee.
(C) After a bill is signed, all disputes pertaining to its implementation are decided by the congressional committee responsible for the bill.
(D) The details of implementing congressional legislation are worked out in the courts on a case-by-case basis.

Here's How to Crack It

9. **A** You should have been able to apply common sense to eliminate (C) and (D) pretty quickly. Congressional committees work on bills *before* they reach the floor for a vote, and this work takes up all their time. They would hardly have time to hear all disputes concerning bills that have already passed. Furthermore, such a system would violate the system of checks and balances, because the responsibility for interpreting laws belongs to the judiciary. All the same, the details of congressional legislation could never be worked out in the courts. There would simply be too many cases for the courts to be able to process them all. Similarly, (B) contradicts the principle of separation of powers. It is the executive branch's responsibility to enforce the law; it is not required to confer with Congress on the manner in which it performs this task. The correct answer, by POE, is (A).

———————————◯———————————

Summary

o   Rest assured that the AP U.S. Government and Politics Exam tests a relatively small amount of information. Be confident: you can review this material fairly quickly and still get a good grade on this exam.

o   Familiarize yourself with the different types of questions that will appear in the multiple-choice section.

o   Remember that most of the questions on this exam are of medium difficulty. The test does not bother with trivial matters or minute exceptions to general trends. The test writers want to know that you understand the general principles underlying U.S. government.

o   Tailor your studying to suit the test's most common topics. Don't spend a lot of time studying civil rights and civil liberties until you have completely reviewed the workings of the federal government and the basics of political behavior.

o   Use POE on all but the easiest questions. Once you have worked on a question, eliminated some answers, and convinced yourself that you cannot eliminate any other incorrect answers, you should guess and move on to the next question.

o   Use common sense.

o   Remember not to leave any questions blank. There is no "guessing penalty" on this exam!

Chapter 2
How to
Approach
Free-Response
Questions

OVERVIEW OF THE FREE-RESPONSE SECTION

You may be surprised to see the words "free response" at the start of this chapter. What is a "free response," anyway? The first thing to be aware of is that this response is hardly free. The College Board wants a very specific type of writing, and it is one that you might not be used to. Forget the idea of crafting a fine piece of writing that convinces the reader of your opinion. Instead, think "just the facts, ma'am." Your basic goal here is to read the questions and answer them to the best of your ability. Don't get too hung up on crafting a perfectly organized essay with transitional phrases—this section of the AP should almost stand for "Answer the Prompt"—just crank out a straightforward, clear answer and show the graders that you know your stuff.

You will have 100 minutes to answer four questions, so be sure to budget your time well. Give as much detail as necessary to answer the question, but no more! Above all, don't worry. So long as you know the basics of American government, this section should be a breeze.

PLANNING AND WRITING YOUR FREE RESPONSE

There are two essential components to writing a successful timed free response. The first is to plan what you are going to write before you start writing. The second is to use a number of tried-and-true writing techniques that will make your response better organized, better thought out, and better written.

Step 1: Know The Question
Read the question carefully and figure out what you are being asked.

Step 2: Brainstorm the Topic
Then, brainstorm for a minute or two. In your test booklet, write down everything that comes to mind about the subject; there is room on the back pages of the booklet and in the blank space at the bottom of the question pages. Think of a question as a lock; this is the point at which you're shaking out your mental pockets to try and find the right key.

Step 3: Match Your Knowledge to the Question

Look at your notes and consider the results of your brainstorming session as you decide which points you will argue in your response. Tailor your argument to the information, but don't make an argument that you know is wrong or with which you disagree. The readers won't know if you're handicapping yourself or writing to your strengths, so stick with what you know so as to maximize your chance of getting full credit on a response: graders only see whether you have a thorough understanding of the topic as written.

Step 4: Answer the Question(s)

Readers are looking for substantive examples, so don't generalize or beat around the bush. **Describe, explain,** and **identify** what's being asked for, and **provide** anything that you're prompted for. If there are multiple parts, clearly label each and address each in turn. In short, be short! (This approach will be a little more in-depth for the argument essay, but we'll get to that in the next section!)

WHAT ARE THE FREE-RESPONSE QUESTIONS LIKE?

The AP U.S. Government and Politics free-response section contains four free-response questions. Each counts equally. The entire free-response section counts as 50% of your examination grade. At least one of the essay prompts will test your knowledge of public policy initiatives. This is most likely to occur in the Concept Application Question.

The Concept Application Question

The Concept Application question features a short passage that outlines a scenario, followed by three related questions. The quote will typically be pertinent to a law or constitutional amendment that you have learned about in your AP Government class.

"There is recognition abroad that we are in many ways a sexist country. Sexism is judging people by their sex when sex doesn't matter. Sexism is intended to rhyme with racism. Both have been used to keep the powers that be in power… Women who get good jobs do it by outsexing the sexism. They persuade the boss that a woman's intuition is needed. Or that women pay more attention to detail. They know it isn't so, but they use the sexist arguments to get around prejudice."

Caroline Bird, "On Being Born Female",
published on November 15, 1968

1. After reading the scenario, respond to A, B, and C below:

    (a) Describe a law which was passed to legally address the problem described in the quote.
    (b) For the law described in Part A, evaluate the extent of its effectiveness.
    (c) In the context of the scenario, explain how the actions of the federal government can be helped or hindered by the states.

Step 1: Know the Question

In the case of a Concept Application question, in which text has been provided, the scenario itself is a part of the question. Read through the scenario, and then after reading Part A, go back through the scenario, underlining key words and determining the central message or theme. In this case, Caroline Bird is defining sexism and comparing it to racism, specifically mentioning the struggle to compete in the workplace.

Step 2: Brainstorm the Topic

Throw out a list of laws and/or constitutional policies that may pertain to sexism, either in general or specifically at the workplace. You might think of the Equal Pay Act of 1963, the Lily Ledbetter Fair Pay Act of 2009, or even Title IX of the Higher Education Act of 1973. If these are unfamiliar, you could even use the Civil Rights Act of 1964, which has undoubtedly promoted more fair treatment for women of color.

Step 3: Match Your Knowledge to the Question

Choose the law or amendment that you know the most about. Note that you're going to have to answer follow-up Part B and Part C about whatever you choose, so stick with the strongest core of your knowledge base. This applies to either/or options like "helped or hindered"; choose the approach that is easiest to defend given your brainstormed knowledge.

Step 4: Answer the Question(s)

Describe the law you've chosen. **Evaluate** its effectiveness. For the final part, **explain** either how a state has hindered or helped the federal government.

The Quantitative Analysis Question

The Quantitative Analysis question will provide you with a chart, graph, or table with numerical data in it. Typically, one or two of the questions will simply ask you to accurately interpret the data as given, while the other remaining question(s) will require your outside knowledge. Here is an example:

As of the printing of this book, the College Board has not yet released any sample responses for the new iteration of their free-response questions. The following accurately describes what the questions will look like and presents a targeted list of strategies based to maximize your score on the rubric for each type of question. However, please be sure to check your online student tools for any late-breaking updates!

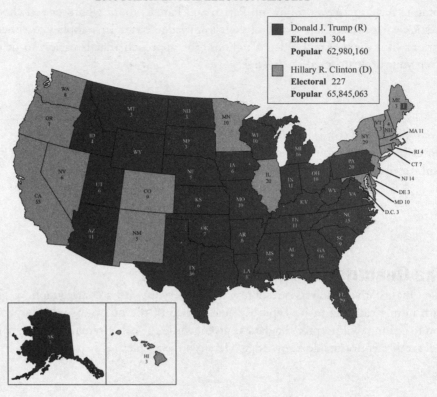

2016 PRESIDENTIAL ELECTION RESULTS

Donald J. Trump (R)
Electoral 304
Popular 62,980,160

Hillary R. Clinton (D)
Electoral 227
Popular 65,845,063

2. Use the information graphic to answer the questions.

    (a) Identify a regional trend in presidential elections
         as illustrated by the graphic.
    (b) Explain the discrepancy in each candidate's
         accrual of electoral votes and popular votes
         in the 2016 presidential election and how
         that discrepancy affected the outcome of the
         election.
    (c) Identify one campaign strategy presidential
         candidates might use to influence the outcome of
         electoral votes in various states or regions.

Step 1: Know the Question

When dealing with a Quantitative Analysis question, the graphic is a part of the
question. Pay close attention to the labels, units, and sidebars provided. In this
case, one shade represents Republican votes, while the other represents Democrat
votes. Note that electoral votes are shown on the map, while the key shows the
popular votes and candidate names. Read through the questions, and circle any
relevant information in the graphic that could be used to answer Part A or Part B.

Step 2: Brainstorm the Topic

You only really need to brainstorm when outside knowledge is required, so just look at Part C. Think about campaign strategies you've learned about in class. Perhaps you have heard of presidential candidates campaigning heavily in swing states while neglecting reliably Republican or Democrat states.

Step 3: Match Your Knowledge to the Question

Michigan, Pennsylvania, and New Hampshire are all swing states. You could point out that Trump campaigned heavily in Michigan and Pennsylvania to capture the swing electoral votes in those states. You could suggest that Clinton did not put enough resources into those states, thus losing the electoral race.

Step 4: Answer the Question(s)

Identify a trend, referring specifically to regions shown in the graphic. **Explain** the difference between electoral votes and popular votes by calling out the electoral worth of each state on the graphic. **Identify**, using everything you've brainstormed, an electoral strategy that may have been used.

The SCOTUS Comparison Question

The SCOTUS Comparison question will require you to read a description of a historical Supreme Court case and then compare or contrast it with another case. Chances are, the case provided in the description will be an obscure case you have not seen before, while the second case will be more familiar, having been covered in your AP Government class. The two cases will be related in topic, but will contain important differences. Your job is to identify the similarities and differences and use them as the primary evidence with which to answer the questions.

Here is an example:

3. The Jehovah's Witnesses are a small Christian
    denomination which has existed in the United States
    since the mid-19th Century. Since they believe that the
    law of God supersedes that of worldly governments,
    they take literally Exodus 20:4, which says: "Thou shalt
    not make unto thee any graven images... thou shalt
    not bow down thyself to them nor serve them." They
    consider that the American flag is an "image" within
    this command and thus their children refuse to recite the
    Pledge of Allegiance or participate in the morning flag
    salute at public schools. In the 1930s and 1940s, children
    of Jehovah's Witnesses throughout the country had been
    disciplined or even expelled from school for taking this
    stand. Parents of such children were prosecuted for
    upholding their children's actions.

    In 1943, the Supreme Court decision in *West Virginia
    State Board of Education v. Barnette* held that the
    Constitution protects students from being forced by
    public schools to salute the American flag or say the
    Pledge of Allegiance in public school. The majority
    opinion in *Barnette* is considered one of the Court's most
    decisive statements regarding the Bill of Rights.

    (a) Identify the constitutional clause that is common
        to both *West Virginia State Board of Education
        v. Barnette* (1943) and *Tinker v. Des Moines
        Independent Community School District*
        (1969).
    (b) Based on the constitutional clause identified
        in part A, describe how *Tinker v. Des Moines
        Independent Community School District* further
        expanded and clarified the rights at stake in
        *West Virginia State Board of Education v.
        Barnette.*
    (c) Describe one circumstance, real or hypothetical,
        in which the rights established by *West Virginia
        State Board of Education v. Barnette* and *Tinker
        v. Des Moines Independent Community School
        District* may still be limited.

Step 1: Know the Question

For a SCOTUS Comparison question, you need to *identify* the known (required)
SCOTUS case and the obscure one described in the prompt, as well as the main
issue covered by the case; in this case, freedom of speech in schools *(Tinker)*. This
is the longest of the essay prompts, so you may want to underline key terms as you
go through, and consult with Part A to assess whether you should be looking for a
similarity or a difference between the two cases—in this case, you want one that is
"common," or similar.

Step 2: Brainstorm the Topic

On a SCOTUS Comparison question, you're given everything you need to know about one case, so you really only need to brainstorm on the second case, the one that was a required Supreme Court case from your class. You also don't need to brainstorm *everything* about that case—only the portions that are similar (or different) from the one that you've been given. Here, the main similarity is freedom of expression by underage school children.

Step 3: Match Your Knowledge

For Part A, you'll want to think about constitutional clauses that apply to both, such as the First Amendment—the freedom of speech. (There might not always be more than one amendment.) You'll also want to think about differences between the two, such as the way in which *Tinker* allowed for discretionary freedom of expression (wearing black armbands to protest the Vietnam War), while *Barnette* was simply concerned with the unconstitutionality of compelling school children to engage in enforced speech (saluting the flag). Finally, for Part C, you'll want to consider various exceptions to the law, such as how schools still restrict speech in certain situations. If nothing comes to mind, remember that you can use hypothetical situations; try to imagine a context in which they could be challenged.

Step 4: Answer the Question(s)

Identify the common constitutional clause, being specific. Describe the differences between how *Tinker* and *Barnette* distinguished those rights. Using either a real-world or hypothetical example, describe how the rights granted by *Tinker* might still be limited.

The Argument Essay

Although the Argument Essay is worth no more than the other three free-response questions, the College Board suggests that you spend up to 40 minutes writing this essay. That's because the directions are more detailed, and because you'll need to rely heavily on primary source material, both of which may require more time and effort. Here is an example:

4. Develop an argument that explains how effectively the United States government has used its legal authority to ensure civil rights for various social groups throughout its history.

   In your essay, you must:

   - Articulate a defensible claim or thesis that responds to the prompt and establishes a line of reasoning

   - Support your claim with at least two pieces of accurate and relevant information:

     ○ At least ONE piece of evidence must be from one of the following foundational documents:
       - Federalist No. 10
       - The Declaration of Independence
       - "Letter from a Birmingham Jail" (MLK)
     ○ Use a second piece of evidence from another foundation document from the list or your study of civil rights:
       - U.S. Constitution
       - Federalist No. 51
       - Federalist No. 78

   - Use reasoning to explain why your evidence supports your claim/thesis

   - Respond to an opposing or alternative perspective using refutation, concession, or rebuttal

Step 1: Know the Question

As opposed to the other free-response questions, which have targeted, specific questions, the Argument Essay largely leaves you to craft an argument on your own. There are still specific tasks, represented by each bullet, but there's no question. That's fine! It just means *you* get to ask it. In this case, rephrase the prompt and ask "When has the United States effectively used its legal authority to ensure civil rights?"

Step 2: Brainstorm the Topic

This step is also a bit different from those of the other free-response questions, because this time, there are restrictions on what you can use. Begin, then, by choosing which documents you'll use as evidence, allowing the one that's provided to help influence the direction of your brainstorming for the second piece of evidence. Perhaps you know "Letter from a Birmingham Jail" like the back of your hand, and perhaps you are well-versed in the Civil Rights Act of 1964. If you use the documents you know best, any argument you choose will be easier to support. Another reason to choose a topic that you're very familiar with is that you'll need to include an opposing perspective, which you should mull over now.

Step 3: Match Your Knowledge to the Question

The heart of your essay is a clear and complete thesis statement, so be sure you have this nailed down before you start writing. Typically, you will have the freedom to argue a "pro" stance, such as "The Federal Government has done an excellent job of defending civil rights throughout our recent history" or a "con" stance, such as "The Federal Government has generally neglected the civil rights of its citizens" or a moderated stance, such as "Despite some setbacks, the defense of the civil rights of all Americans is making greater strides over time." Choose the argument that you feel most comfortable with; you won't get any extra points for attempting a more nuanced, trickier essay. Because there's less structure here than there was on the other free-responses, you may also want to briefly outline how you'll connect each piece of evidence to your thesis statement.

Step 4: Answer the Question(s)

The prompt for the essay changes for each test, as do the foundational documents that you can choose between, but the directions themselves are largely the same. That means that you should always expect to have to **articulate** a thesis, **support** that thesis with evidence (**explaining** each connection in detail), and use **refutation, concession,** or **rebuttal** to respond to the opposing point of view.

AS YOU ARE WRITING

Here are some general tips to keep in mind as you write.

- **Keep sentences as simple as possible.** Long sentences get convoluted very quickly and may give both you and your graders a headache.

- **Use appropriate political science terminology.** Just as a picture is worth a thousand words, so too is the right word. That said, don't overdo it. Good writing doesn't have to be complicated, and you should only be using political terms because they help you more succinctly state your point. *Never* use a word if you are unsure of its meaning or proper usage. A malapropism may give your graders a good laugh, but it won't earn you any points and may cost you points, especially if it changes the intended meaning of your response.

- **Write clearly and neatly.** Here's an easy way to put graders in a good mood. Graders look at a lot of chicken scratches; it strains their eyes and makes them grumpy. Also keep in mind that they have as little as two minutes to read each response. Neatly written essays make them happy. When you cross out, do it neatly. Write in blue or black ink. If you're making any major changes—for example, if you want to insert a paragraph in the middle of your response—make sure you indicate them clearly.

- **Define your terms.** Most questions require you to use terms that mean different things to different people. One person's "liberal" is another person's "conservative" and yet another person's "radical." The folks who grade the test want to know what you think these terms mean. When you use them, define them. Take particular care to define any such terms that appear in the question. Almost all official College Board materials stress this point, so don't forget: define any term that you suspect can be defined in more than one way.

- **Use structural indicators to organize your paragraphs.** Another way to clarify your intentions is to organize your response around structural indicators. For example, if you are making a number of related points, number them ("First…Second…Finally…"). If you are attempting to compare and contrast two viewpoints, use the indicators "on the one hand" and "on the other hand" or "whereas."

- **Stick to your outline.** Unless you get an absolutely brilliant idea after you've brainstormed and while you're in the middle of writing, don't deviate from your outline. If you do, you risk muddying your response, or forgetting to answer the actual question. (That's why planning is so important!)

- **Back up your ideas with examples.** When a part of a question calls for evidence or reasoning, be prepared to provide it, and remember to always be specific, especially when indicating data points on the Quantitative Analysis question. Don't just throw half-baked ideas out there and hope that the reader will connect the dots for you. You will score big points if you substantiate your claims with facts, and remember that at least in the SCOTUS Comparison, you may be able to use hypothetical situations to illustrate your point, if no real-world ones spring to mind.

- **Answer each part of the question directly.** You can label each part of a question that you're responding to, but to make sure you stay on track and help the reader follow, it helps to restate that question in your response. For instance, if asked how Jefferson's concern about term limits is relevant today, begin by restating the question: "Jefferson's concern is relevant (or irrelevant) today."

- **Don't panic.** As you scan the four questions, you may well come to rest on the one that deals with a subject your teacher didn't cover or you didn't get around to studying. Don't worry: everyone finds some questions harder than others. To build your confidence, answer the question you find easiest before turning to the intimidating one.

- **Watch your time.** You need to average about 20 minutes per question for the first three prompts, with about 40 minutes devoted to the Argument Essay. The biggest mistake you can make, with the exception of skipping a question entirely, is failing to leave yourself enough time to answer all four questions. It's okay to spend as much as 25 minutes on a given question, but you'd better make it worthwhile. (You also probably don't want to spend that much time on the first essay or you'll feel rushed while writing the remaining three.)

- **If you draw a total blank on a question, take a deep breath and ask yourself what you do know about the topic.** You may realize that you know more than you think. Try to figure out what the question is asking and/or how you can approach it. Remember that you can get partial credit if you're only able to answer some parts correctly.

Summary

o   Use the four-step approach so that you stay on target for each free-response question.

o   Read each part carefully and be sure that you address each of them.

o   Mark up the question. You may bracket the core of the question, underline the operative words such as identify, discuss, describe, and analyze, or circle limiters like, "since 1992," "give one example," and "list three."

o   Look out for questions that require a definition of a term. If they ask for a definition, write one, and even if they don't, be sure that you understand what it means.

o   Always back up your statements with evidence.

o   Don't start writing until you have brainstormed and chosen a thesis if required. Consider writing a brief outline at least for the Argument Essay.

o   Write clearly and neatly. Don't use sentences that are too long. Toss in a couple of political science terms that you know you won't misuse. When in doubt, stick to simple syntax and vocabulary.

o   Take a watch to the exam and check it several times throughout the section so that you internalize how long you should be taking for each question.

o   Every piece of data that supports your argument should be linked to it. Do not just list information without relating it to the point you are trying to make.

Chapter 3
Using Time
Effectively to
Maximize Points

Very few students stop to think about how to improve their test-taking skills. Most assume that if they study hard, they will test well, and if they do not study, they will do poorly. Most students continue to believe this even after experience teaches them otherwise. Have you ever studied really hard for an exam, and then blown it on test day? Have you ever aced an exam for which you thought you weren't well prepared? Most students have had one, if not both, of these experiences. The lesson should be clear: factors other than your level of preparation influence your final test score. This chapter will provide you with some insights that will help you perform better on the AP U.S. Government and Politics Exam, as well as on other exams.

PACING AND TIMING

A big part of scoring well on an exam is working at a consistent pace. The worst mistake that inexperienced or unsavvy test takers make is to come to a question that stumps them, and rather than just skip it, they panic and stall. Time stands still when you're working on a question you cannot answer, and it is not unusual for students to waste five minutes on a single question (especially a question involving a graph or the word EXCEPT) because they are too stubborn to cut their losses. It is important to be aware of how much time you have spent on any given question and on the section on which you are working. There are several ways to improve your pacing and timing for the test.

- **Know your average pace.** While you prepare for your test, try to gauge how long you take on five, ten, or twenty questions. Knowing how long you spend on average per question will help you identify how many questions you can answer effectively and how best to pace yourself for the test.

- **Have a watch or clock nearby.** You are permitted to have a watch or clock nearby to help you keep track of time. It is important to remember, however, that constantly checking the clock is in itself a waste of time and can be distracting. Devise a plan. Try checking the clock after every fifteen or twenty questions to see if you are keeping the correct pace or whether you need to speed up; this will ensure that you're cognizant of the time while not permitting you to fall into the trap of dwelling on it.

- **Know when to move on.** Since all questions are scored equally, investing appreciable amounts of time on a single question is inefficient and can potentially deprive you of the chance to answer easier questions later on. If you are able to eliminate answer choices, do so, but don't worry about picking a random answer and moving on if you cannot find the correct answer. Remember, tests are like marathons; you do best when you work through them at a steady pace. You can always come back to a question you don't know. When you do, very often you will find that your previous mental block is gone, and you will wonder why the question perplexed you the first time around (as you gleefully move on to the next question). Even if you still don't know the answer, you will not have wasted valuable time that you could have spent on easier questions.

- **Be selective.** You don't have to do any of the questions in a given section in order. If you are stumped by an essay or multiple-choice question, skip it or choose a different one. In the section below, you will see that you may not have to answer every question correctly to achieve your desired score. Select the questions or essays that you can answer and work on them first. This will make you more efficient and give you the greatest chance of answering the most questions correctly.

- **Use Process of Elimination on multiple-choice questions.** Many times, one or more answer choices can be eliminated. Every answer choice that can be eliminated increases the odds that you will answer the question correctly. The section on multiple-choice questions will go through strategies to find these incorrect answer choices and increase your odds of choosing the correct answer.

Remember, when all the questions on a test are of equal value, no one question is that important. Your overall goal for pacing is to get the most questions correct. Finally, you should set a realistic goal for your final score. In the next section, we will break down how to achieve your desired score and ways of pacing yourself to do so.

GETTING THE SCORE YOU WANT

Depending on the score you need, it may be in your best interest not to try to work through every question. Check with the schools to which you are applying. Do you need a 3 to earn credit for the test? If you get a raw score of 43 (out of 60) on the multiple-choice section and do as well on the essays, you will get a 3.

AP exams in all subjects no longer include a guessing penalty of a quarter of a point for every incorrect answer. Instead, students are assessed solely on the total number of correct answers. A lot of AP materials, even those you receive in your AP class, may not include this information. It is really important to remember that if you are running out of time, you should fill in all the bubbles before the time for the multiple-choice section is up. Even if you don't plan to spend a lot of time on every question and even if you have no idea what the correct answer is, you need to fill something in.

Based on the most recent information available from the College Board, out of 120 points total for the four free-response and multiple-choice questions, students needed at least 93 points to get a score of 5, 82 points for a 4, 66 points for a 3, and 48 points for a 2.

There are multiple ways to achieve your desired score. It is important to remember that guessing is no longer penalized and that you must put in energy and effort on the essays to perform well.

TEST ANXIETY

Everybody experiences anxiety before and during an exam. To a certain extent, test anxiety can be helpful. Some people find that they perform more quickly and efficiently under stress. If you have ever pulled an all-nighter to write a paper and ended up doing good work, you know the feeling.

However, too much stress is definitely a bad thing. Hyperventilating during the test, for example, almost always leads to a lower score. If you find that you stress out during exams, here are a few preemptive actions you can take.

- **Take a reality check.** Evaluate your situation before the test begins. If you have studied hard, remind yourself that you are well prepared. Remember that many others taking the test are not as well prepared, and (in your classes, at least) you are being graded against them, so you have an advantage. If you didn't study, accept the fact that you will probably not ace the test. Make sure you get to every question that you know something about. Don't stress out or fixate on how much you don't know. Your job is to score as high as you can by maximizing the benefits of what you do know. In either scenario, it is best to think of a test as if it were a game. How can you get the most points in the time allotted to you? Always answer questions you can answer easily and quickly before you answer those that will take more time.

- **Try to relax.** Slow, deep breathing works for almost everyone. Close your eyes, take a few, slow, deep breaths, and concentrate on nothing but your inhalation and exhalation for a few seconds. This is a basic form of meditation, and it should help you to clear your mind of stress and, as a result, concentrate better on the test. If you have ever taken yoga classes, you probably know some other good relaxation techniques. Use them when you can (obviously, anything that requires leaving your seat and, say, assuming a handstand position won't be allowed by any but the most free-spirited proctors).

- **Eliminate as many surprises as you can.** Make sure you know where the test will be given, when it starts, what type of questions are going to be asked, and how long the test will take. You don't want to be worrying about any of these things on test day or, even worse, after the test has already begun.

The best way to avoid stress is to study both the test material and the test itself. Congratulations! By buying or reading this book, you are taking a major step toward a stress-free AP U.S. Government and Politics Exam.

REFLECT

Think about what you learned in Part IV, and respond to the following questions:

- How much time will you spend on multiple-choice questions?

- How will you change your approach to multiple-choice questions?

- What is your multiple-choice guessing strategy?

- How much time will you spend on the free-response questions?

- How will you change your approach to the free-response questions?

- Will you seek further help, outside of this book (such as a teacher, tutor, or AP Students), on how to approach multiple-choice questions, free-response questions, or a pacing strategy?

Part V
Content Review for the AP U.S. Government and Politics Exam

Chapter 4
The Constitutional Underpinnings

CONCEPTS

- Why did the Articles of Confederation fail?
- What was the immediate impact of Shays' Rebellion?
- What motivated the framers of the Constitution? Were they elitists or pragmatists?
- Why did the framers create a republican form of government?
- Why did the framers create a federal system of government?
- What is the purpose of checks and balances and the separation of powers?
- Why are plurality systems democratic but unstable?

ENLIGHTENMENT PHILOSOPHIES

The framers of the Constitution lived in a unique time when new ideas on how government should be organized and run challenged conventional wisdom regarding the roles of people and their governments. The Enlightenment was an 18th-century philosophical movement that began in Western Europe with roots in the Scientific Revolution. The focus was on the use of reason rather than tradition to solve social dilemmas.

Major Enlightenment Philosophers

Thomas Hobbes: Hobbes's famous work *Leviathan* (1660) argued that if humans were left to their own devices, chaos and violence would ensue. In a state of nature, life would be "solitary, poor, nasty, brutish, and short." He argued that the best way to protect life was to give total power to an absolute monarch because man cannot be trusted to rule himself.

John Locke: While Hobbes was concerned primarily with the protection of life, Locke went further and argued in his *Second Treatise on Civil Government* (1690) that liberty and property also needed to be respected. According to Locke, life, liberty, and property were natural rights granted by God; it was the duty of all governments to respect and protect these rights. If the government did not, Locke contended, the citizens have the right of revolution.

Charles de Montesquieu: Montesquieu was a French philosopher who greatly influenced the founders. His *De l'Esprit des Lois* (*The Spirit of the Laws*, 1748) advocated for the separation of power into three branches of government.

Jean-Jacques Rousseau: Rousseau argued in *The Social Contract* (1762) that the only good government was one that was freely formed with the consent of the people. This consent was shown by a powerful agreement among people.

Enlightenment philosophers favored democracy over absolute monarchy. Here are some of the forms a democracy can take:

- **Participatory democracy** emphasizes broad participation in politics and civil society by citizens at various levels of socioeconomic status.
- **Pluralist democracy** implies organized group-based activism by citizens with common interests all striving for the same political goals.
- An **elite democracy,** on the other hand, would discourage participation by the majority of citizens and cede power to the educated and/or wealthy.

The American Founding Fathers were most politically influenced by Enlightenment thought in their promotion of Republicanism. Republicanism espouses individual liberty and God-given rights, believes that all governmental power is derived from the people, rejects aristocracy, and encourages broad-based civic participation in political affairs. American Republicanism is characterized by **representative democracy,** the principle of elected officials representing a group of people, as in the U.S. Congress and state legislatures. Direct democracy is not the primary mode of governance in the United States, although many states do allow for referendums (direct voting by the people). Also, most towns in New England still require a direct vote by the people on budgetary and legislative matters. Perhaps the stability of the American system of democracy is its use of diverse systems at different levels of government.

> Many Enlightenment philosophers promoted the idea of **popular sovereignty,** the notion that the authority of a government is created and sustained by the consent of its people, through their elected representatives. Benjamin Franklin once said, "In free governments, the rulers are the servants and the people their superiors and sovereigns."

The Declaration of Independence

Although the American colonies and Great Britain had already been involved in armed conflict for more than one year, the Declaration of Independence was a formal declaration of war between the two groups. The majority of the document outlines the various injustices perpetrated by King George III against the colonies, which author Thomas Jefferson uses to explain why the colonies are declaring their independence. Not only a foundational document for the United States, in the following centuries other nations would use it as a template when declaring their independence from colonial powers.

You can read The Declaration of Independence in full at https://www.archives.gov/founding-docs/declaration-transcript.

THE WEAKNESS OF THE ARTICLES OF CONFEDERATION

The first government of the newly born United States of America was formed under the **Articles of Confederation**, the predecessor to the Constitution. These Articles were informally followed from 1776 to 1781 when they were ratified and so named. The government under the Articles achieved some notable accomplishments, including the following:

ARTICLES OF CONFEDERATION

Set the precedent of **federalism**, whereby the states and central government shared governing responsibilities	Negotiated the treaty that ended the Revolutionary War (on favorable terms for the United States' victorious army)	Established the **Northwest Ordinance**, creating methods by which new states would enter the Union

However, the Articles of Confederation suffered from insurmountable weaknesses that placed the newly independent states at risk. The year 1783 was the official end of the American Revolution and the post-revolution transitional period was marked by states being wholly unprepared to manage their own affairs. By 1787, trade between the states was in decline, the value of money was dropping, potential threats from foreign enemies were growing, and there was the real threat of social disorder from groups within the country. The inability of the state of Massachusetts to effectively deal with **Shays' Rebellion**, a six-month rebellion in which more than 1,000 armed farmers attacked a federal arsenal to protest the foreclosure of farms in the western part of the state, was a major concern at the Constitutional Convention. The nation's leaders began to see the necessity of a stronger central government, as Shays' Rebellion frightened the statesmen and exposed the weakness of the Articles of Confederation.

The federal government under the Articles

- could not draft soldiers
- was completely dependent on the state legislatures for revenue—the federal government was not permitted to tax citizens
- could not pay off the Revolutionary War debt
- could not control interstate trade
- had no Supreme Court to interpret law
- had no executive branch to enforce national law
- had no national currency

Review Source Documents

Many students mix up the Constitution with the Declaration of Independence. Be sure to read through the Constitution (found at the back of this book) and the Declaration of Independence a few times before your exam.

- had no control over import and export taxes imposed between states
- needed unanimity to amend the Articles
- needed approval from 9 out of 13 states to pass legislation (69% majority)

These deficiencies of the Articles of Confederation were the direct causes for calling a convention. But amending the articles became so difficult that James Madison did not have difficulty persuading the other delegates that a complete rewrite was necessary. The result was the **Constitution,** and the convention came to be known as the **Constitutional Convention**.

The Constitutional Convention

When the framers of the Constitution met in Philadelphia in 1787, they were divided over their views of the appropriate power and responsibilities of government. Some saw the current government, formed under the Articles of Confederation, as weak and ineffective, while others believed that changes to the Articles would be infringements on the responsibilities of state governments and intrusions into the lives of citizens. Some historians (such as Charles Beard) see the convention as an elitist conspiracy to protect the wealth of the rich, while others see the convention as a meeting of political pragmatists who knew that by protecting everyone's property and rights, they could best protect their own. Today, the generally accepted view is that the framers were pragmatists.

The delegates agreed that a stronger central government was necessary but were fearful of the corrupting influences of power. How to control the federal legislature was a central theme at the convention. The two main plans presented at the convention resulted in a compromise.

The Virginia Plan

The large states seized the agenda at the beginning of the convention and proposed the **Virginia Plan**, a recipe for a strong government with each state represented proportionately to its population.

The New Jersey Plan

The small states worried that a government dominated by the large states would be overly strong, so they proposed the **New Jersey Plan**, under which each state would be represented equally.

The Great Compromise

The Great (or "Connecticut") **Compromise** created the solution: a **bicameral** (two-house) legislature with a House of Representatives, based on population, and a Senate, with equal representation for all states.

Compromises, Compromises

Each state had its own interests to pursue and protect, which led to some key issues being temporarily tabled so as to ratify the Constitution. For instance, despite moral objections, delegates at the Constitutional Convention agreed that the international slave trade could not be ended until at least 1808. And while southern states—who heavily relied on foreign trade—opposed tariffs being placed by Congress on exported goods, they did concede a tax on imports, something that would be a major issue of contention down the road when determining states' rights.

Another major conflict arose over the representation of slaves. (Remember that slaves could not vote then.) Northerners felt that slaves should not be counted when determining each state's number of electoral votes, while Southerners disagreed. The "solution" was the infamous **Three-Fifths Compromise**, in which the decision was made that slaves would count as three-fifths of a person when apportioning seats in the House of Representatives.

Under the Articles of Confederation there was no executive authority to enforce laws. The framers of the Constitution corrected that problem by addressing the issue of a chief executive, or president. Under the Constitution, the executive is the enforcer of law and a second check on the power of the legislature. Before bills become law, they require presidential approval, and the president has the power to veto acts of the legislature. However, presidential power is not absolute. Congress can override a presidential veto if two-thirds of both houses of the legislature vote to do so.

In order to arbitrate disputes between the Congress and the president, between states, and between the states and the central government, the framers created the Supreme Court.

Despite all of the compromises that were reached at the convention, acceptance of the Constitution was by no means assured. It had to be submitted to the states for ratification. Supporters and opponents of the Constitution broke into two camps, **Federalists** and **Anti-Federalists**. Alexander Hamilton, James Madison, and John Jay wrote a series of newspaper articles supporting the Constitution, collectively known as *The Federalist Papers*. These essays are the primary source for understanding the original intent of the framers. They were designed to persuade the states of the wisdom of a strong central government coupled with autonomous political power retained by the states.

The Anti-Federalists opposed the creation of a stronger national government, arguing that a Constitution would threaten citizens' personal liberties and effectively make the president a king. Keep in mind that only 12 years prior, these people had declared independence from Britain, and many were fearful that a large government would recreate that same state of tyrannical control from which they had just escaped.

The opposition to the Constitution centered on the lack of a **Bill of Rights** that would protect the rights of individuals from government infringement. Once the Federalists guaranteed that a Bill of Rights would be added to the Constitution immediately after ratification, opposition diminished, and the Constitution became the foundation of American government.

The Federalist Papers and Anti-Federalist Dissent

Brutus No. 1

Basic Philosophy—Brutus No. 1 was the first publication that began the series of essays known as the *Federalist* and *Anti-Federalist Papers*. In Brutus No. 1, the anonymous author posed a series of questions about and critiques of the then-proposed Constitution. Main critiques included that the proposed national government had too much power, a standing army could diminish liberty, and that representatives would not truly represent the people.

You can read Brutus No. 1 in full at http://teachingamericanhistory.org/library/document/brutus-i.

Major Dissent—*The Federalist Papers* were an attempt to answer the questions and assuage the concerns posed by Brutus and other Anti-Federalist writers.

Federalist No. 10

Basic Philosophy—James Madison addressed the dangers of factionalism and how to protect minority factions in a nation founded on majority rule. Madison argued that a large republic ensures multiple factions so as to avoid any one faction taking control, which could lead to a suppression of minority opinion.

You can read *Federalist No. 10* in full at http://teachingamericanhistory.org/library/document/federalist-no-10/.

Major Dissent—Anti-Federalists argued that Madison's claims were naïve, as a nation with multiple factions would never form the "perfect union" proclaimed in the Constitution. Anti-federalists believed that no nation larger than one of the states could survive for long. They believed that states' separate interests would tear them apart, as happened during the American Civil War.

Federalist No. 51

Basic Philosophy—James Madison argued that separation of powers and checks and balances would guarantee that no one faction will take total control of the national government. Also, separation of powers would make the national government more efficient, as each branch had specific responsibilities.

Major Dissent—Anti-Federalists claimed that there was no perfect way to separate powers and that eventually, one branch of government would hold more power.

You can read *Federalist No. 51* in full at http://teachingamericanhistory.org/library/document/federalist-no-51/.

Federalist No. 70

Basic Philosophy—Alexander Hamilton argued that the Executive Branch should consist of a single person, a president. Hamilton looked to the British monarchy as an example; the king had significant power but was checked by the House of Commons. Hamilton went a step further by proposing term limits as another check on the executive's power.

Major Dissent—Anti-Federalist critics claimed that with executive power vested in one person, only the president's "minions" would influence him. Other Anti-Federalists were alarmed at the prospect of giving control of the military to a single person.

You can read *Federalist No. 70* in full at http://teachingamericanhistory.org/library/document/federalist-no-70/.

Federalist No. 78

Basic Philosophy—Alexander Hamilton addressed Anti-Federalist critiques on the power of the federal judiciary by arguing that under the Constitution, the judicial branch would have the least amount of power. Even so, Hamilton reaffirmed that the Judicial Branch would have the power of judicial review, acting as a check on Congress.

Major Dissent—Anti-Federalists argued that a federal judiciary would overshadow the states' judicial systems, making state courts all but powerless. Also, Anti-Federalists claimed that federal judges' lifetime appointments could lead to corruption.

You can read *Federalist No. 78* in full at http://teachingamericanhistory.org/library/document/federalist-no-78/.

THE CONSTITUTION AS AN INSTRUMENT OF GOVERNMENT

The Constitution is vague and skeletal in form, containing only about 5,000 words. It was intended to be a blueprint for the structure of government and a guide for guaranteeing the rights of citizens. It was written to allow change, anticipating unknown needs of future generations, through amendments that require widespread support. The branches of government have all grown and evolved since the ratification of the Constitution.

You can find the full text of the Constitution at the end of this book.

- The first three articles of the Constitution set up the threefold separation of powers that are the **legislative**, **executive**, and **judicial** branches. More on that in a few pages.

- The **necessary and proper clause** of the Constitution (Article I, Section 8) allows Congress to "make all laws" that appear "necessary and proper" to implement its delegated powers. This is also called the **elastic clause.** For example, there is nothing in the Constitution that creates the Federal Reserve System, which is the central bank for the United States. Neither is there any mention of a cabinet in the executive branch. The Federal District Courts and the Courts of Appeals were both created by congressional elaboration.

- "The executive power shall be vested in a President of the United States of America" has given presidents the power to issue **executive orders,** which have the same effect as law, bypass Congress in policy making and are not mentioned in the Constitution. Presidents use them as part of the enforcement duties of the executive branch. **Executive agreements** between heads of countries have many of the same elements as treaties. These agreements bypass the ratification power of the Senate but are not mentioned in the Constitution. An extreme example of an executive order is Executive Order 9066, in which Franklin D. Roosevelt ordered people removed from a military zone. It was no coincidence that these people were Japanese American and German American. This order paved the way for all Japanese Americans on the West Coast to be sent to internment camps for the duration of World War II. Thousands of German Americans and Italian Americans were also sent to internment camps under executive order.

- When the Supreme Court decided the case of *Marbury v. Madison* in 1803, it drastically increased its own power by granting itself the ability to overturn laws passed by the legislature, also known as **judicial review.**

- Finally, custom and usage have changed the system to meet differing needs. The political party system, with its organization, technology, and fund-raising capabilities, was created from custom and usage. The rules used in Congress were also created from custom and usage.

Federalism

Central to the Constitution is the idea that the United States government is a federal government. The term **federalism** describes a system of government under which the national government and local governments (state governments, in the case of the United States) share powers. Other federal governments include Germany, Switzerland, and Australia. Contrast this with a **confederation**, a system in which many decisions are made by an external member-state legislation; decisions on day-to-day matters are not taken by simple majority but by special majorities, consensus, or unanimity—and changes to the Constitution require unanimity. But let's get back to federalism for now.

The Supreme Court (which we'll discuss in depth later) handed down a few important decisions concerning the relationship between the national government and local governments. Know these two, in particular, for your exam:

- *McCulloch v. Maryland* (1819). The Court ruled that the states did not have the power to tax the national bank (and, by extension, the federal government). This decision reinforced the supremacy clause of the Constitution, which states that the Constitution "and the laws of the United States which shall be made in pursuance thereof...shall be the supreme law of the land; and the judges in every state shall be bound thereby, anything in the Constitution or laws of any State to the contrary notwithstanding."

- *Gibbons v. Ogden* (1824). The Court ruled that the state of New York could not grant a steamship company a monopoly to operate on an interstate waterway, even though that waterway ran through New York. The ruling increased federal power over interstate commerce by implying that anything concerning interstate trade could potentially be regulated by the federal government.

Powers Under Federalism

Delegated or Enumerated Powers

Delegated, or **enumerated**, **powers** are those that belong to the national government only. These powers include

- printing money
- regulating interstate and international trade
- making treaties and conducting foreign policy
- declaring war

Reserved Powers

Powers that belong exclusively to the states are called **reserved powers**. According to the Tenth Amendment, these powers include any that the Constitution neither specifically grants to the national government nor denies to the state governments. These powers are not listed in the Constitution; in fact, they are made up of all powers not mentioned in the Constitution. These powers include

- o   the power to issue licenses
- o   the regulation of intrastate (within the states) business
- o   the responsibility to run and pay for federal elections

Concurrent Powers

Concurrent powers are those that are shared by federal and state governments. These powers include

- o   the power to collect taxes
- o   the power to build roads
- o   the power to operate courts of law
- o   the power to borrow money

The Constitution specifies which powers are denied to the national government and which powers are denied to the states. Those powers are listed on the next page.

The Constitution also obliges the federal government to guarantee the states a republican form of government and protection against foreign invasion and domestic rebellion. The federal government must also prevent the states from subdividing or combining to form new states without congressional consent. The states, in turn, are required by the Constitution to accept the court judgments, licenses, contracts, and other civil acts of all the other states; this obligation is contained in the "**full faith and credit**" **clause.** The states may not refuse police protection or access to their courts to a U.S. citizen just because that person lives in a different state; this provision appears in the **privileges and immunities clause.** Finally, the states usually must return fugitives to the states from which they have fled; this process is called **extradition.**

The **supremacy clause** of the Constitution requires conflicts between federal law and state law to be resolved in favor of federal law. State laws that violate the Constitution, federal laws, or international treaties can be invalidated through the supremacy clause.

The nature of federalism has changed over time. For the first part of the nation's history, the federal and state governments remained separate and independent. The relationship between the national and state governments during this period is called **dual federalism**. What little contact most Americans had with government occurred on the state level, as the national government concerned itself primarily with international trade; the construction of roads, harbors, and railways; and the distribution of public land in the West.

The Federal Government Does Not Have the Power to	**The State Governments Do Not Have the Power to**
• suspend the writ of *habeas corpus*, (which protects against illegal imprisonment), except in times of national crisis • pass *ex post facto* (retroactive) laws or issuance of bills of attainder (which declare an individual guilty of a capital offense without a trial) • impose export taxes • use money from the treasury without the passage and approval of an appropriations bill • grant titles of nobility	• enter into treaties with foreign countries • declare war • maintain a standing army • print money • pass *ex post facto* (retroactive) laws or issuance of bills of attainder (which declare an individual guilty of a capital offense without a trial) • grant titles of nobility • impose import or export duties

As with all parts of the Constitution, the definition of federalism is in the eye of the beholder. Ideological **States' Righters** define federalism as a relationship in which the states retain most of the political power. **Nationalists** often see the federal government as being supreme in all matters and ultimately in control.

Categorical Grants
Examples of categorical grants include Head Start, Medicaid, and the Food Stamp Program.

Most federal government programs, such as those to aid the poor, clean the environment, improve education, and protect the handicapped, are administered through the states. The federal government pays for these programs through grants-in-aid, which are outright gifts of money to the states. Nationalists prefer to tie strings to the grants, ensuring that the federal government maintains control over the money. States' Righters want no strings attached, leaving decisions about how the grant money is to be used to state and local governments, whom they believe know how best to spend it.

Nationalists like **categorical grants**, aid with strict provisions from the federal government on how it may be spent. States' Righters like **block grants**, which permit the state to experiment and use the money as they see fit. In the final analysis, however, the federal government can use a number of techniques, including direct orders and preemption, to force the states to abide by federal law. The federal government can also use a crossover sanction, which requires a state to do something before a grant will be awarded. An example would be to raise the drinking age to 21 before federal highway money to build state roads is released.

Advantages of Federalism	Disadvantages of Federalism
• Mass participation: Constituents of all ages, backgrounds, races, and religions can participate by voting on both local and national issues.	• Lack of consistency: Differing policies on issues like gun control, capital punishment, and local taxes can clog the court system and create inequality in states.
• Regional autonomy: States retain some rights and have choices about public policy issues such as gun control, property rights, abortion, and euthanasia.	• Inefficiency: Federalism can lead to duplication of government and inefficient, overlapping, or contradictory policies in different parts of the country.
• Government at many levels: Politicians are in touch with the concerns of their constituents.	• Bureaucracy: Power can be spread out amongst so many groups; it can result in corruption and a stalemate.
• Innovative methods: States can be laboratories for government experimentation, to see if policies are feasible.	

Separation of Powers

The framers of the Constitution decided that no one faction of the government should be able to acquire too much power. To prevent this, they borrowed the concept of the **separation of powers** from the French political philosopher **Charles de Montesquieu**. The framers delegated different but equally important tasks to the three branches of government. The **legislative branch** (Congress) makes the laws; the **executive branch**, led by the president, enforces the laws; and the **judicial branch** interprets the laws.

Separation of powers also prevents a person from serving in more than one branch of the government at the same time. For example, a congressperson (legislative branch) may not simultaneously be either a judge (judicial branch) or a cabinet member (executive branch). If a congressperson were appointed to one of these positions, he or she would first have to resign his or her seat in Congress.

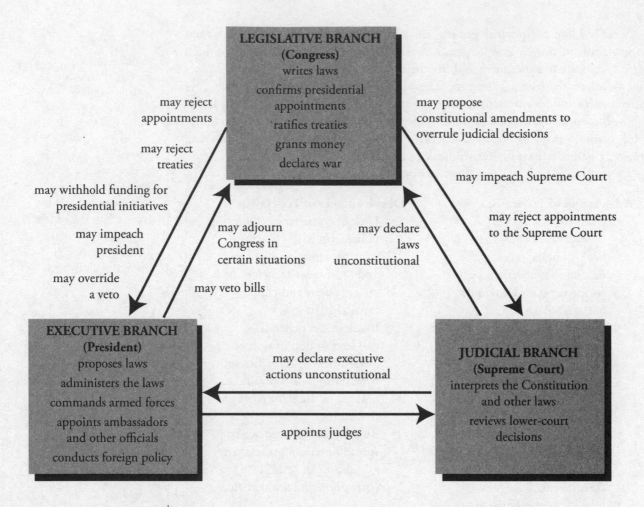

LEGISLATIVE BRANCH
(Congress)
writes laws
confirms presidential
appointments
ratifies treaties
grants money
declares war

may reject
appointments

may reject
treaties

may withhold funding for
presidential initiatives

may impeach
president

may override
a veto

may adjourn
Congress in
certain situations

may veto bills

may propose
constitutional amendments to
overrule judicial decisions

may impeach Supreme Court

may reject appointments
to the Supreme Court

may declare
laws
unconstitutional

EXECUTIVE BRANCH
(President)
proposes laws
administers the laws
commands armed forces
appoints ambassadors
and other officials
conducts foreign policy

may declare executive
actions unconstitutional

appoints judges

JUDICIAL BRANCH
(Supreme Court)
interprets the Constitution
and other laws
reviews lower-court
decisions

The System of Checks and Balances

The system of **checks and balances** is another constitutional safeguard designed to prevent any one branch of government from becoming dominant. The system of checks and balances requires the different branches of government to share power and cooperate with one another to accomplish anything of importance.

- **Nomination of federal judges, cabinet officials, and ambassadors.** The president chooses nominees for these positions. However, the president's nominees must be approved by the Senate.

- **Negotiation of treaties.** The president is empowered to negotiate treaties. No treaty can go into effect, however, until it is approved by two-thirds of the Senate.

- **Enactment of legislation.** Only Congress may pass laws. However, the president has the power to **veto**, or reject, legislation. The president's veto power encourages the legislature to consider the president's position on a law, and to negotiate with the president to

Note the use of the word "encourages." As can be seen with regards to President Obama's support of the Affordable Care Act, the legislative bodies still have the freedom to choose their own approach to a law.

prevent a veto. Congress can also check the president's veto by **overriding** the veto, but to do so it must pass the same law with a two-thirds majority in both houses (a congressional override is difficult, but not impossible). If Congress succeeds in overriding the president's veto, the legislation becomes law regardless of the president's position. Finally, the courts may determine the constitutionality of the law. Thus, the courts have the power to overturn laws passed by Congress and approved by the president (only on constitutional grounds, however; judges may not overturn laws simply because they don't like them).

AMENDMENT PROCESS

One reason that the Constitution has lasted more than 200 years is that it is flexible. (Think of the elastic clause!) Many of its provisions require interpretation, allowing the document to become more conservative or progressive as the times warrant. Furthermore, the Constitution can be changed through **amendments** (the addition of provisions to the document).

To amend the Constitution, a proposed amendment must be introduced to both houses of Congress and approved by a two-thirds majority in each. The amendment is then passed on to each of the fifty state legislatures. Three-fourths of the state legislatures must **ratify** (approve) the amendment for it to become part of the Constitution. The states themselves are allowed to determine the number of votes required to ratify an amendment. Most states require a simple majority of their legislatures, but seven states require either three-fifths or two-thirds majorities. Also, rather than use the state legislatures, Congress can mandate that each state use a **ratifying convention**, with delegates expressly elected to vote on the proposed amendment. This method was once used to ratify the Twenty-First Amendment, which ended Prohibition in 1933.

The Constitution allows for a second means of amendment. Two-thirds of the state legislatures could petition Congress to call a **constitutional convention**. Because no constitutional convention has ever taken place, nobody knows for certain how extensively conventioneers would be allowed to alter the Constitution. Could they rewrite it entirely, or would they be restricted to amendments mentioned specifically in their petitions for a convention? Fear that a constitutional convention could attempt drastic alterations has persuaded many state legislators to oppose any call for a convention. There are ongoing movements in many states to call a constitutional convention to add a balanced budget amendment to the Constitution. While about 30 state legislatures have approved a convention, the movement has not yet met the bar of 34 states required to call the convention.

Proposal Methods	Ratification Methods
• Proposed amendment wins $\frac{2}{3}$ majority in the House and Senate. • Used for all 27 amendments.	• $\frac{3}{4}$ of all state legislatures approve of the amendment. • Used 26 times (not for Twenty-first Amendment).
• A constitutional convention is called by $\frac{2}{3}$ of state legislatures. Any amendment can now be proposed at the convention. • This method has never been used.	• $\frac{3}{4}$ of special state-ratifying conventions approve the amendment. • Used only once, for the Twenty-first Amendment.

AMENDMENTS

The Bill of Rights (December 15, 1791)

The first ten amendments were added to the Constitution within three years of its ratification. These amendments are known collectively as the Bill of Rights. Originally written by James Madison, many provisions of the Bill of Rights have been expanded and clarified over the years.

The First Amendment

Supreme Court Justice (1932–1937) Benjamin Cardozo said that the First Amendment of the Bill of Rights contains "the fundamental principles of liberty and justice which lie at the base of all of our civil and political institutions."

- **Freedom of religion.** The government may not interfere with an individual's right to practice his or her faith as described in the **free exercise clause**. Furthermore, as stated in the **establishment clause**, Congress may not establish an official church of the United States nor give a particular faith or sect preferential treatment over others. This constitutional provision is usually referred to as the separation of church and state.
- **Freedom of speech and freedom of the press**. Congress may not pass a law that prevents citizens from expressing their opinions, either in speech or in writing. Nevertheless, the Supreme Court has placed some limits on these freedoms. Speech or writing intended to incite violence or used to intentionally slander or libel is not protected. Justice Oliver Wendell Holmes articulated the **clear and present danger test**, in which the government has the right to interfere in free speech if it

poses a threat to others, in the case of *Schenck v. United States* (1917). Nevertheless, criticism of the government and its politics is protected. When it comes to censoring the press, there are few instances in which the government can use **prior restraint**—crossing out sections of an article before publication. These strong protections for the press were established in the case of *Near v. Minnesota* (1931).

- **Freedom of assembly and freedom to petition the government**. The Constitution protects the people's rights to assemble peacefully, to hold demonstrations, and to ask the government for changes in policy. Rallies and demonstrations that encourage or incite violence and those that do not seek official sanction to trespass on public property are not protected.

The Second Amendment

The Second Amendment to the Constitution, which protects citizens' rights to bear arms, has led to a debate over whether the Constitution protects citizens' rights to bear arms under all circumstances, or only when those citizens serve in "well-regulated militias." Thus far, the Supreme Court's rulings on the Second Amendment have upheld the individual right to keep and bear arms, while allowing for wide variations in gun laws from state to state and in large cities. Future court decisions are likely to revolve around concerns about public safety and the ways in which governmental regulation of firearms may promote or interfere with public safety and individual rights.

The Third Amendment

The most antiquated of all the amendments—though important at the time of its creation—the Third Amendment forbids the quartering of soldiers and the direct public support of armed forces. It was a direct reaction to the British practice of using civilian support to conduct military operations.

The Fourth Amendment

The Fourth Amendment places restrictions on government agencies regarding criminal or civil procedural investigations and does much to protect an individual's "person, house, papers, and effects against unreasonable searches and seizures." This amendment was most dramatically reviewed in the 20th century, as evidenced in *Mapp v. Ohio* (1961). Questions regarding the use of probable cause, traffic-stop and stop-and-frisk searches, and the use of search warrants have led to challenges regarding the interpretation of the **exclusionary rule** regarding evidence seized without proper procedures. In its original form, the exclusionary rule holds that all evidence unlawfully gathered must be excluded from judicial proceedings. In recent times, the primacy of the Fourth Amendment has been challenged by the ease with which government agencies can gather data on citizens digitally through such methods as wiretapping, bulk collection of phone records, or computer hacking. Fears of internal and external terrorism have led some Americans to support the Patriot Act, USA Freedom Act, and warrantless searches at airports, while others fear that government intrusion into privacy may confer too much power to an anonymous elite.

The Fifth Amendment

The Fifth Amendment does the most to protect an individual from the broad powers of the federal government. It provides a guarantee of a **grand jury** when a suspect is held for a capital or other "infamous" crime. It eliminates the possibility of a person being maliciously prosecuted for the same crime again and again by prohibiting **double jeopardy**. It establishes the right of the government to seize property for public use under the auspices of **eminent domain** but only if such seizure can be "justly compensated." Nor may defendants be forced to testify against themselves if on trial, thus prohibiting **self-incrimination** (commonly known as "pleading the fifth"). The most significant attribute of the Fifth Amendment is its mandate that the federal government not deprive an individual of "life, liberty, or property by any level unless **due process of law** is applied."

The Sixth Amendment

This amendment allows persons accused of a crime to be prosecuted by an impartial jury in a "speedy" public trial. Individuals have the right to be informed of their charges, to confront witnesses, to subpoena witnesses for their defense, and to have a lawyer for their defense. The sixth amendment forms the basis for **habeas corpus**, which protects against unlawful imprisonment and ensures that a person cannot be held indefinitely without being formally charged before a judge or in a court, or without a legal reason to extend his or her detention.

The Miranda rights, which you may be familiar with ("You have the right to remain silent..."), help to maintain both the Fifth and Sixth Amendments. They remind the accused that they do not have to incriminate themselves (Fifth) and that they are guaranteed the right to representation (Sixth). These rights were cemented as a result of the landmark Supreme Court decision in *Miranda v. Arizona* (1966).

The Seventh Amendment

Although statutory, or written, law has come to replace or supersede common law, which is based on past court decisions, the Seventh Amendment allows for trial by jury in common-law cases.

The Eighth Amendment

The Eighth Amendment prohibits excessive bail in federal cases. Yet its most significant challenges have arisen from the clause that prohibits "cruel and unusual punishment." **Capital punishment** is one of the most contentious issues of the modern day. At issue is whether it constitutes "cruel and unusual punishment." Federal and state Supreme Courts have taken different positions on this debate.

The Ninth Amendment

The Ninth Amendment reaffirms the principles of a limited federal government. "The enumeration in the Constitution, of certain rights, shall not be construed to deny or disparage others retained by the people" means that rights not specifically mentioned in the Constitution are still protected—everyone has the right to brush their hair, for example—even though that right is mentioned nowhere in the Bill of Rights. Although somewhat vague in its premise, the Ninth Amendment has led to the implied right to privacy and other questions regarding individual rights not identified or even understood at the time of the creation of the Constitution.

The Tenth Amendment

The Tenth Amendment defines the relationship between the states and the national government under the concept of federalism. It states that when powers are not defined or delegated by the Constitution, the states have **reserved power** to make their own individual judgments—so long as they do not infringe on the explicit rules of the Constitution and the federal government. State issues such as the death penalty, speed limit, and drinking age are within the jurisdiction of the states to decide so long as they do not contradict the Constitution.

Early Amendments (1795–1804)

The Eleventh Amendment (1795)

This amendment was passed as a response to the Supreme Court ruling of *Chisholm v. Georgia* (1793), which held that states did not enjoy sovereign immunity from lawsuits brought by residents of other states. In order to overrule *Chisholm*, the Eleventh Amendment provides that states may not be sued in federal court by citizens of another state or country without the consent of the states being sued.

The Twelfth Amendment (1804)

Originally, under Article II of the Constitution, those selected as electors for choosing the president got to cast *two* votes. The candidate who got the highest number of votes won the presidency, while the runner-up got the vice presidency as a consolation prize. The Twelfth Amendment was created following the debacle of the election of 1800—a tie between Thomas Jefferson and Aaron Burr, who split the Republican vote. This amendment ensured that electors would now have to cast separate votes for the president and the vice president.

In *Hans v. Louisiana* (1890), the Supreme Court held that the Eleventh Amendment establishes that states possess sovereign immunity and are therefore generally immune from being sued in federal court without their consent. This issue has been revisited and states sovereign immunity has been strengthened by cases including *Blatchford v. Native Village of Noatak* (1991) and *Alden v. Maine* (1999).

The Civil War, Civil Rights, Civil Liberties Amendments (1865–1870)

The Thirteenth Amendment (1865)

This amendment prohibited the institution of slavery except as punishment for a convicted crime, and was a direct result of the Union victory in the Civil War.

The Fourteenth Amendment (1868)

Remember, the Bill of Rights did not originally apply to state law. After the Civil War, Northerners pushed for a constitutional amendment that would prevent the South from denying equal rights to the newly freed slaves. The Fourteenth Amendment was designed to accomplish this purpose, stating that

No state shall make or enforce any law which shall abridge the privileges or immunities of citizens of the United States; nor shall any state deprive any person of life, liberty, or property, without due process of law; nor deny to any person within its jurisdiction the equal protection of the laws.

The Fourteenth Amendment expanded the right to due process to all Americans; however, it did not immediately apply the protections of the Bill of Rights to all state laws. Instead, the Supreme Court has used the "due process" and "equal protection" clauses to extend most of the Bill of Rights protections but has done so on a case-by-case basis. This process of incorporating some of the Bill of Rights protections to state law is called **selective incorporation**.

The Fifteenth Amendment (1870)

The Fifteenth Amendment granted voting rights to males of all races, and was originally designed to extend voting rights to newly freed male slaves. Ultimately, the Supreme Court and southern states later narrowed, and in some cases eliminated, the provisions of this amendment during the late 19th and early 20th centuries. Voter rights were only later made secure by the passage of the Twenty-Fourth Amendment and the Voting Rights Act of 1965.

Progressive Era Amendments (1913–1920)

The Sixteenth Amendment (1913)

Before the passage of this amendment, most revenue was gathered through tariffs that placed a large burden on the poor. The Sixteenth Amendment gave Congress the power to collect taxes on income, which allowed for the creation of a **progressive income tax** that fell more on the rich.

The Seventeenth Amendment (1913)

This amendment provided for the direct election of United States senators. Previously, senators had been selected by the state legislatures. The Seventeenth Amendment shifted the responsibility for choosing senators from the legislatures to the general voting public.

The Eighteenth Amendment (1920)

Known as the Prohibition amendment, this amendment prohibited the manufacture, sale, and transportation of alcohol in or out of the United States.

The Nineteenth Amendment (1920)

This amendment granted voting rights to all American women.

Later Amendments (1933–1992)

The Twentieth Amendment (1933)

Before the passage of the Twentieth Amendment, there was a long gap in between when the new president was elected (early November) and when he took office (March 4). This gap proved especially damaging to the nation, first in 1860–1861, when southern states seceded as Lincoln waited to take office, and again in 1932–1933 when the nation was in the grip of the Great Depression and anxiously waiting for Franklin Delano Roosevelt (FDR) to take the reins. As a result, this amendment clearly defined the procedures regarding the specifics of presidential and legislative terms and shortened the amount of time between presidential election and inauguration (now January 20).

The Twenty-first Amendment (1933)

Prohibition had largely led to the rise of organized crime and widespread law-breaking. The Twenty-first Amendment recognized the failure of this government experiment and repealed prohibition, allowing for the legalization of the sale of alcohol.

The Twenty-second Amendment (1951)

In response to FDR's unprecedented four presidential election victories, this amendment limited the president to two terms.

The Twenty-third Amendment (1961)

This amendment allowed the residents of Washington, D.C., to vote in presidential elections, bringing the total national electoral count to 538.

The Twenty-fourth Amendment (1964)

The Twenty-fourth Amendment eliminated the racially discriminatory practice of forcing African Americans to pay poll taxes when attempting to vote in Southern state elections.

The Twenty-fifth Amendment (1967)

Following the assassination of John Kennedy and given the age of his successor, Lyndon Johnson, this amendment provided clarity regarding the selection of a new vice president should the position become vacant. The Twenty-fifth Amendment also formally permitted the vice president to assume the presidency temporarily in the event of a presidential disability.

The Twenty-sixth Amendment (1971)

In response to the number of young people fighting in the Vietnam War, the Twenty-sixth Amendment lowered the voting age from 21 to 18.

The Twenty-seventh Amendment (1992)

This is a sleeper amendment that was passed more than 200 years after it was first proposed. If Congress votes itself a pay increase, that increase cannot take effect until after the next election.

Informal Changes to the Constitution

Some changes to the Constitution have been initiated either by changes in custom or interpretation of the document. Sometimes, these informal changes gradually give way to more formal changes. For example, when George Washington became president, he served two terms and elected not to serve a third term. Every president after Washington continued this custom until Franklin Roosevelt was elected president four times. Because of Franklin Roosevelt's four terms in office, the Twenty-second Amendment to the Constitution was proposed and ratified. In this case, an informal custom became a formal change.

STATE AND LOCAL GOVERNMENTS

The Constitution does not stipulate the form state governments must take. The states are instead free to form whatever governments they choose, provided that the government is defined by a state constitution and that the constitution is approved by Congress. However, most state governments are structured after the federal government.

All states have an executive branch led by a **governor**, whose duties to the state are similar to the president's duties to the nation. Governors direct state executive agencies, which oversee areas such as education, roads, and policing. They command the state National Guard and may grant **pardons** and **reprieves.** Most have the power to appoint state judges, with the "advice and consent" of one of the state's legislative bodies. Governors have veto power over acts of the state legislature.

An Exception
Nebraska has a unicameral legislature, meaning that they have one legislative chamber or house.

All states but one have bicameral legislatures modeled after the House of Representatives and the Senate. In the same way that Congress enacts federal law, the state legislatures enact state law. The legislatures have the power to **override** the **gubernatorial veto** (the word *gubernatorial* means *relating to the governor*). Governors have many of the same executive powers as presidents. However, many governors may use a **line-item veto** to reject only parts of bills. Presidents were denied this power by the Supreme Court under the ruling that a federal line-item veto would take too much power away from the legislative branch. We'll discuss line-item vetoes in greater detail in Chapter 8.

All states also have state judiciaries to interpret state law. These judicial systems consist of trial courts and appeals courts, as does the federal judiciary. They hear both criminal cases (in which an individual is accused of a crime) and civil cases (in which disputing parties can sue to receive compensation).

KEY TERMS

- Articles of Confederation
- Northwest Ordinance
- federalism
- Shays' Rebellion
- Constitution
- Constitutional Convention (of 1787)
- Virginia Plan
- New Jersey Plan
- Great Compromise
- bicameral legislature
- Three-Fifths Compromise
- Federalists
- Anti-Federalists
- *The Federalist Papers*
- Bill of Rights
- necessary and proper clause (elastic clause)
- presidential practice
- executive order
- executive agreement
- judicial review
- confederation
- delegated powers
- reserved powers
- concurrent powers
- full faith and credit clause
- privileges and immunities clause
- extradition
- supremacy clause
- dual federalism
- States' Righters
- Nationalists
- categorical grants
- block grants
- separation of powers
- Charles de Montesquieu
- legislative branch
- executive branch
- judicial branch
- checks and balances
- veto
- override
- amendment
- ratify
- ratifying convention
- constitutional convention
- First Amendment
- free exercise clause
- establishment clause
- clear and present danger test
- exclusionary rule
- grand jury
- double jeopardy
- eminent domain
- self-incrimination
- due process of law
- habeas corpus
- capital punishment
- selective incorporation
- Sixteenth Amendment
- progressive income tax
- Twenty-second Amendment
- governor
- pardons
- reprieves
- gubernatorial veto
- line-item veto

Summary

o   Remember that the Articles of Confederation were ultimately too weak to serve as a viable governing constitution for the new nation.

o   Know the important philosophers that influenced the framers: Hobbes, Locke, Montesquieu, and Rousseau.

o   The Constitutional Convention in Philadelphia resulted in a new governing document that sought to balance the autonomy of the states with a stronger federal government.

o   The vagueness of some sections of the Constitution along with elements like the elastic clause make the document adaptable to changing times.

o   The United States, through the Constitution, was the first nation to practice federalism: a balance of power between the states and the federal government.

o   In keeping with the principles of Montesquieu, the Founders created a government split into three branches and gave each branch the power to check the other two.

o   Try to remember all twenty-seven amendments by era: the Bill of Rights, the early amendments, the Civil War amendments, the Progressive Era amendments, and the later amendments.

o   Many powers that are not formally declared in the Constitution have been taken on by the president and Congress—you should be aware of this "unwritten Constitution."

o   Know a bit about how state and local governments function and how they interact with the federal government.

Chapter 4 Drill

See Chapter 11 for answers and explanations.

Questions 1 and 2 refer to the passage below.

The United States in Congress assembled shall never engage in a war, nor grant letters of marque or reprisal in time of peace, nor enter into any treaties or alliances, nor coin money, nor regulate the value thereof, nor ascertain the sums and expenses necessary for the defense and welfare of the United States, or any of them, nor emit bills, nor borrow money on the credit of the United States, nor appropriate money, nor agree upon the number of vessels of war, to be built or purchased, or the number of land or sea forces to be raised, nor appoint a commander in chief of the army or navy, unless nine States assent to the same.

—The Articles of Confederation, 1781

1. Which of the following statements best illustrates the central idea of this excerpt from The Articles of Confederation?

   (A) States kept their sovereignty under the Articles of Confederation.
   (B) States had the authority to declare war without the approval of the national government.
   (C) Congress was the only branch of government.
   (D) A majority of states had to agree on major decisions affecting the new nation.

2. The excerpt best supports which of the following arguments?

   (A) The Articles of Confederation created a strong national government.
   (B) The Articles of Confederation gave more power to Congress than the states.
   (C) The Articles of Confederation created an inefficient national government.
   (D) The Articles of Confederation gave Congress a different set of powers than the Constitution.

3. Which of the following is an accurate comparison between the New Jersey Plan and the Virginia Plan?

	Virginia Plan	**New Jersey Plan**
(A)	Equal representation in Congress	Representation in Congress passed on population
(B)	Bicameral legislature	Unicameral legislature
(C)	Supported by smaller states	Supported by larger states
(D)	President elected by the people	President elected by the Electoral College

4. Which principle of American government establishes concurrent state and national governments?

   (A) Federalism
   (B) Separation of powers
   (C) Checks and balances
   (D) Limited government

5. The Fifth Amendment to the Bill of Rights protects which right of American citizens?

   (A) Restriction against interferences in free speech
   (B) Restriction against unreasonable searches and seizures
   (C) Restriction against double jeopardy
   (D) Restriction against cruel and unusual punishment

6. Which of the following statements best illustrates the significance of Shays' Rebellion in American history?

   (A) It led to the overthrow of British rule.
   (B) It scared American elites, leading to the adoption of the Constitution.
   (C) It led to the enactment of slavery in the South.
   (D) It narrowly avoided overthrowing the government of Vermont.

7. Which of the following decided the issue of the representation of slaves?

   (A) Three-Fifths Compromise
   (B) Connecticut Compromise
   (C) Commerce and Slave-Trade Compromise
   (D) Bill of Rights

REFLECT

Respond to the following questions:

- For which content topics discussed in this chapter do you feel you have achieved sufficient mastery to answer multiple-choice questions correctly?

- For which content topics discussed in this chapter do you feel you have achieved sufficient mastery to discuss effectively in an essay?

- For which content topics discussed in this chapter do you feel you need more work before you can answer multiple-choice questions correctly?

- For which content topics discussed in this chapter do you feel you need more work before you can discuss effectively in an essay?

- What parts of this chapter are you going to re-review?

- Will you seek further help, outside of this book (such as a teacher, tutor, or AP Students), on any of the content in this chapter—and, if so, on what content?

Chapter 5
Public Opinion and the Media

CONCEPTS

- What is public opinion?
- What is the public agenda, and how is the agenda shaped?
- How is public opinion measured?
- What role does the media play in shaping public opinion?
- What effect does the media have on individual political beliefs and voting behavior?

Public opinion, simply put, is how people feel about things. Pollsters measure the public's opinion of everything from television programs to commercial products to political issues. Networks, companies, and politicians commission these polls because they seek the approval of the public.

Obviously, public opinion is not uniform. Even the most popular television shows attract a minority of all Americans. Furthermore, many programs are designed to receive favorable ratings from a specific subgroup of society rather than from the public at large. Networks, for example, seek high ratings from young, middle-class audiences, as these are the audiences most sought after by advertisers. Because advertisers are less interested in senior citizens, networks seek their approval less aggressively.

The same holds true for political issues. Most Americans—the **general public**—care more about the political issues that affect their day-to-day lives directly. A political issue does not have to interest the majority of Americans, then, to be considered important by politicians. If an issue is of enough importance to a smaller group—the **issue public**—to cause those voters to become more politically active, that issue may well become an important political issue. Furthermore, very few politicians seek the approval of the general public as a whole. With the exception of the president, all politicians have much smaller constituencies, and they measure the public opinion of these constituencies in order to appeal to them. Members of the House of Representatives, for example, are interested primarily in the concerns of their home districts, which are often quite different from the concerns of the general public.

CHARACTERISTICS OF PUBLIC OPINION

Those who measure public opinion are not just interested in the direction of public opinion—that is, how the public is feeling at a given moment. They also want to know how strongly the public feels and how likely people are to change their minds. That is why they try to gauge the following characteristics of public opinion:

- **Saliency.** The saliency of an issue is the degree to which it is important to a particular individual or group. For example, Social

Security is an issue with high salience for senior citizens. Among young voters, Social Security has a much lower salience.

- **Intensity.** How strongly do people feel about a particular issue? When the intensity of a group's opinion is high, that group can wield political influence far beyond their numbers.

- **Stability.** Public opinion on issues changes over time. Some dimensions of public opinion, such as support for democracy and a controlled free-market economy, remain relatively stable. Others, like presidential approval ratings, can change quickly, as was the case during the last two years of George H. W. Bush's administration. During the Gulf War (January 1991), President Bush recorded the highest approval ratings of any president since 1945. Less than two years later, the majority of Americans showed their disapproval of his performance as president by voting against him.

In the United States, public opinion is measured regularly through elections. Elections measure public opinion indirectly, however, because votes for—or against—candidates can rarely be translated into clear and specific opinions. Referenda measure the public's opinion on specific issues (a **referendum** submits to popular vote to accept or reject a measure passed by a legislative body). Public opinion is measured most frequently and directly by **public opinion polls.**

POLLS MEASURE PUBLIC OPINION

Public opinion polls are designed to determine public opinion by asking questions of a much smaller group. Pollsters achieve this through **random sampling**, a method that allows them to poll a representative cross section of the public. When polling by phone, pollsters use a computer that dials numbers randomly. When conducting **exit polls** at polling places on election day, they target voting districts that collectively represent the voting public and randomly poll voters who are leaving the voting place. This method discourages bias, which may occur if pollsters were to approach only those voters who seemed most friendly or anxious to participate.

> Polling Accuracy
> When performed correctly, polls can measure the opinions of 300 million Americans by polling a mere 1,500 of them within about a 5% margin of error.

For a poll to accurately reflect public opinion, its questions must be carefully worded. A poll that asks, "Do you approve or disapprove of the death penalty?" would likely yield a very different response from one that asks, "Would you want the death penalty imposed on someone who killed your parents?" Most pollsters try to phrase questions objectively. Polls generally ask multiple-choice questions, which are closed-ended, as opposed to open-ended questions (such as, "Explain why you approve or disapprove of the death penalty"). Closed-ended questions yield results that are more easily quantifiable, providing a more accurate read of the direction and intensity of public opinion.

Even with those controls, polls cannot be 100% accurate. Polling organizations know how accurate their polls are and include this information with the poll results. The accuracy is measured as a sampling error and appears as a percentage with a plus and minus sign to the left (for example, ±4%). The **sampling error** tells how far off the poll results may be. Suppose a poll indicated that 60% of Americans favored the death penalty. If that poll had a sampling error of ±4%, the actual percentage of Americans favoring the death penalty could be anywhere between 56 and 64%. Generally, the more respondents a poll surveys, the lower the sampling error.

The best-known poll is the Gallup poll. Many major newspapers and television networks conduct public opinion polls, as do academic and public interest institutions.

WHERE DOES PUBLIC OPINION COME FROM?

Public opinion is made up of the views of individuals. Individuals develop their political attitudes through a process called **political socialization.** Why, and when, do they change? What factors influence a person's political beliefs?

The first factor that influences individual political beliefs is **family.** Most people eventually affiliate with the same political party as their parents. Children's political beliefs are also greatly affected by the moral and ethical values they learn from their parents. Political values learned in childhood stay with many Americans throughout their entire lives. Also important is their **location**—people born in rural states may develop political views that are more socially conservative than those of city dwellers.

As children grow, other factors influence their political socialization. In **school** they learn about history and government and are exposed to the political perspectives of teachers and peers. **Religious institutions** have a similar influence on many Americans. **Mass media** such as television, radio, magazines, and the Web further inform political attitudes. In general, however, youth is a time when many Americans pay relatively little attention to and have little interest in political issues. This is because most political issues have little direct impact on their day-to-day lives.

Those who progress to **higher education** often find themselves questioning their social and political assumptions for the first time. As a result, college can be a time of radical change in an individual's political beliefs. Studies have shown that students retain many of the political attitudes they acquire in college throughout their lives.

As individuals reach adulthood, **real-life experiences** become the primary influence on their political beliefs. Family responsibilities and property ownership tend to make people more conservative. Conversely, individuals who experience bias based on their socioeconomic status, race, or gender may grow more liberal or more cynical about government. Adults continue to be influenced by participation in religious organizations, by the attitudes of their peers, and by what they learn through the news media.

POLITICAL IDEOLOGIES

The terms *liberal* and *conservative* in the previous paragraph refer to the predominant ideologies in the United States. An **ideology** is a coherent set of thoughts and beliefs about politics and government.

The three most common political ideologies in the United States are the following:

- **Conservative.** Conservatives stress that individuals should be responsible for their own well-being and should not rely on government assistance. As a result, they tend to oppose government interference in the private sector. They also oppose most federal regulations, preferring that the market determine costs and acceptable business practices (laissez-faire economics). Social conservatives, who make up a powerful wing of the conservative population, do support government action on social issues. In a 2015 Gallup poll, 37% of Americans considered themselves to be conservatives.

- **Liberal.** Liberals believe that the government should be used in a limited way to remedy the social and economic injustices of the marketplace. They tend to support government regulation of the economy. They also support government efforts to redress past social injustices through programs such as affirmative action. Most liberals believe the government should strictly enforce the separation of church and state, and therefore oppose school-sponsored prayer and proposed bans on abortions, which they perceive as motivated by religious beliefs. In a 2014 Gallup poll, 24% of Americans considered themselves to be liberal.

- **Moderate (or Independent).** The beliefs of moderates do not constitute a coherent ideology. Instead, moderates view themselves as pragmatists who apply common sense rather than philosophical principles to political problems. Moderates once made up the largest part of the American public, but with the financial crisis of 2008–2009, polls have shown a small decline in this number. Indeed, a 2014 Gallup poll found that 35% of Americans considered themselves to be moderate.

Compared with citizens of other Western democracies, Americans have fewer main ideological groups. The many extreme political parties that exist in Europe, ranging from right-wing nationalists to left-leaning communists, are practically nonexistent in the United States. Furthermore, perhaps because of the paucity of viable groups, Americans readily vote outside of their self-professed political beliefs. In 2008, for example, 20% of self-identified conservative voters chose the more liberal Barack Obama over conservative Republican candidate John McCain due to the economic crisis and negative perception of Republican incumbent George W. Bush.

Americans who are strongly ideological tend to be the most politically active citizens. They are more likely than other Americans to join political organizations and participate in political activities, such as rallies and boycotts. One result of this phenomenon is that candidates in the presidential primaries must perform a balancing act. To win the primaries, they must first appeal to the more ideological party members. Then in the general elections, candidates must move back to the political center or risk alienating the general voting public.

See the next chapter for a more detailed explanation of political beliefs by party.

Determining Factors in Ideological and Political Behavior

Although there is no one-to-one correlation between people's backgrounds and their political beliefs, people who share certain traits tend to share political beliefs. Here are some of the factors that influence people's ideological and political attitudes.

- **Race/ethnicity.** Racial and ethnic groups who disproportionately populate the lower income levels tend to be more liberal than other Americans. Blacks and Hispanics have been more likely than other Americans to support liberal social programs, for example. There are exceptions to these rules, however: Cuban Americans, for one, have tended to be conservative.

- **Religion.** Among the various religious groups in the United States, Jews and African-American Protestants are generally the most liberal. Catholics also lean toward the political left, although many are conservative on social issues. Devout white Protestants tend to be more conservative. This is particularly true in the South, where white Protestants who attend church regularly are among the nation's strongest supporters of the Republican Party.

- **Gender.** Women tend to be more liberal than men. They are more likely to vote Democratic, more likely to support government social welfare programs, and less likely to support increases in military spending.

- **Income level.** Americans in higher income brackets tend to be more supportive of liberal goals such as racial and sexual equality. They also support greater international cooperation. However, they tend to be more fiscally conservative. Poorer Americans, conversely, are generally more conservative on all issues except those concerning social welfare.

- **Region.** Regional differences arise from different economic and social interests. The ethnic and racial mix of the East Coast has made it the most liberal region of the country (making these "blue states"). In the more religious South, conservatism is predominant (making these "red states"). The West Coast, toward which many Americans continue to migrate, is the most polarized, with strong liberal and conservative contingencies scattered up and down the coast; though, this region has leaned more to the left in recent years. Liberals tend to congregate in cities; elsewhere, small town and more rural voters are generally conservative.

PUBLIC OPINION AND THE MASS MEDIA

The **news media** play an important role in the development of public opinion. News media include all of the following:

- news broadcasts on television (particularly 24-hour cable news networks), radio, and the Internet
- newspapers
- news magazines, such as *Time*
- magazine broadcast programs, such as *60 Minutes* and *20/20*
- newsmaker interview programs, such as *Meet the Press* and *The Daily Show* (which may be a comedy show, but has hosted many political guests and approached interviewing those guests seriously)
- political talk radio and podcasts
- websites, blogs, news aggregators, and online forums, such as *The Huffington Post, Drudge Report,* and *Politico*
- social media such as Facebook, Twitter, Tumblr, and Reddit

These media provide most Americans with their most extensive exposure to politicians and the government. In many ways, they act as an intermediary between the people and the government, constantly questioning the motives and purposes of government actions and then reporting their findings to the public.

Throughout American history, public exposure to news media has consistently increased, both through higher literacy rates and through the expansion of news sources available in print, broadcast, and online. As a result, the media have played an increasingly significant role over the years in shaping public opinion.

The Media and the Public Agenda

The most important role the media play is in setting the **public agenda.** By deciding which news stories to cover and which to ignore, and by returning to some stories night after night while allowing others to die after a few reports, the news media play an important part in determining the relative importance of political issues. This power of the media is limited by the public's inherent interest in a story, however. Prior to American involvement in Bosnia, constant coverage of the crisis there did little to raise public awareness of or interest in the story, because many Americans perceived the crisis as too remote to be of interest. In general, the process of setting the national agenda is a dynamic one. The media generally try to report stories that they believe will interest the public, and often there is a domino effect: as interest grows, coverage increases, and the story becomes more important.

Less clear is whether the media have the power to alter public opinion. It is generally believed that the media affect public opinion only when news coverage is extensive and is either predominantly negative or positive. For example, a constant barrage of negative images broadcast from Vietnam in the 1960s is credited with having turned many Americans against the war.

The news media can also alter public opinion when it is volatile: studies have demonstrated, for example, that public approval of the president is quite volatile and changes depending on whether news coverage of the president is positive or negative. In most other instances, however, the media do not greatly impact public opinion. This is in part because the news media cover many stories simultaneously, thus diluting their ability to influence public opinion on any single issue. It is also due in part to the fact that most Americans choose those news media that reinforce their political beliefs. For example, conservative magazines such as the *National Review* are read almost exclusively by conservatives; liberal magazines, such as *The Nation*, are read primarily by liberals and progressives.

In addition to the news media, social media have become crucial tools for major grassroots political movements, both within the United States and abroad. Facebook, Twitter, Tumblr, Reddit, and other such social media sites can act as both a shaper and an indicator of public opinion, mostly with younger demographics (ages 18–25).

Are the News Media Biased?

Critics from both ends of the political spectrum claim that the news media interject their political beliefs into their reports. It seems that not a day goes by without political pundits accusing FOX of being wildly conservative, and MSNBC of pushing a liberal agenda. Conservatives cite polls that have consistently shown that news reporters are more likely to hold liberal views and vote Democratic than are average Americans. Liberals point out that the major news media are owned by large, conservative companies. They argue that these companies exert pressure on the networks to downplay or ignore stories that reflect badly on the companies or the economic and political forces that support them.

Many studies have shown that there is less ideological bias in news reporting than is claimed by critics, either in the stories news organizations choose to report or in the way they report them. Over the course of American history, the news media have in fact grown markedly less biased. Most newspapers in the 18th and 19th centuries were openly partisan; today, many news organizations attempt to maintain journalistic integrity by remaining as objective as possible.

Commercial concerns reinforce this trend toward objectivity. Biased reporting may appeal strongly to one segment of the population, but it would just as surely alienate another segment. Seeking to offend the fewest possible audience members, most news organizations attempt to weed out bias and represent both sides of every story in their reports.

This does not mean, however, that the news media achieve complete objectivity, which is impossible. News organizations must make hundreds of decisions each day about what to report and how prominently to report it. Many local newspapers, for example, ignore all but the most major international stories, and not because they are not newsworthy but rather because their readers are generally uninterested in such stories. Network news broadcasts shy away from more complex stories, both because of time constraints and out of fear that they may bore viewers and listeners.

Time and space constraints also result in bias in news reporting. Time and space concerns affect all news organizations, but they are most acutely felt by television news programs, which report up to 20 stories during their 18 minutes of broadcast time (some half-hour programs feature as many as 12 minutes of advertising!). News broadcasts increasingly use short sound bites to summarize information, with presidential candidates' sound bites decreasing in length from about 40 seconds (in 1968) to about 7.3 seconds today.

Finally, news reports can be biased by the sources that reporters use for their information. Reporters in Washington, D.C., must rely heavily on politicians and government sources for information, for example. The effect of this reliance is complicated. On one hand, reporters try to not offend their government sources with uncomplimentary reports, because they will need to return to those sources for future stories. Furthermore, there is the danger that reporters in Washington will become too close to the people and events they cover, resulting in bias. On the other hand, reporters must maintain their credibility and so must demonstrate their independence. They cannot consistently file favorable reports on the subjects they cover and expect to remain credible to the viewer. Moreover, surveys have demonstrated that reporters are more skeptical about the motives of politicians than average Americans are. This skepticism is reflected in their reporting. This may in part explain why public confidence in the government has decreased as the news media have grown more prominent.

Most modern politicians understand the power of the media and, accordingly, attempt to influence coverage. They stage events that yield appealing photographs (photo ops) and provide voluminous documented information in support of their positions (press releases). They plan appearances on shows with specific audience demographics that they are seeking, such as *The Daily Show* if they are seeking the youth vote. One famous photo op was President George W. Bush's speech aboard the USS Abraham Lincoln on May 1, 2003. A banner reading "Mission Accomplished" hung behind the president as he spoke, and it caused much controversy, as that was the final day of combat operations in Iraq. Many politicians felt that the banner was irresponsible and misleading, because casualties have continued for many years afterward. Attempts to manipulate media reports have grown more frequent and more sophisticated in recent years. Many politicians have studied the masterful way in which Ronald Reagan handled press coverage and have attempted to copy his successes.

The Audience Factor
A primary source of media bias is the media's need for an immediate audience appeal.

KEY TERMS

- public opinion
- general public
- issue public
- saliency
- intensity
- stability
- referendum
- public opinion polls
- random sampling
- exit polls
- sampling error
- political socialization
- ideology
- conservative
- liberal
- moderate (Independent)
- news media
- public agenda

Summary

- Public opinion is measured by looking at saliency, intensity, and stability.

- Data about what people think come from polls, and many politicians base their decisions on polling data.

- Political socialization is the term used to describe how people learn about politics as they grow and mature.

- There are three basic political ideologies in America: conservative, liberal, and moderate.

- Know which factors tend to lead to which ideologies. For example, a black woman in Chicago is more likely to be liberal than a white man from the rural South.

- The media plays a major role in the perception of government by placing certain policies and news events in the spotlight. This is also known as creating a public agenda.

Chapter 5 Drill

See Chapter 11 for answers and explanations.

Questions 1 and 2 refer to the table below:

RELIGION OF ADULTS IN THE U.S.

Year	1990	2001	2008
Total adult population	175,440	207,983	228,182
Christian	151,225	159,514	173,402
Other religion	5,853	7,740	8,796
No religion	14,331	29,481	34,169
Other response	N/A	57	45
No response	4,031	11,246	11,815

1. Which of the following describes a trend in the table above?

   (A) America's adult population declined between 1990 and 2008.
   (B) The number of American who follow no religion more than doubled between 1990 and 2008.
   (C) All groups grew between 1990 and 2008.
   (D) The number of American Christians declined between 1990 and 2001.

2. If the trends in the table continue at the same rate, what is the best conclusion that can be drawn about the changing nature of political socialization in America?

   (A) "Other Religions" will become a dominant force in political socialization.
   (B) Fewer Americans will experience political socialization in a religious setting.
   (C) Political socialization will become a thing of the past.
   (D) Religion will become Americans' primary method of political socialization.

3. Which of the following is an accurate comparison between moderates and conservatives?

	Conservative	Moderate
(A)	Smallest voting block	Largest voting block
(B)	Back abortion rights	Rarely change their minds on political issues
(C)	Support affirmative action	Always vote the same way
(D)	Oppose government regulation	View themselves as pragmatists

4. Which of the following issues carries the most intensity with the American public?

   (A) Charter schools
   (B) Indian affairs
   (C) NASA's budget
   (D) Social Security

5. Which of the following is generally a factor in determining someone's ideological behavior?

   (A) Birth order
   (B) Gender
   (C) Sport preference
   (D) Age

6. In which of the following ways could a politician most likely generate positive media stories?

   (A) Change positions on a controversial issue
   (B) Appear in photographs with military veterans
   (C) Divorce a spouse with different political views
   (D) Solicit political donations from foreign governments

7. Which of the following is considered to have low stability in U.S. public opinion?

   (A) Presidential approval ratings
   (B) Support for an incumbent U.S. House Representative running unopposed
   (C) Support for Social Security benefits
   (D) U.S. Supreme Court approval ratings

REFLECT

Respond to the following questions:

- For which content topics discussed in this chapter do you feel you have achieved sufficient mastery to answer multiple-choice questions correctly?

- For which content topics discussed in this chapter do you feel you have achieved sufficient mastery to discuss effectively in an essay?

- For which content topics discussed in this chapter do you feel you need more work before you can answer multiple-choice questions correctly?

- For which content topics discussed in this chapter do you feel you need more work before you can discuss effectively in an essay?

- What parts of this chapter are you going to re-review?

- Will you seek further help, outside of this book (such as a teacher, tutor, or AP Students), on any of the content in this chapter—and, if so, on what content?

Chapter 6
Linkage Institutions

CONCEPTS

- What coalitions make up the two main political parties in the United States?
- Why do third parties so often fail in U.S. politics?
- What effect has dealignment had on political parties?
- Are there serious policy differences between Democrats and Republicans?
- Who supports the two parties and why?
- How does the Constitution control special interests?
- How have interest groups helped to democratize the U.S. political system?
- Why are interest groups a threat to democracy?
- What role do interest groups play in setting the political agenda?
- What techniques do PACs use to get their messages across?
- How do interest groups achieve and exert their influence?

In the previous chapter we reviewed how individuals develop their political beliefs. Few political acts, however, are the work of a single person. Rather, most politically active people work within groups to achieve common political goals. The AP U.S. Government and Politics Exam expects you to know about four types of linkage institutions. They are **political parties, interest groups, political action committees (PACs),** and **527 groups.** This chapter reviews everything you need to know about the organization and activities of these groups.

POLITICAL PARTIES

No Partying
The framers of the Constitution disliked political parties and hoped to prevent them.

As we've mentioned, few successful political accomplishments are the work of one person. More often, such a person joins with other like-minded individuals to form organizations that try to influence the outcomes of elections and legislative struggles. **Political parties** are unique among these groups in that they play a formal role in both of these processes. Although they are not mentioned in the Constitution, political parties became a mainstay of U.S. elections by the year 1800. Parties arose in the United States as a means of uniting those who shared political ideals, enabling them to elect like-minded representatives and pursue similar legislative goals. To those ends, parties endorse candidates for office and assist in their election efforts. In return for this support, parties expect candidates to remain loyal to goals defined by the party leadership.

The United States has two major political parties: Democrats and Republicans. This **two-party** or **bipartisan system** is reinforced by the nation's electoral system. U.S. election rules, which have been agreed upon by members of the two parties, also make it difficult for all but the two major parties to win a place on the ballot, further strengthening the two-party system.

Party Characteristics

Don't forget these facts about political parties.

- Parties serve as intermediaries between the people and the government.

- Parties are made up of grassroots members, activist members, and leadership.

- Parties are organized to raise money, present positions on policy, and get their candidates elected to office.

- Parties were created outside of the Constitution—they are not even mentioned in the document but were developed in the 1790s.

The major purpose of political parties is to get candidates elected to office. In the past, candidates were chosen by the party hierarchy, with little or no public input. However, since 1960, more states have passed laws requiring parties to select candidates through state-run **primary elections**. These primaries have reduced the power of political parties. Candidates must raise their own money for primaries, campaigning for their party's nomination with little to no support from the party itself. If the parties don't control the money, they can't control the candidates. This levels the playing field, but multiple candidates for the nomination can splinter the party membership.

Functions of Modern Political Parties

Political scientists identify three major subdivisions of political parties.

- **The party among the electorate.** Voters enroll in and identify with political parties. They generally vote for candidates who represent their party.

- **The party in government.** Government officials belong to political parties. They act together to pursue common goals, although regional and ideological differences sometimes subvert their efforts.

- **The party organization.** A group of people who are neither elected officials nor average voters, the party organization is made up of political professionals who recruit candidates and voters, organize campaign events, and raise money to promote the party.

Political parties perform all of the following functions:

- **Recruit and nominate candidates.** The parties are the major players in electoral politics. They seek out candidates to run in their primary elections. They also create the rules by which candidates seek their nominations. In nearly all elections, nomination by one of the major parties is a prerequisite to victory. For example, in the 2008 Democratic primary, Barack Obama and Hillary Clinton continued to campaign until Obama had enough delegates to secure the nomination, at which point the Democratic party formally announced him as their candidate.

- **Educate and mobilize voters.** Political parties fund propaganda campaigns to persuade voters to choose their candidates. They send mailings, hold rallies, and run advertisements. They target regions in which their support is strong and campaign to persuade voters in those regions to vote on election day.

- **Provide campaign funds and support.** The national parties have committees dedicated to raising funds for House and Senate campaigns. State parties also raise funds for candidates for both state and national office. Although most candidates rely primarily on their own personal campaign support staff, they also need the help of the state or national party organizations.

- **Organize government activity.** Parties act as an organizing force in government. The House and Senate organize their leadership and committee systems strictly along party lines, as do state legislatures.

- **Provide balance through opposition of two parties.** Each party serves as a check on the other by constantly watching for and exposing weakness and hypocrisy. The minority party (provided a single party controls both the White House and the Congress) performs the role of the *loyal opposition*, constantly critiquing the performance of the party in power.

- **Reduce conflict and tension in society.** The two-party system promotes compromise and negotiation in two ways: by encouraging parties to accommodate voters and encouraging voters to accept compromises in policy. The Republican Party, for example, includes both religious social conservatives and libertarians. To assemble winning coalitions, the party must somehow appease both groups. The groups, in turn, must be willing to compromise if they wish to prevent the Democrats from prevailing.

U.S. political parties are not hierarchical. The national party organization and each of the state and local organizations are largely autonomous and serve different functions; one does not necessarily take orders from the other.

Party committees are organized by geographic subdivisions. Locally, committees at the precinct, town, ward, and electoral district levels coordinate get-out-the-vote drives, door-to-door canvassing, and leaflet distribution. These party committees are staffed mostly by volunteers, and their work is largely concentrated around election time. The next largest geographic grouping is the county. County committees coordinate efforts in local elections and organize the efforts of committees on the precinct level. They also send representatives to each polling place to monitor voting procedures.

State committees raise money and provide volunteers to staff campaign events. They provide support to candidates for both state and national offices. National legislative elections, however, are also the responsibility of the powerful congressional district and senatorial committees. These committees, chaired by incumbents and staffed by professionals, are part of the national party organization. They are most likely to become involved in these legislative elections when the possibility exists of gaining or losing a seat. Because incumbents usually run for reelection and are often reelected easily, the congressional and senatorial committees are active in a minority of election efforts during each electoral cycle.

The national party plans the **national conventions** held every four years to nominate a presidential candidate. It sponsors polls to keep party members informed of public opinion and manages issue-oriented advertising and propaganda.

Are Parties in Decline?

Some political scientists believe that the parties are no longer as powerful or as significant as they once were. Prior to 1968, one party typically controlled both the executive and legislative branches of government. Since that year, however, there have been only a few years of one-party control of these branches (1977 to 1980, 1992 to 1994, 2002 to 2005, 2008 to 2010, and 2016 to 2018). Americans are voting a split ticket (see Chapter 7) more frequently than ever before. They are more likely to consider the merits and positions of a particular candidate than to merely consider his or her party affiliation. As a result, no one party dominates government, and officials with different political agendas are elected to work together. As shown in the following graph (see the next page), more and more Americans are identifying as independent rather than with a single political party.

Increasingly, modern candidates have taken control of their own election campaigns, relying less on party support than did past candidates. They are now able to appeal directly to the public through television and the Internet. This has left the parties—which once wielded great power over the electoral process—with less power. In their place, media consultants have become the chief movers and shakers in political campaigns.

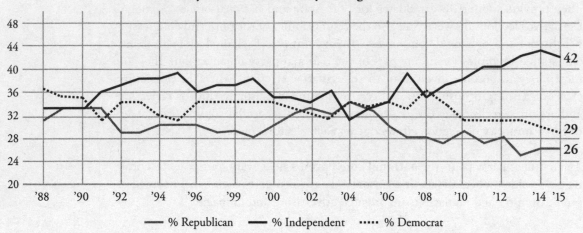

— % Republican   — % Independent   ····· % Democrat

Party Coalitions

Political parties consist of combinations of groups, which consist of combinations of individuals. The larger the coalition, the more likely the candidate will win. Party candidates and party positions on policy are designed to attract more groups of voters, putting together a winning **coalition.**

In the presidential elections of 2008 and 2012, the Republican coalition included the following:

- veterans' groups and military supporters
- religious conservatives
- libertarians
- opponents of gay marriage
- opponents of affirmative action
- supporters of the development of natural resources on public lands
- rural dwellers

In the same elections, the Democratic coalition included the following:

- disaffected moderate Republicans
- pro-choicers
- African and Hispanic Americans
- members and supporters of labor unions
- gay rights supporters
- people with lower incomes
- city dwellers
- feminists
- environmentalists

While there are always exceptions to the rule, the two parties tend to rely on these groups as a base of support. Regionally, it appears that the east and west coasts and the upper Midwest are more Democratic, while the South and lower Midwest are more Republican.

Ideological Differences Between the Parties

While there are general ideological differences between the two parties, there are also a number of similarities. Neither party, for example, questions the validity of the nation's capitalist economic system.

Although both parties tend to be centrist, there are nevertheless differences in the ways the two parties view the role of government. The greatest ideological differences are between the liberals in the Democratic Party and the conservatives in the Republican Party, the so-called **party bases.** While appealing to the independent centrist voter during election campaigns, each party counts on its base to get out and vote. Party leaders must use great care in choosing policy positions so they do not lose their party base. They must also avoid alienating the moderates of the party by taking extreme left or right positions.

Democrats Tend to Be...	Republicans Tend to Be...
Less disposed to spend on defense	More disposed to spend on defense
Less disposed to use vouchers, or other public funds, to enable certain students to attend private/charter schools	More disposed to use vouchers for private or charter schools and to give governmental aid to parochial schools
More disposed to spend money to advance social-welfare programs	Less disposed to spend money on social-welfare programs
More disposed to use government money for public education	Less disposed to use government money for public education
More disposed to grant tax relief to targeted programs such as the lower and middle classes	More disposed to grant tax relief to everyone, including the wealthy and corporations
Against private ownership of assault weapons and supportive of broader regulations on the ownership of firearms	Less disposed to regulate firearms

Party Realignment

Party **realignment** occurs when the coalitions making up the two parties fall apart, such as when many of the groups that make up the majority party defect to the minority party. Realignments are very rare and usually occur as a result of some major traumatic event, such as an economic depression or a war. They are signaled by what is called a **critical election,** when a new party comes to dominate politics. Realignments occur over a period of time and show permanence. The New Deal coalition of the 1930s lasted for decades. There have been no realignments since the 1930s.

Depression Politics

The last realignment took place in 1932 as a result of the Great Depression, when the Republican Party became the minority party and the Democratic party became the majority party, with overwhelming numbers of Democrats being elected to every branch of government at every level.

The trend today seems to be toward dealignment. **Dealignment** is usually a result of party members becoming disaffected as a result of some policy position taken by the party. These disaffected party members join no political party and vote for the candidate rather than the party he or she belongs to. Since the 1960s, membership in the Democratic Party has declined significantly, while the number of Republicans has declined modestly. During the same time period, the number of voters self-identifying as independents has increased dramatically.

Third Parties

New parties are occasionally formed in the United States. Unless and until these parties reach the level of a major party, they are called third parties. Third parties form to represent constituencies that feel disenfranchised from both of the major parties. These so-called **splinter** or **bolter parties** usually unite around a feeling that the major parties are not responding to the demands of some segment of the electorate. The Reform Party, under whose banner Ross Perot ran for president in 1996, was an example of a splinter party whose constituency was fed up with "politics as usual."

Sometimes third parties form to represent an ideology considered too radical by the mainstream parties. These **doctrinal parties** reject the prevailing attitudes and policies of the political system. The Socialist Party and Libertarian Party are examples. **Single-issue parties** are formed to promote one principle. The American Independent Party, which sponsored the segregationist candidacy of George C. Wallace in 1968, is an example. Third parties can have a major impact on elections, especially in tight races. The Green Party, which favors strict environmental policies, more government social programs, and controls over big business, ran Ralph Nader for president in 2000. Some analysts have suggested, based on voter patterns and polls, that if Nader had not run, Al Gore would have received a greater number of votes, which would have allowed him to win the election against George W. Bush.

Third-party candidates should not be confused with **Independent candidates.** Independent candidates run without party affiliation. It is very difficult for

Independent candidates to overcome the money and organization of the two major parties. Eugene McCarthy, an anti-Vietnam War candidate in 1968, and John Anderson, a fiscal conservative and social liberal in 1980, are two examples.

Why Third Parties Fail

The failure of third parties to elect presidential and other candidates to office is a direct result of an American political system designed to support only two major parties. National campaigns in countries using equal, single-member, plurality voting-district systems (like the United States) require huge sums of money and vast organizations. Also, in American presidential elections, almost all states have a winner-take-all system for electoral votes; the candidate who receives the most votes, even if it is only by one, wins all of the votes in that state. Because the losers get no electoral votes, the electoral count does not always accurately reflect the popular vote. During the 2000 presidential election (which featured the Florida voting controversy), Al Gore won the popular vote by about 500,000 votes nationwide, but George W. Bush was found to have won the Florida electorate, giving him all of Florida's 25 electoral votes and ultimately the presidency. Similarly, during the 2016 presidential election, Hillary Clinton won the popular vote by approximately 2.9 million votes, but Donald Trump won the Electoral College, winning him the presidential election.

INTEREST GROUPS

Interest groups are organizations dedicated to a particular political goal or to a set of unified goals. Group members often share a common bond, either religious (Christian Coalition), racial (National Association for the Advancement of Colored People), or professional (American Medical Association). In other cases, they simply share a common interest, such as the environment (Sierra Club) or political reform (Common Cause). In any case, they are similar to political parties in that they try to influence the outcome of elections and legislation. Unlike political parties, however, they do not nominate candidates, nor do they normally try to address a wide range of issues.

When interest groups try to influence legislators, we say they are **lobbying** for a bill or issue. The term originated with the historical practice of early lobbyists; they waited in the lobby of the capitol so they could catch legislators coming in and out of session. Today, most lobbyists are highly paid professionals. A number are former legislators, whose experience and friendships in the Capitol make them particularly effective.

There are literally thousands of interest groups in the United States. Most groups fall under one of the following categories:

- **Economic groups.** Economic groups are formed to promote and protect members' economic interests. They include peak business groups such as the U.S. Chamber of Commerce, which represents the interests of all businesspeople. Other groups represent specific

All For Many, But All For One
If you're curious, the two states that do not have this winner-take-all system are Maine and Nebraska, and both proportionately distribute their votes by congressional district. The 2008 presidential election between Barack Obama and John McCain was the first time Nebraska's electoral vote was split, and the 2016 presidential election between Donald Trump and Hillary Clinton was the first time Maine's electoral vote was split.

One For All, Even When All For None
The purpose of an interest group is to advocate for a benefit that is in the best interests of its membership. The free rider problem, however, occurs when the beneficiaries of the interest group fail to participate in political action or give financial support. For instance, a professional organization will fight for the general goals of those in its profession, even those who are not formal members of the group. Those beneficiaries go along for a "free ride" because they reap the benefits of actions taken on their behalf, but do not share the burden of supporting the interest group.

trades and industries; among these are the American Farm Bureau Federation and the American Nuclear Energy Council. Labor groups such as the AFL-CIO and the United Auto Workers represent union members. Professional groups include the American Medical Association and the American Bar Association. Most economic groups have existed a long time and have developed strong ties with legislators and bureaucrats. They are also very large, highly influential, and extremely well funded, and either represent or employ large constituencies. As a result, they are usually the most powerful interest groups in Washington, D.C.

- **Public interest groups.** Public interest groups are nonprofit organizations that are generally organized around a well-defined set of public policy issues. Consumer groups usually work to promote safer products and more informative labeling; the most prominent of these groups is Public Citizen, led by **Ralph Nader**. Environmental groups, such as the Sierra Club, advocate preservation of wildlife and wilderness areas. Religious groups such as the Christian Coalition attempt to influence public policy in such a way as to promote or protect their beliefs. Other groups promote causes such as women's rights, minority rights, and political reform. Single-issue groups like the National Rifle Association (NRA) and Mothers Against Drunk Driving (MADD) are often among the most powerful public interest groups because of the intensity of their supporters. Single-issue constituents are more likely than other voters to use a single issue as a litmus test for candidates. Thus, a candidate who advocates gun control runs the risk of losing the votes of all three million NRA members.

- **Government interest groups.** Most states and many cities and other localities maintain lobbying organizations in the nation's capital. A separate group represents the nation's governors, and yet another represents mayors. Most foreign governments and businesses lobby the government as well.

How Interest Groups Influence Government

Interest groups use a number of tactics to disseminate information and persuade Congress, the president, the judiciary, and federal bureaucrats. Those tactics include the following:

- **Direct lobbying.** Representatives of the interest group meet privately with government officials to suggest legislation and to present arguments supporting their positions. Lobbyists are often the source for a great deal of information to young congressmen who are trying to learn about new bills. Some would argue that the lobbyists need to give relatively good information to those congressmen in order to maintain a good relationship with them so that they can lobby them later on their issues.

- **Testifying before Congress.** Interest groups provide expert witnesses at committee hearings.

- **Socializing.** Social events in Washington, D.C., are often political events as well. Interest groups hold social functions and members attend other functions to meet and forge relationships with government officials.

- **Political donations.** Interest groups provide financial support to candidates and parties that champion their causes. Corporations, trade groups, and often unions do so by forming political action committees (PACs) and super PACs for that purpose.

- **Endorsements.** Many groups announce their support for specific candidates. Some groups rate legislators on the basis of their voting records; a high rating constitutes an implicit endorsement of that candidate.

- **Court action.** Interest groups file lawsuits or **class action suits** to protect and advance their interests. They will also submit *amicus curiae* (friend of the court) **briefs** in lawsuits to which they are not a party so that judges may consider their advice in respect to matters of law that directly affect the case in question.

- **Rallying their membership.** Public interest groups often engage in grassroots campaigning by contacting members and asking them to write, phone, or email their legislators in support of a particular program or piece of legislation. In addition, members may engage in demonstrations and rallies promoting their cause.

- **Propaganda.** Interest groups send out press releases and run advertisements promoting their views.

Limits on Lobbying

Several laws limit the scope of lobbyists' activities. Most are ineffective, but stronger efforts to regulate lobbying run the risk of violating the First Amendment right to free speech. The 1946 Federal Regulation of Lobbying Act was intended to allow the government to monitor lobbying activities by requiring lobbyists to register with the government and publicly disclose their salaries, expenses, and the nature of their activities in Washington, D.C.

Other laws prohibit, for limited amounts of time, certain lobbying activities by former government officials. These laws are meant to counteract the appearance of **influence peddling**, the practice of using personal friendships and inside information to get political advantage. Former legislators must wait one year before lobbying Congress directly, for example. However, they may lobby the executive branch immediately after leaving office. Some groups complain of a "revolving door" that pushes former federal employees into jobs as lobbyists and consultants. A limit similar to that of the former legislators also applies to former executive officials. It prevents them from lobbying for five years after they leave the agency that employed them. These limits were determined in *Buckley v. Valeo* (1976), the case that equated donations with free speech. In this ruling, the Supreme Court upheld federal limits on campaign contributions and ruled that donating money to influence elections is a form of constitutionally protected free speech.

Finally, federal laws prohibiting campaign contributions from corporations, unions, and trade associations can be sidestepped through the formation of a political action committee or PAC.

> ### Changes to Campaign Financing
> In January of 2010, the Supreme Court changed many of the campaign finance rules in the case of *Citizens United v. Federal Election Commission*. The court ruled that corporations have a First Amendment right to expressly support political candidates for Congress and the White House. The ruling struck down restrictions that had prevented corporations from spending company money directly on campaign advertising right before an election. In the near future, this groundbreaking case will surely cause many changes in the financing of election campaigns. It is still important to learn how and why these groups function by reading the following sections.

POLITICAL ACTION COMMITTEES (PACS) AND SUPER PACS

The 1974 **Federal Election Campaign Act (FECA)** allowed corporations, unions, and trade associations to form political action committees as a means of raising campaign funds. FECA set restrictions on contributors and contributions, and stipulated that corporate, union, and trade PACs must raise money from employees and members and may not simply draw it from their treasuries. Corporations, unions, and trade associations are not the only groups that form PACs. Many other interest groups form PACs to collect and distribute contributions, as do legislators (these are referred to as leadership PACs). After that change, the **Bipartisan Campaign Reform Act (BCRA) of 2002** (also known as the **McCain-Feingold Act**) further regulated campaign finance and PAC regulated campaign finance and PAC donations by prohibiting unregulated contributions (soft money) to national political parties and limited the use of corporate and union money for ads discussing political issues within 60 days of a general election and 30 days of a primary. Then in 2010, in ***Citizens United v. Federal Election Commission***, the Supreme Court overturned BCRA's limits on PAC fundraising for "corporate independent expenditures." Under the terms of the *Citizens United* decision, PACs that donate to specific candidates must operate under limits on their contributors and their donations, but PACs that do not donate to specific candidates—as long as they do not directly coordinate with specific candidates—

are not limited in their fundraising. In this context, political donations are considered free speech. These unlimited PACs have come to be known as **Super PACs** and are generally financed by the ultra-rich; however, because of disclosure laws affecting such Super PACs, it can be difficult to identify donors.

For regular PACs, donations from single-candidate PACs to individual candidates cannot exceed $2,500 ($5,000 for a multi-candidate PAC). Such PACs' donations to national political committees cannot exceed $15,000 from multi-candidate PACs and $30,800 from single-candidate PACs. Though Super PACs avoid limits by not directly or officially coordinating with specific candidates, the *Citizens United* decision is vague on what constitutes coordination.

> ## Hard vs. Soft: We're Not Talking About Water
> For the exam, you should be familiar with the terms "hard money" and "soft money." "Hard money" refers to tightly regulated contributions to candidates, while "soft money" refers to unregulated, unlimited contributions to political parties for general party-building activities such as get-out-the vote drives, voter registration efforts, and ads that say "Vote for Democrats" or "Vote for Republicans." Potential uses of soft money were limited by Congress with the passage of the McCain-Feingold Act.

527 GROUPS

A 527 group (named after the section of the tax code that allows them) is a tax-exempt organization that promotes a political agenda, although they cannot expressly advocate for or against a specific candidate. The term is generally used to refer to political organizations that are not regulated by the **FEC (Federal Election Commission)** and are not subject to the same contribution limits as PACs. They avoid regulation by the FEC because 527s are "political organizations" but are not registered as "political committees" subject to campaign finance law contribution limits. Sounds confusing, huh? The line between issue advocacy and candidate advocacy is a huge source of contention and disagreement. The BCRA changed **soft money** rules to make establishing new 527s a more attractive option than traditional PACs and allowing outside organizations to circumvent the hard money limits of the BCRA. The *Citizens United* decision, however, makes Super PACs another viable alternative for avoiding such limits.

KEY TERMS

- political parties
- interest groups
- political action committees (PACs)
- Super PACs
- 527 groups
- two-party (bipartisan) system
- primary elections
- splinter (bolter) parties
- doctrinal parties
- single-issue parties
- Independent candidates
- national convention
- split-ticket voting
- divided government
- dealignment
- coalition
- realignment
- critical election
- lobbying
- class action suits
- *amicus curiae* briefs
- influence peddling
- Federal Action Campaign Act
- Bipartisan Campaign Reform Act (McCain-Feingold Act)
- *Citizens United v. Federal Election Commission*
- Federal Election Commission (FEC)
- soft money

Summary

o Though they are not mentioned in the Constitution, political parties have become an integral part of American government. They may embrace a wide variety of ideologies, but ultimately both parties share the same goal: to be elected by any means necessary.

o American history has been marked by numerous third parties that have challenged the prevailing duopoly. If it is popular enough, a third party may influence the two major parties to adopt its ideas.

o Parties serve many functions in American democracy: they recruit and fund candidates, educate voters, provide a loyal opposition, and run the government—all while mitigating societal tension.

o When we look at parties, they often turn out to be broad coalitions of disparate ideologies and groups. The Republican Party, for example, blends libertarians who are hostile to government regulation with religious conservatives who want government to play a greater role in enforcing public morality.

o Generally speaking, Democrats tend to be in favor of government regulation of industry, redistribution of government money to the poor, and social freedom. Republicans tend to want to empower business to free itself from government rules, encourage people to earn money with assistance from the state, and want more social and moral controls on society.

o Interest groups are large organizations with strong policy goals, but they are different from political parties in that they do not change their ideologies. These groups try to control the political process by hiring lobbyists to influence legislators and by giving them money as well.

o When labor unions or corporations want to fund candidates, they do so by forming Political Action Committees, or PACs. PACs and Super PACs provide a means to funnel money to a candidate of choice and are regulated by the Federal Election Commission (FEC).

o 527 groups are not regulated by the FEC, and the nature of these groups is a source of great contention. They have become a way for organizations to avoid hard money limits, and their spending has ballooned in recent years, despite efforts to limit and regulate outside money in elections.

Chapter 6 Drill

See Chapter 11 for answers and explanations.

Questions 1 and 2 refer to the passage below.

"However [political parties] may now and then answer popular ends, they are likely in the course of time and things, to become potent engines, by which cunning, ambitious, and unprincipled men will be enable to subvert the power of the people and to usurp for themselves the reins of government, destroying afterwards the very engines which have lifted them to unjust dominion. Towards the preservation of your government, and the permanency of your present happy state, it is requisite, not only that you steadily discountenance irregular oppositions to its acknowledged authority, but also that you resist with care the spirit of innovation upon its principles, however specious the pretexts."

—George Washington, Farewell Address, 1796

1. Which of the following statements best reflects Washington's message in the passage?

   (A) Political parties are a natural part of American political life.
   (B) Political parties never work in the interests of the American people.
   (C) Political parties are run by moral men.
   (D) Political parties manipulate the government to ensure their grasp on power.

2. Someone arguing that Washington's message is coming true would point to which of the following events in American political history?

   (A) The Federal Action Campaign Act
   (B) The Bipartisan Campaign Reform Act (McCain-Feingold Act)
   (C) *Citizens United v. Federal Election Commission*
   (D) The creation of the Federal Election Commission

3. Which of the following is an accurate comparison between a political party and an interest group?

	Political Party	Interest Group
(A)	Organize government activity	Undergo realignment every few decades
(B)	Direct lobbying	Reduce conflict and tension in society
(C)	Nominate candidates for office	Make endorsements
(D)	Educate and mobilize voters	Help coordinate the campaign of a presidential candidate

4. Which of the following could be defined as a "splinter" party?

   (A) The Libertarian Party
   (B) The Socialist Labor Party
   (C) The Communist Party
   (D) The Reform Party

5. Which of the following people would most likely be a Democrat?

   (A) A Cuban American
   (B) An evangelical Christian
   (C) A white Southerner
   (D) A Mexican American

6. Political Action Committees (PACs) allow unions and corporations to perform which of the following actions?

   (A) Run their own members for political office
   (B) Funnel unlimited amounts of money to candidates of their choice.
   (C) Have a voice in government.
   (D) Sit down together to work out their differences.

7. Which of the following events in the 20th century caused the Democratic Party to undergo a party realignment?

   (A) World War I
   (B) The Great Depression
   (C) World War II
   (D) The assassination of President Kennedy

REFLECT

Respond to the following questions:

- For which content topics discussed in this chapter do you feel you have achieved sufficient mastery to answer multiple-choice questions correctly?

- For which content topics discussed in this chapter do you feel you have achieved sufficient mastery to discuss effectively in an essay?

- For which content topics discussed in this chapter do you feel you need more work before you can answer multiple-choice questions correctly?

- For which content topics discussed in this chapter do you feel you need more work before you can discuss effectively in an essay?

- What parts of this chapter are you going to re-review?

- Will you seek further help, outside of this book (such as a teacher, tutor, or AP Students), on any of the content in this chapter—and, if so, on what content?

Chapter 7
Elections

CONCEPTS

- Does the media place too much emphasis on irrelevant issues in presidential campaigns?

- Why do incumbents win at such high rates?

- Why is voter turnout so low in the United States?

- What is the impact of primary elections, and who votes in them?

- Why do political parties have such a difficult time holding their coalitions together?

- Why are soft money contributions considered a threat to the election process?

- Why did the Supreme Court have a problem with the imposition of spending limits on PACs?

- Has the Federal Election Campaign Reform Act succeeded in fulfilling the intent of the legislation?

- What accounts for the so-called gender gap?

The federal government holds elections every two years. Each election gives voters the chance to select a new representative in the House of Representatives. Every other election allows them to vote for president. Each of a state's two seats in the Senate is contested every six years; as a result, state voters select a senator in two out of every three federal elections.

To cut expenses and to encourage voter turnout, states often hold their elections at the same time as federal elections. Thus, voters choose not only federal officials at election time, but also state legislators, judges, the governor, and local officials. They may also be asked to vote on referenda and state bond issues.

Thus, many officeholders are chosen and many issues are decided during each election. When the AP U.S. Government and Politics Exam asks about elections, however, it nearly always focuses on the presidential election. This chapter will do the same.

There is one exception to this rule. The AP U.S. Government and Politics Exam always asks at least one question about the **incumbent advantage.** Be sure you know the following two facts, as they will almost certainly be tested on the exam: (1) representatives who run for reelection win approximately 90% of the time; and (2) while incumbent senators have a tremendous electoral advantage, House incumbents have an even greater advantage. Senators must run statewide, and they almost always face a serious challenger. On the other hand, House members run in their home districts, where constituents are often overwhelmingly of one party due to **gerrymandering** (partisan redrawing of congressional district borders). In such races, victory in the primary election virtually guarantees victory in the general election. In fact, each year a number of House incumbents run for reelection unopposed.

THE ELECTION CYCLE

Elections consist of two phases: **nominations**, during which the parties choose their candidates for the general elections, and **general elections**, during which voters decide who will hold elective office.

The majority of states (39) use primary elections to select presidential nominees. All states use some form of primary election to select legislative and state nominees. These elections are usually held between early February and late spring of an election year, with the Iowa caucus and New Hampshire primary enjoying the coveted "first-in-the-nation" position. Each state sets its own rules for these elections, and there is considerable variation in primary procedures from state to state. There are several types of primaries.

- **Closed primary.** This is the most common type. In a closed primary, voting is restricted to registered members of a political party. Voters may vote only for candidates running for the nomination of their declared party. Democrats choose among the candidates for the Democratic nomination, while Republicans choose among Republican hopefuls.

- **Open primary.** In open primaries, voters may vote only in one party's primary, but they may vote in whichever party primary they choose. Voters select the party primary in which they wish to participate in the privacy of the voting booth. Critics argue that open primaries allow voters to sabotage their opponents' primaries by crossing party lines to vote for the candidate *least* likely to win the general election. This is likely to happen only when there are no close contests in one party, however.

- **Blanket primary.** Blanket primaries use the same procedure as the general elections. In blanket primaries, voters may vote for one candidate per office of either party.

In primary voting for legislators and state officials, the candidate who receives a **plurality** (greatest number of votes, but not more than half the total votes cast) or majority (more than half) in each primary is declared the winner. Some states require the winner to receive a minimum percentage of the vote, however. If no candidate receives the required share of votes, a **runoff primary** is held between the top two. Runoffs occur most often when many challengers vie for an open office, especially when none of them are well known.

In primary elections for the presidency, voters also choose **delegates** pledged to a particular presidential candidate. Winning delegates attend their party's national convention. Some states select presidential convention delegates at **state caucuses** and **conventions.** This process begins with local meetings of party members, who select representatives to send to statewide party meetings. Compared with primaries, the state caucus and convention process usually attracts fewer participants. Those who participate tend to be more politically active and better informed than typical voters.

The Democratic Party uses a third method to choose some delegates to its national convention. It grants automatic delegate status to many elected party leaders, including congresspersons and important state leaders. These **superdelegates** generally support the front-runner. Critics complain that the superdelegates dilute the importance of the primary elections by making it easier for the party elite to control the nominating process. The Republican Party does not have superdelegates. To promote diversity within the delegate pool, the **McGovern-Fraser Commission** was created in 1968. It recommended that delegates be represented by the proportion of their population in each state.

General elections for federal office are held on the Tuesday after the first Monday of November. Elections in which the president is being chosen are called **presidential elections.** Those that occur between presidential elections are called **midterm elections.**

First Steps Toward Nomination

Nearly all elected officials first receive the endorsement, or nomination, of one of the two major parties. Nominees usually have extensive backgrounds in government. Some presidential candidates are current or former members of the Senate. Many have served as governors. Gubernatorial experience allows candidates to claim executive abilities, because governors serve many of the same government functions in their states as the president does in the federal government. Governors also have the advantage of being able to run as Washington outsiders, as opposed to senators, who usually have extensive federal experience (and whose voting records are often used against them). At a time when public distrust of Washington is high, outsider status can be a significant benefit. Bill Clinton and George W. Bush successfully exploited this factor in their presidential campaigns. Because Barack Obama had been a senator for only four years (as opposed to other candidates like Joe Biden, who had a 36-year tenure in 2008, or Rick Santorum, who had 16 years in 2012), he was also able to successfully campaign as an outsider in 2008.

On occasion, the major parties will pursue a candidate with little or no government experience. Such candidates are usually popular and well-respected figures, often from the military. World War II General Dwight Eisenhower was such a candidate in his successful 1952 campaign. More recently, the Republican nominee for the 2016 presidential race (and eventual winner) was Donald Trump, a businessman with no prior experience in government. Trump used his outsider status as a campaign selling point, which was successful with many voting demographics.

A presidential run is an all-consuming endeavor that must begin up to two years before the first primary. As a result, most candidates devote themselves to the effort full time. Jimmy Carter and Ronald Reagan both left their governorships before running for the presidency; Bob Dole retired from the Senate in 1996 to commit himself more fully to his campaign. Others have remained in office and run successful campaigns. Bill Clinton and George W. Bush are two candidates who remained governors while successfully seeking their party's nomination. Chris Christie made his recent White House run while he remained governor of New Jersey, and numerous New Jersey newspapers called for his resignation, claiming that he had neglected his gubernatorial duties while campaigning. Presidents running for reelection and vice presidents seeking the presidency benefit from the prestige of their offices.

Those considering a run for the presidency must first seek support among the party organizations. They must especially seek the aid of influential donors to the party because elections are extremely expensive. Candidates spend much of the early stages of the nomination process meeting with potential donors, establishing PACs to raise funds (more about fundraising below), and campaigning for the endorsements of important political groups and leaders. This entire process is often referred to as testing the waters.

In the year before the first primaries, potential candidates attempt to increase their public profile. They schedule public appearances and attempt to attract media coverage by taking stands on current issues and discussing the goals of their projected presidencies. Candidates are particularly vulnerable to the media during this period. Since the public knows little about most potential candidates, negative reports or media spin can quickly scuttle a campaign (see Newt Gingrich in 2012). As primary season begins, candidates try to raise as much money as possible and to garner as many votes in the primaries as possible, in an effort to win the nomination. Candidates who can't raise their own money and don't get enough votes are quickly forced out of the race. The candidates also begin to assemble campaign personnel—advisors, political consultants, public relations experts, speechwriters, fund-raisers, lawyers, and office administrators—who will help manage the campaign.

Elections and the Elite
Many campaigns fail when testing the waters, long before the public is ever aware of them, due to lack of interest among the political elite.

On occasion, wealthy candidates have attempted to run for the presidency without needing, or using, federal matching funds. Ross Perot in 1992 and Steve Forbes in 1996 used their own money to campaign, but both campaigns failed. Ross Perot's 1992 campaign spent more money than the Democratic and Republican candidates combined.

The following chart summarizes the nomination process.

Steps Toward Presidential Nomination

1 Approximately two years before the presidential election, candidates begin preparing for the first primary election, during which they will attempt to win the official nomination of their party.

Candidates seek support from party organizations.

Candidates campaign for the endorsements of political groups and leaders.

Candidates seek financial aid from donors and establish PACs to raise funds.

2 In the year before the first primaries, candidates attempt to increase their public profiles by scheduling public appearances in an effort to attract media coverage.

Candidates who don't raise enough money or receive enough votes are forced out of the race.

3 Candidates begin to assemble campaign personnel—advisors, political consultants, public relations experts, speechwriters, fund-raisers, lawyers, and office administrators—to help manage the campaign.

4 Primary season begins in the presidential election year.

Endorse, Endorse, Of Course, Of Course
At some point during the campaign, candidates will likely pursue endorsements from other politicians and news organizations. This extra publicity can help them in all other steps.

Financing Campaigns

A successful presidential campaign requires much more than an appealing candidate. It needs a huge supporting staff, jets and buses, and the resources to hire consultants, pollsters, and advertising agencies. It should come as no surprise, then, that one of the most important skills a candidate can possess is the ability to raise money.

Presidential candidates who meet certain prerequisites may receive federal funding. Primary candidates who receive more than 10% of the vote in an election may apply for **federal matching funds.** These funds essentially double all campaign contributions of $250 and less by matching them. To receive matching funds, candidates must agree to obey federal spending limits. Any candidate who receives less than 10% of the vote in two consecutive primaries loses his or her eligibility for matching funds until he or she wins more than 10% of the vote in another primary.

The federal government funds the general election campaigns of the two major presidential candidates, provided those candidates agree not to accept and spend other donations (an exception is made for up to $50,000 of the candidate's own money). The year 2004 was the first election in which both major party nominees declined public matching funds during the primaries. Independents do not receive federal funding for their campaigns. (In 2008, John McCain accepted matching funds while Barack Obama did not. In the subsequent 2012 race, neither Obama nor Mitt Romney accepted matching funds.) In the 2016 election, only one presidential contender sought and qualified for public financing (Martin O'Malley).

Despite attempts at campaign finance reform, the trend toward high levels of election spending has continued through the 1990s and into the first decade of the 21st century. In the 2004 election, George W. Bush raised $272.5 million and John Kerry raised $250.3 million. Both candidates refused matching funds to avoid all spending limits. This precedent-setting high, however, was swiftly broken in light of the ability for corporations and unions to now donate directly and without limits. The combined expenditures for the 2012 campaign that set Mitt Romney against Obama totaled over $7 billion dollars—just about 14 times as much in only eight years. Without any sort of cap, future candidates may raise even more.

There is currently no public financing of congressional campaigns, and there are no spending limits for congressional candidates. There are, however, limits on the amounts that individuals and political committees may donate to candidates. These limits were revised by the Bipartisan Campaign Reform Act (BCRA) in 2002 as shown in the following table.

Setting Limits
In 2016, the federal spending limit was $48.07 million for the primary elections and $96.14 million for the general election.

	To a Candidate	To a National Party	To a Political Committee	Total per 2 Calendar Years
Individual may give	$2,700	$33,900	$5,000	no limit
Multi-candidate PAC may give	$5,000	$15,000	$5,000	no limit
Non-multi-candidate PAC committee may give	$2,700	$33,900	$5,000	no limit

Many Americans believe that the current campaign finance system has a corrupting effect on government, and a talking point among many of the candidates within the 2016 election has been that the public financing system is broken. Efforts to change the system, however, run into several obstacles. The Supreme Court ruled in *Buckley v. Valeo* (1976) that mandatory spending limits on campaigns violate candidates' First Amendment rights to free expression. Furthermore, the system currently benefits incumbents, in that the incumbent's job description is basically the stuff of reelections: meetings, events, talking to voters, photo ops, and so on. Accordingly, legislators are reluctant to make changes because changes would make their reelection more difficult. The permissible donations listed in the above table will change if campaign finance reform is enacted.

Primary Season

By January 1 of election year, candidates are campaigning widely among the public. From this point on, candidates participate in debates, campaign from state to state delivering their "stump speeches" (so called because campaigning is often referred to as "stumping"), and choreograph media events—in an effort to draw positive media coverage of their campaigns.

The earliest primaries (New Hampshire's is a prime example) provide a great boost to the campaigns of whoever wins, increasing the candidate's media exposure and making all-important fund-raising chores easier. Major financial contributors usually desert the campaigns of the losers in early primaries. Furthermore, candidates who receive less than 10% of the vote in two successive primaries lose their eligibility for crucial federal matching funds. As a result, those who fare poorly in early primaries usually have to drop out of the race long before the majority of delegates have been selected.

Because early primaries are perceived to have grown increasingly important in recent years, many states have pushed forward the date of their primary elections. Many states even hold their primaries all on the same day in early March (called **Super Tuesday**). Large states such as New York and California have moved their primaries forward in hopes of having a greater influence on which candidates win the nominations. Political analysts refer to this strategy as **front-loading**, and the result has been to place increased pressure on candidates to succeed early.

Critics argue that it unnecessarily forces voters to choose early in the election process, before they have gotten a chance to know the candidates well.

Primary elections and state caucuses continue into late spring. In many recent elections, however, the party nominee has been decided long before the last elections. Mitt Romney's nomination in 2012 is an example of that very phenomenon.

National Conventions

After the primary season has ended, both parties hold national conventions to confirm their nominee. When no candidate has received the pledge of a majority of convention delegates, conventions decide who the nominee will be; such conventions are called **brokered conventions**. The parties have designed their primary systems to prevent brokered conventions, which can divide the party and cost it the election. The most recent brokered conventions are 1952 for Democrats (Adlai Stevenson) and 1948 for Republicans (Thomas Dewey) making them seem, at least for now, like historical relics.

One of the main purposes of a national convention, in fact, is to unify the party. Primary elections can damage each party, as candidates attack one another and thereby expose rifts within the party membership. Another main purpose of conventions is to make a show of party unity for political gain. Both parties' conventions are nationally televised and are widely covered by the news media. Not surprisingly, most of what occurs on the convention stage is choreographed to appeal to the party faithful and undecided voters watching at home.

That does not mean that conventions are placid affairs, however. Conventions are the site of many political negotiations, as different factions of the party attempt to win concessions in return for their full support during the general election. There are often intense battles over the party **platform**, a statement of purpose and party goals, which, ironically, has little concrete significance. The conventions also offer some political drama, as nominees sometimes wait until the convention to announce their choice of running mates.

The greatest impact conventions can have on general election results is negative. In 1968, for example, rioting outside the Democratic convention in Chicago created a bad impression among voters, especially when contrasted with the unified display at the Republican convention in Miami weeks later. In 1992, ultraconservatives were able to control key elements of the Republican convention. The image the convention created was one of an angry and activist party, which frightened voters and hurt President Bush's reelection campaign. Under normal circumstances, however, conventions usually help their candidates considerably. Polls taken immediately after conventions show the candidates' approval ratings up significantly. This rise in public approval is called a **post-convention bump**.

Nonetheless, it is important to note that national conventions have been altered dramatically in the last century. Until about mid-century, conventions and convention delegates actually selected and nominated the candidate. With the adoption of primary elections, conventions have been transformed into mere coronations with the nominees generally being determined before the convention begins (as with Clinton and Trump in 2016).

The General Election and the Electoral College

The remaining candidates continue to campaign for the general election in much the same way as they campaigned during the primaries: holding rallies, participating in debates, running campaign advertisements, and pursuing positive media coverage. There are several key differences between the primaries and the general election. First, during the primaries, candidates run against members of their own party. Because primary candidates are often in general agreement about big-picture issues, their campaigns focus instead on the subtler differences between them. During the general elections, candidates often emphasize the general policy and philosophical differences between the two parties. Put simply, a candidate courts his or her political base during the primary season and then usually attempts to move toward the center in the general election to win undecided votes in hopes of securing the majority.

Candidates planning their campaign strategies must consider the nature of the **Electoral College.** This institution was created by the framers of the Constitution as a means of insulating the government from the whims of a less-educated public. Critics feel this system is antiquated, but no one has successfully proposed an amendment to change it. Presidential elections therefore continue to be determined not by the final popular vote but by this institution. Each state is given a number of electors equal to the sum of its federal legislators (senators plus representatives). The winner of the presidential election in each state wins all of that state's electors[1] (which is why it is often referred to as a **winner-take-all system**).

The Electoral College places greater emphasis on election results in large states. Victory by a single vote in California wins a candidate all of that state's 55 electoral votes; a similar margin of victory in Vermont yields only three electoral votes. Despite the number of votes at stake in the large states, candidates will often devote the bulk of their time to "swing" states—areas in which polling indicates a close race. This is the reason that during the 2016 presidential election, states like Ohio, Colorado, and New Hampshire were inundated with political ads while large states whose voters generally go with one party, such as New York, California, and Texas, were relatively quiet. Finally, candidates consider each other's electoral strategies in planning their campaigns. In 1968, the Democratic Party relied on the support of its Southern base. Republican Richard Nixon realized that this support was weakening and campaigned aggressively in the region. Nixon's

---

[1] The two exceptions are Maine and Nebraska, which give two electoral votes to the candidate who wins a plurality of the statewide vote, and one vote to the winner of each of the state's congressional districts. Maine has four electoral votes; Nebraska has five.

"Southern strategy" worked in enough Southern states to swing the election to the Republicans.

MEDIA INFLUENCE ON ELECTIONS

With approximately 240 million Americans of voting age, it is clear that candidates cannot come into direct contact with even a small portion of the electorate. Instead, they must rely on the media to get their political message across.

- **News media** provide many voters with daily campaign information. While most news programs occasionally report on the candidates' positions on the issues, they concentrate on the candidates' standing in the polls, or the horse race aspect of the election. This is because news directors prefer information that can be communicated quickly and that changes regularly, such as public opinion poll results. In contrast, candidates' positions on issues are often complex. Furthermore, they rarely change. Therefore, news programs may report such information once during an election, but they do not report it repeatedly as they do with poll results. As a result, the attention of the network news audience is focused on the campaign game rather than on the candidates' political agendas.

- **Campaign advertisements** provide another, more controlled look at the candidates. Through advertising, candidates attempt to build a positive image with the public. In many cases, they also try to belittle their opponents through negative advertising. Negative advertising works best when the public knows little about a candidate. In 1988, for example, Democratic candidate Michael Dukakis was the subject of several effective negative advertisements. Although he led in the polls prior to the ads, Dukakis's support was weak, as most voters knew little about him. The negative advertisements were effective in destroying Dukakis's lead by portraying him as weak, incompetent, and soft on crime.

ELECTION DAY

Of the 240 million Americans of voting age, around 200 million are registered to vote. In the 2016 election, though, around 139 million actually turned out to vote (57.9% of the country). **Voter turnout** is even lower for midterm elections: approximately 36.4% of all eligible voters participated in 2014. American voter turnout rates are among the lowest of all Western democracies.

Certain patterns are detectable in American voters' behavior. The likelihood that an individual will vote corresponds closely to his or her level of education: the more educated a person is, the more likely he or she is to vote. Age is also a factor:

turnout rates are highest among Americans over the age of 40, and lowest among those under the age of 20.

Voter turnout is also influenced in part by how close a race is. Voters are less likely to vote when they believe they know who will win the election. Such was the case in 1996, when many Americans were certain that Bill Clinton would be reelected. Remember, however, that many federal and state offices are up for grabs on election day. A closely contested race in any of those elections can be enough to motivate voters to participate. Voter turnout can also be affected by various legislation. The National Voter Registration Act (1993), also known as The Motor Voter Act, made voting easier by allowing voter registration at the time someone applies for a driver's license. Conversely, the photo ID laws enacted in some areas at the state level depress voter turnout by requiring voters to show a photo ID before voting. These photo ID laws are controversial, with those who are for them saying it reduces voter fraud and those who are against them saying it decreases voting by impoverished Americans.

On election day, the media report not only election results but also the results of exit polls that break down the vote by age, gender, race, income level, region, and nearly every other demographic imaginable. They do so in an effort to determine the meaning of the results. Why did voters choose one candidate over another? How satisfied were voters with the choices presented them? Were the voters sending a clear message—a **mandate**—or not? Winners search the results for evidence of a mandate. In 1992, Bill Clinton interpreted his victory as a mandate for a more active and progressive federal government. Several historic failures—on efforts to integrate homosexuals in the military and to establish nationalized health care— demonstrated that voter mandates are not always so clear. The voters' message has become more difficult to discern as **split-ticket voting**—voting for a presidential candidate of one party and legislators of the other—has grown more common.

> **Split-ticket voting** leads to **divided government**, when one party controls the Senate or House or both and the other controls the White House. An example of this comes from the composition of the government in 2015: following the 2014 elections, Republicans had House and Senate majorities, while Democrats controlled the White House. This can create policy gridlock because these two branches are often at odds with each other. Conversely, it can cause them to work together in the creation of moderate public policy. Lastly, it encourages party **dealignment** because voters do not align with their parties as uniformly as they once did.

Who Do You Think You/ They Are?

Voting tends to be motivated by one or more of the following factors:

- **Rational**—A voter believes the candidate will support policies that further the voter's own personal interest
- **Retrospective**—A voter chooses a candidate based on the candidate's political track record or that of the candidate's political party
- **Prospective**—A voter chooses a candidate based on hopes of what that candidate may accomplish in the future
- **Party-Line**—A voter selects all available candidates within a certain party, regardless of their individual merits

KEY TERMS

- incumbent advantage
- gerrymandering
- nominations
- general elections
- closed primary
- open primary
- blanket primary
- plurality
- runoff primary
- caucus
- delegates
- superdelegates
- McGovern-Fraser Commission
- federal matching funds
- Super Tuesday
- front-loading
- platform
- post-convention bump
- Electoral College
- winner-take-all system
- voter turnout
- mandate

Summary

o   Elections consist of two phases: nominations and the general election. Most nominations are made through party primaries. These can be open, closed, or blanket.

o   Candidates need the backing of the major parties along with a compelling back story before they can hope to make a strong campaign for national office.

o   Campaign finance was restricted by a complicated web of regulations defined by the election laws of the 1970s along with the 2002 Bipartisan Campaign Reform Act, but new laws were passed in 2010.

o   Before the general elections, the candidates need to win their party primaries, which often involves energizing the base. Later, candidates may have to repudiate some of the more radical statements they made to court primary voters in order to win more moderate voters in the general election.

o   Nominating conventions used to be where the party nominees were selected, but now they are symbolic coronations of the candidate who has already been selected through the primary process. Still, delegates assemble, cheer, and argue over the drafting of the party platform.

o   Presidential candidates must win each state's electors, which is done by getting a plurality of all the voters in that state. This method causes candidates to spend most of their time in "swing" or "battleground" states and can also result in the winner of the popular vote losing the election (as was the case with Al Gore in the election of 2000).

o   After all the voting is done, pollsters, the parties, and the media try their best to determine why the people voted the way they did. Exit polls and surveys are the tools used to decipher these factors.

Chapter 7 Drill

See Chapter 11 for answers and explanations.

Questions 1 and 2 refer to the table below.

RESULTS OF THE 1992 PRESIDENTIAL ELECTION

Presidential Candidate	Popular Vote	Percentage of Vote	Electoral Vote
George H.W. Bush	39,104,550	37.5%	168
Bill Clinton	44,909,806	43.0%	370
Ross Perot	19,743,821	18.9%	0

1. Which of the following statements does the information in the table above support?

   (A) George H.W. Bush lost his reelection campaign in 1992.
   (B) There was no strong third-party candidate in 1992.
   (C) Ross Perot took votes away from both Bush and Clinton.
   (D) Bill Clinton barely won the electoral vote.

2. Someone would use this table as evidence to support which of the following opinions?

   (A) Ross Perot would have been a better president than Bush or Clinton.
   (B) The Electoral College is an undemocratic tool in modern elections.
   (C) The Electoral College is the simplest way to decide who becomes president.
   (D) Clinton ran a poor campaign during the general election.

3. Which of the following is an accurate comparison between a presidential candidate's actions during the primary and general elections?

	Primary Election	General Election
(A)	Criticize policies of members of the other party	Criticize policies of members of own party
(B)	Focus on convention delegates	Focus on the electoral map
(C)	Campaign to all Americans	Campaign to the base
(D)	Plan the convention	Cultivate superdelegates

4. Which of the following describes an open Republican primary?

   (A) Only Republicans can vote.
   (B) Only Democrats can vote.
   (C) Only Republicans and Democrats can vote.
   (D) Every registered voter can vote.

5. At a nominating convention, which committee decides the positions that the political party will take?

   (A) Platform Committee
   (B) Credentials Committee
   (C) Rules Committee
   (D) Ideology Committee

6. Which of the following people is most likely to vote in a general election?

   (A) A 25-year-old high school dropout
   (B) A 65-year-old college professor
   (C) A 19-year-old college student
   (D) A 30-year old college graduate

7. Which of the following statements is true about presidential primaries?

   (A) All delegates in a primary are awarded to the winning candidate.
   (B) Voters in primaries all show up at the same time to discuss candidates and then vote.
   (C) Most states use primaries to award delegates to presidential candidates.
   (D) Voters in primaries choose representatives to vote for them.

REFLECT

Respond to the following questions:

- For which content topics discussed in this chapter do you feel you have achieved sufficient mastery to answer multiple-choice questions correctly?

- For which content topics discussed in this chapter do you feel you have achieved sufficient mastery to discuss effectively in an essay?

- For which content topics discussed in this chapter do you feel you need more work before you can answer multiple-choice questions correctly?

- For which content topics discussed in this chapter do you feel you need more work before you can discuss effectively in an essay?

- What parts of this chapter are you going to re-review?

- Will you seek further help, outside of this book (such as a teacher, tutor, or AP Students), on any of the content in this chapter—and, if so, on what content?

Chapter 8
Institutions of
Government

CONGRESS

Concepts

- Why do congressional incumbents have an advantage over challengers?
- Why did the Supreme Court strike down majority-minority voting districts?
- Why does Congress continue to maintain the seniority system?
- What is it about the way Congress operates that promotes factionalism?
- Why has it been argued that Congress contributes to the fragmentation of policy making?
- Why do we hate Congress but love our congressperson?
- Why would members of Congress vote against campaign finance reform?
- Why would members of the Senate engage in a filibuster?
- Why is the House Rules Committee so important?
- How does politics enter into the nomination process for independent agencies and the judiciary?
- What impact has the high cost of campaigning had on the legislative process?
- What are the powers of the leaders in the House and Senate?

Congressional Structure

Congress is the bicameral (two-house) legislature responsible for writing the laws of the nation. Congress also serves other functions, such as overseeing the bureaucracy, consensus building, clarifying policy, legitimizing, and expressing diversity. It is made up of a **House of Representatives** of 435 members and a **Senate** of 100 members.

Every 10 years, a **census** is taken by the federal government to count the population to determine the number of each state's **congressional districts**. Each state must then redraw its congressional boundaries to ensure that each district is equal in population. Congressional **redistricting** is done by each state legislature. Therefore, the political party in control of the state legislature controls how the districts are drawn. As much as is legally possible, the legislature will **gerrymander** the district boundaries to give the majority party an advantage in future elections. This is true in every state with the exception of Iowa, which uses an independent commission to form districts. In some states, such as Alaska and Wyoming, the populations are so small that the entire state becomes a congressional district; all states are guaranteed at least one seat in the House.

Congressional Elections

Elections for all the 435 seats of the House of Representatives occur every two years. House members must reside in the district they represent, be a citizen of the state, and be at least 25 years old. Election to the House takes place within each congressional district. The constituencies of representatives are relatively small compared with those of senators, and the House incumbent election rates are very high, averaging more than 90%. Many House members have safe seats and are not seriously challenged for reelection.

Elections for one-third of the Senate occur every two years, with a senator's term lasting six years. Prospective senators must be at least 30 years old. Every state is guaranteed two senators, elected on a staggered basis in statewide elections. Senate elections are generally more competitive, expensive, high profile, and draw candidates from other elected offices.

Essential Case: *Shaw v. Reno* (1993)

Facts: After the 1990 national census, the federal government reapportioned seats in the House of Representatives to reflect changes in the population. The North Carolina legislature began to redraw its congressional map.

Issue: The proposal the North Carolina legislature submitted to the Department of Justice suggested that the state legislature was attempting to use gerrymandering to isolate African American voters into the 12th Congressional District. White voters living in the 12th sued. When a federal District Court dismissed their lawsuit, the case went to the Supreme Court.

Holding: In a 5-4 decision, the Supreme Court ruled that North Carolina's 12th Congressional District was a clear case of the state using racial bias in its congressional map. Dissenting justices noted that it was not the Court's place to make this determination, as the plaintiffs were not African American. North Carolina was forced to redraw its congressional map.

Important Voting Rights Court Cases

Smith v. Allwright (1944). The denying of African Americans the right to vote in a primary election was found to be a violation of the Fifteenth Amendment.

Wesberry v. Sanders (1963). Ordered House districts to be as equal as possible—enshrined the principle of "one man, one vote."

Buckley v. Valeo (1976). The court ruled that giving money to a political campaign was a form of free speech and threw out some stringent federal regulations on fund-raising and election spending.

Miller v. Johnson (1995). Race cannot be the sole or predominant factor in redrawing legislative district boundaries.

U.S. Term Limits v. Thornton (1995). States cannot set term limits on members of Congress.

Bush v. Gore (2000). Florida's recount in the election of 2000 was ruled to be a violation of the Fourteenth Amendment's equal protection clause.

Shelby County v. Holder (2013). Invalidated part of the Voting Rights Act of 1965, clearing the way for the expansion of photo ID laws.

Congressional Districts and Representation

Descriptive representation means that the elected legislature should reflect the demographic characteristics of the constituency. Minorities and women have always been underrepresented in Congress and state legislatures, which is the reason that the **Voting Rights Act of 1965** encouraged states to take measures to increase minority representation in Congress. Into the early 1980s, little progress had been made. Women and minority groups continued to be underrepresented. In 1982, Congress amended the Voting Rights Act to encourage states to create majority-minority districts, concentrating black and Hispanic populations into distinct congressional districts. These districts were created to make it more feasible for minority candidates to get elected.

Following the 1990 census, many states redrew their congressional districts, which resulted in an increase of black representation by 50% and Hispanic membership by 70%. Various districts were drawn to conform to the Voting Rights Act. However, the shape of these districts was sometimes quite bizarre. North Carolina District 12, for example, stretched in a narrow band 160 miles down Interstate Highway 85. A Duke University professor joined with four other white plaintiffs to challenge the constitutionality of District 12. In *Shaw v. Reno* (1993), the Supreme Court surprised many with a split decision. The court invalidated the district in question because its boundaries were neither contiguous nor compact and were drawn with the intent to discriminate through the use of racial gerrymandering. The court ruled that any racial gerrymandering by the state required a compelling state interest, and it did not see such a compelling interest in this district. On the other hand, the Supreme Court has heard other redistricting cases like this one, and has upheld the redistricting or simply declined to take the challenge. The following maps show how the individual counties voted for the 2012 and 2016 elections.

Compare the results shown on the next page to the actual outcomes to get an idea of where there might be a disparity between counties and the districts that are sometimes seemingly arbitrarily created through them.

2012 Presidential Election Map by County

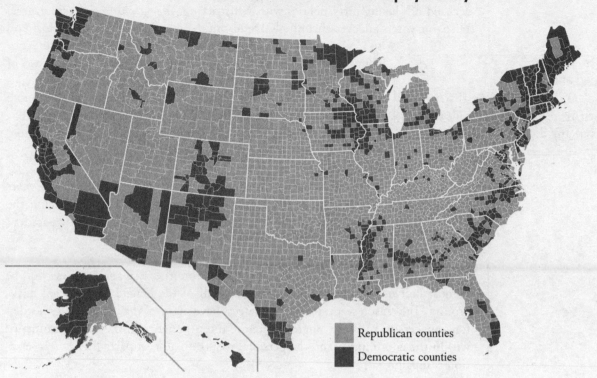

Republican counties

Democratic counties

2016 Presidential Election Map by County

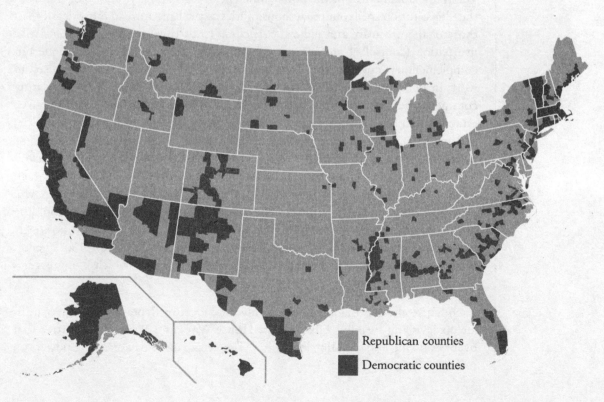

Republican counties

Democratic counties

Legislators in North Carolina, Georgia, Texas, and many other states have been accused of playing dirty politics with redistricting. Black and (to a lesser degree) Hispanic voters are overwhelmingly Democrat. (Cuban Americans in Florida tend to vote Republican.) Critics claim that Republican-controlled state legislatures were not motivated by any sense of duty. Instead, they stand accused of trying to remove racial-minority Democrats from other districts to ensure that more Republicans get elected. The political trade-off was to create a guaranteed Democratic district and at the same time gain more Republican seats from the surrounding districts.

> **Packing and Cracking**
> To isolate minorities in the district is known as "packing." To divide them across many districts is "cracking."

To add to the representation controversy, population shifts in the last 20 years have given additional seats in the House to southern states while reducing the number from other regions. In addition, suburban representation has increased, at the expense of both rural and urban areas.

Finally, Congress draws its members primarily from the legal and business worlds. Almost half of the House and more than half of the Senate have a legal background. The reason seems to be that lawyers have many of the prerequisites needed for a successful run for Congress: interest and experience in the law, prominence within the community, and the personal wealth to at least partially fund an election campaign.

Congressional Powers

The framers had a fear of the power inherent in legislatures. Because of that fear, the Constitution spells out the responsibilities of the legislature in more detail than those of the executive and judicial branches. To further guard against legislative usurpation (control of one house over the other), both houses have unique but complementary powers. The delegated powers, which require both houses to work in concert with each other, include taxing, borrowing money, regulating commerce, raising an army, creating and making rules for the federal courts, establishing naturalization laws, establishing post offices, providing for a militia, and making any law that is deemed necessary and proper for carrying out these powers. In Article I, Section 9, Clause 7 (the appropriations clause) and Article I, Section 8, Clause 1 (the taxing and spending clause), the Congress is given much control over budgetary spending. The power of the purse, as this is known, gives Congress power to influence the president or bureaucrats by withholding or putting conditions on funding. The power of the purse can be used positively to promote certain programs or negatively to diminish the power of an agency. Historically, the power of the purse has been a key tool by which Congress has limited executive power.

Each house also has unique powers. Only the House of Representatives may initiate tax laws and spending bills. It is the **House Ways and Means Committee** that oversees taxing and spending legislation. The Senate has only amending powers on revenue bills.

The Senate's unique powers include confirmation of presidential nominations to the federal courts and ambassadorships to foreign countries. The Senate must also ratify all treaties signed by the president.

There are also restrictions on congressional actions. Congress may not pass **bills of attainder** (laws that find people guilty of a crime and sentence them to prison without a trial) or *ex post facto* **laws** (that punish people for actions that occurred before the behavior was made criminal) and may not levy export taxes or grant titles of nobility. These same prohibitions apply to states.

The Nonlegislative Tasks of Congress

Congress's primary responsibility is to fulfill the legal needs of the nation by writing laws. However, Congress also performs other equally important functions. These include the following:

- **Oversight.** Through its committees and subcommittees, Congress reviews the work of the federal agencies. This helps check the executive branch. It investigates charges of corruption and waste, and it holds hearings where experts and citizens discuss the government's problems and suggest solutions. All committee chairs have the power to subpoena (legally compel) witnesses to appear and testify. It is also the role of the Senate to confirm the members of the president's cabinet as well as to approve nominees for all positions in the federal court system.

- **Public education.** Committee hearings and floor debates increase public awareness of government and societal problems. Floor debates over issues such as gun control, tax cuts, Social Security reform, health care reform, and sending armed troops abroad all help to focus national attention.

- **Representing constituents within the government**. As representatives of their electorates, also known as **politicos,** members of Congress not only vote on laws but also help constituents in their dealings with the government. They receive and can act on complaints about federal services, sponsor voters who seek scholarships or federal contracts, and solicit constituents' suggestions on how to improve the government. In performing this last task, some members of Congress consider themselves delegates whose job it is to mirror the views of their home districts. This is known as the Delegate Model or representational view. Others see themselves as trustees who should consider their constituents' views but should ultimately use their best judgment as experts when deciding how to vote. This is known as the Trustee Model, or attitudinal view.

The Legislative Process

The legislative process is, by design, slow and complicated. This is to prevent Congress from acting hastily. The framers intended for the process to foster compromise. The result has been that the final versions of bills are often radically different from the initial versions. Without compromise there would be no legislative process.

As many as 10,000 bills are introduced on the floor of Congress each year. Some are written by members of Congress and their staffs; others are drafted by the executive branch and are introduced by a sympathetic member of Congress. Many are suggested or written by interest groups and their lawyers. Regardless of who authors a bill, a bill can be proposed only by a member of Congress. Whoever introduces a bill is called the **sponsor** of the bill.

The legislative process requires the two houses to work cooperatively with each other. All bills must pass both houses in exactly the same form. While the bills must be the same, the debate and voting processes in the two houses differ. Because there are 435 members of the House of Representatives, the process by which bills are debated is limited. The Senate, which is smaller, has fewer rules governing the legislative process.

Unlike the Senate, the House has a **Rules Committee,** which is responsible for determining how long a bill will be debated and, whether to allow an open or closed rule for amending the bill. Open rules allow amendments; closed rules prohibit amendments. When Republicans gained control of the House of Representatives in 1994, they promised most bills would be debated under open rules. Allowing 435 members an opportunity to add amendments to bills became so cumbersome, however, that the House leadership returned to the closed rule process. Because the House Rules Committee controls crucial aspects of the legislative process, it is considered the most powerful committee in the House. The Rules Committee can kill a bill by delaying a vote or by making it easy for opponents to add **poison-pill** (or "**killer**") **amendments**. The House Rules Committee can also bring bills up for an immediate floor vote.

While the House strictly controls debate, the Senate does not. There are no time restraints placed on senators. A **filibuster** is a tactic used to delay a vote on a bill and tie up the work of the Senate, usually by a senator making a speech that continues for hours on the Senate floor. A filibuster can also happen without actual continuous speeches, although the senate majority leader may require an actual traditional filibuster if he or she so chooses. The only way to end a filibuster is to vote for **cloture**, but this requires the votes of sixty members, which is difficult to achieve when the two parties are evenly represented.

The Senate has no closed rules for amending legislation. Amendments, called riders, do not have to be relevant to a bill. This allows individual senators an opportunity to add amendments, such as "pet" issues or projects for their home state, or to prohibit the actions of executive agencies. "Pet project" riders designed to bring federal money to a home state are called **pork barrels. Earmarks**—provisions within legislation that appropriate money to a specific project—appear

Meat Lovers
"Bringing home the bacon" is one of the reasons incumbent reelection rates are so high. The members of both houses love pork-barrel legislation.

in appropriation bills and authorization bills. There are a few groups that monitor earmarking in the U.S. Congress, but earmarks are no longer allowed by the House.

After debates, bills usually end up passing the House and Senate in different forms, so both versions are sent to a **conference committee**. The members of these conference committees come from the respective committees of the two houses that wrote the bill. The conference committee tries to negotiate a compromise bill, acceptable to both houses of Congress. Once a compromise version has been written, the bill is returned to the two houses for a vote. Failure to pass a bill from a conference committee will kill a bill. If the bill is passed in both houses, it is sent to the White House for the president's signature.

The president has options. If he does nothing for 10 days, the bill becomes law without his signature. If a congressional session ends during those 10 days, the president must sign every bill into law. If he doesn't, the bill will be **pocket vetoed**, requiring the bill go through the entire legislative process again. If there are more than 10 days left in a congressional session, and a president wants to prevent a bill from becoming law, he may veto the entire bill. The president must then give his reasons in writing and return the bill to the house of origination.

At that point, Congress has choices. The two houses may make the required changes, or they may attempt to override the president's veto by a two-thirds vote. If the bill passes both houses by the required two-thirds vote, the bill becomes law without the president's signature. If the house of origination (where the bill was originally introduced) does nothing with the presidential veto, the bill is dead.

In 1996, Congress gave the president the **line-item veto,** empowering the president to veto individual parts of a bill. The constitutionality of the line-item veto was immediately challenged in the Supreme Court (*Clinton v. New York City*). The court struck down the line-item veto as an unconstitutional delegation of legislative authority to the president.

Congress has also attempted to give itself veto power over the actions of the president. In specific instances, Congress would write legislation giving the president broad powers to act but reserve the right to void presidential actions by a vote of one or both houses. This legislative veto was declared unconstitutional by the Supreme Court in *INS v. Chadha* (1983). The only form of veto mentioned in the Constitution is that used by the president.

More Than Just a Bill
A signing statement is a written message issued by the president when he signs a bill into law. The statements typically begin as "This bill, which I have signed today and continue with several paragraphs of commentary. Signing statements have recently become controversial, having been used extensively by Presidents George W. Bush and Barack Obama. Critics fear that signing statements may function as attempts to modify the law or undermine the principle of separation of powers.

The following chart summarizes the legislative process.

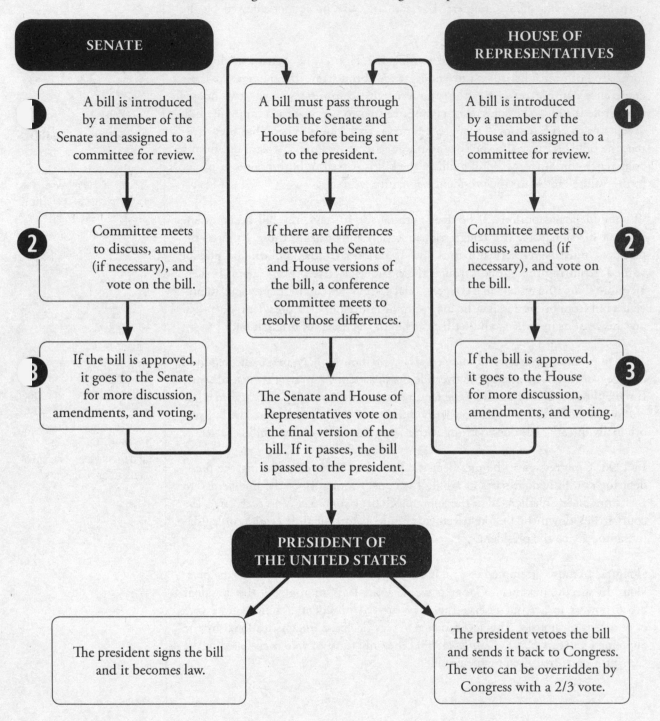

SENATE

HOUSE OF REPRESENTATIVES

1 — A bill is introduced by a member of the Senate and assigned to a committee for review.

A bill must pass through both the Senate and House before being sent to the president.

A bill is introduced by a member of the House and assigned to a committee for review. — 1

2 — Committee meets to discuss, amend (if necessary), and vote on the bill.

If there are differences between the Senate and House versions of the bill, a conference committee meets to resolve those differences.

Committee meets to discuss, amend (if necessary), and vote on the bill. — 2

3 — If the bill is approved, it goes to the Senate for more discussion, amendments, and voting.

The Senate and House of Representatives vote on the final version of the bill. If it passes, the bill is passed to the president.

If the bill is approved, it goes to the House for more discussion, amendments, and voting. — 3

PRESIDENT OF THE UNITED STATES

The president signs the bill and it becomes law.

The president vetoes the bill and sends it back to Congress. The veto can be overridden by Congress with a 2/3 vote.

Legislation by Committee

Most of the legislative business of Congress occurs in committees. Who serves on which committee and what position they hold is determined by a number of factors. The majority party of each house holds all the committee chairs. The majority party will also hold a majority of the seats on each committee, effectively controlling all the business of the committee. On the important committees, the majority usually holds two-thirds of the committee seats.

Generally, the committee member of the majority party with the most seniority becomes the chair and the senior member from the minority party becomes the ranking member. The ranking member becomes chair if the minority party becomes the majority party. This happened in 2001 when a member of the Republican-controlled Senate left the Republican Party to become an Independent. All Democrat ranking members of Senate committees became the chairs, while the Republican chairs became the ranking members. The same principle applies in the House of Representatives.

Committee assignments in the House and Senate are determined by the House and Senate leadership and a caucus of the two political parties. Members of Congress attempt to get on the committees that will allow them to do the most constituent service and help them get reelected. For example, representatives and senators from farm states try to get assigned to agriculture committees.

Committees serve as mini-legislatures, performing the tasks of investigating and debating bills that, due to time constraints, could never otherwise receive the consideration of Congress. Often, the congressional committee assigns the bill to an even smaller group, called a **subcommittee,** for initial consideration. Recently, there has been a proliferation of subcommittees. Subcommittees often determine how money is spent and have therefore become very powerful.

The fate of a new bill depends on much more than its content. The membership of the committee and subcommittee that first considers the bill is crucial. Bill sponsors attempt to draft bills in such a way as to steer them toward sympathetic committees. Supporters of a bill must also decide which house of Congress should consider their bill first, because with the exception of revenue bills, federal bills may originate in either house. To build political momentum, supporters attempt to have the bill introduced in the house most sympathetic to their cause.

The House has more committees than the Senate. House members, however, tend to become more specialized because they serve on fewer committees. As a result, they are considered to have more expertise than senators.

There are four types of committees in Congress.

1. **Standing committees** are permanent, specialized committees. Examples include the House Ways and Means Committee, the Senate Judiciary Committee, and the Senate Armed Services Committee. There are twenty standing committees in the House and seventeen in the Senate.

2. **Joint committees** are made up of members of both the House and the Senate. These committees are normally used for communicating to the public or for investigations but generally do not send bills to the floor for votes.

3. **Select committees** are temporary committees organized in each house for some special purpose. These committees usually carry out investigations for the purpose of writing special legislation. The House Watergate Committee and the Senate Select Committee on Unfair Campaign Practices are examples from the Nixon era. The work of these committees eventually led to campaign reform.

4. **Conference committees** are temporary and include members from the committees of the two houses who were responsible for writing a bill. These committees try to negotiate compromise bills, which are then submitted to the two houses for an up or down vote without amendments. Once a compromise bill has been negotiated, the conference committee disbands.

Most bills die almost immediately in a subcommittee due to lack of interest from committee members; unless a committee member takes a special interest in a bill, the bill will either be quickly rejected or ignored until it dies a natural death at the end of the congressional session.

Committees and subcommittees function by calling interested parties and expert witnesses who have some information to give. Lobbyists often testify as expert witnesses. Congress can subpoena reluctant witnesses, forcing them to appear in hearings and can grant immunity to compel them to testify. Once their investigations have concluded, committees begin amending and rewriting sections of bills in meetings called markup sessions.

Committees will sometimes refuse to vote a bill out, hoping to keep it from being considered by the House. A bill stuck in a House or Senate committee is said to be **pigeonholed.** The parliamentary mechanism to force a bill out of committee for a floor vote is called a **discharge petition.**

Committees have responsibilities in addition to writing laws. For example, they are responsible for the oversight of many bureaucratic agencies and departments. Heads of regulatory agencies, which are responsible for enforcing the laws, often appear to give testimony before congressional committees with oversight jurisdiction. If the agency has not followed the intent of the law, the agency head will be in for a rough time. A recent example comes from a congressional investigation of the Secret Service and subsequent resignation by Director Julia Pierson after multiple security lapses involving President Obama and the White House.

Committees also hear testimony from agency heads pleading for money and personnel. Congressional budget cutting and agency reorganization can have a profound impact on an agency's ability to carry out its responsibilities. This is one way that Congress can use the budget to shape policy.

Congressional Leadership

The House

The leader of the House of Representatives is the **Speaker**, who is chosen by the majority party in a special election. The Speaker is powerful because he or she can direct floor debate and has influence over committee assignments and over the Rules Committee. The Speaker can also control which bills go to which committees. The **majority leader** of the House keeps party members in line and helps determine party policy and the party's legislative agenda. The **minority leader** keeps the minority party members in line and helps determine the minority party's legislative agenda. The House majority and minority whips also help their respective party leaders keep the members loyal to the party's legislative agenda. They coordinate members of each party and help garner support for proposed legislation.

The Senate

The vice president is the president of the Senate, and this is his only constitutionally delegated responsibility. However, the vice president is rarely on the floor of the Senate and votes only to break a tie. When the vice president is absent during Senate sessions, the **president *pro tempore*** is the presiding officer. The president *pro tempore* is largely an honorary position and is usually given to the most senior member of the majority party of the Senate. The majority leader has the real power in the Senate because he or she controls the legislative agenda and acts as a power broker and policy initiator. The minority leader can act as a power broker but usually cannot initiate policy or control the agenda.

Why Do They Vote That Way?

Congresspersons are always cross-pressured to influence their vote. These pressures come from their own party and from the opposition. It also comes from the president through jawboning (trying to influence) and from their colleagues by logrolling ("you help me on this bill, and I'll help you on yours"). PACs try to influence votes through contributions, as do constituents and interest groups.

Personal ideology and religious beliefs can also impact their judgment. The most important factor in determining the vote of a congressperson is party affiliation. Members of Congress usually—but not always—vote with their parties.

NOTABLE LEGISLATION

National Growth, Expansion, and Institution Building

- **Northwest Ordinance (1787, 1789).** One of the few successes of the Articles of Confederation, providing clear guidelines for the settlement of new territories and a path to statehood. Reaffirmed by Congress under the Constitution in 1789.

Regulation of Government and Industry

- **Pendleton Act (1883).** Eliminated the spoils system of patronage in selection for government jobs and set up an exam-based merit system for qualified candidates.
- **Sherman Anti-Trust Act (1890).** Provided Congress with authority to regulate and break up monopolies—or trusts—in the United States. Abused, however, to break up labor unions.
- **Hatch Act (1939).** Permitted government employees to vote in government elections but forbade them from participating in partisan politics.
- **Freedom of Information Act (1966).** Declassified government documents for public use.
- **Air Quality Act (1967).** The beginning of a series of acts to regulate impacts on the environment.
- **Federal Election Campaign Acts (1971, 1974).** Established the Federal Election Commission and required disclosures of contributions and expenditures, as well as limitations on contributions and presidential election expenditures.
- **War Powers Act (1973).** Limited president's power to use troops overseas in hostilities, put a time limit on use, and gave Congress final power to withdraw troops. Since 1973, all presidents have declared this act unconstitutional and it has been repeatedly ignored.
- **Budget and Impoundment Control Act (1974).** Established congressional budget committees and the Congressional Budget Office, as well as gave Congress the power to prevent the president from refusing to fund congressional initiatives (known as "impoundment").
- **Gramm-Rudman-Hollings Bill (1985).** Set budget reduction targets to balance the budget. Failed to eliminate loopholes.

Rights and Freedoms

- **Espionage Act (1917), Sedition Act (1918).** Severely curtailed the civil liberties of Americans during wartime and greatly increased the power of the federal government in controlling public activity. The Sedition Act was repealed by Congress in 1921.

- **Immigration Act (1924).** This law stringently limited the number of immigrants admitted into the United States and set strict quotas for entry.

- **Voting Rights Act (1965).** Suspended literacy tests, empowered federal officials to register voters, and prohibited states from changing voting procedures without federal permission.

- **Age Discrimination in Employment Act (1967).** Banned age discrimination in jobs unless age is related to job performance.

- **Civil Rights Act** or **Fair Housing Act (1968).** Title II banned discrimination in public places on the basis of race, color, national origin, or religion. Title VII prohibited employment discrimination based on gender.

- **Title IX Education Act (1972).** Prohibited gender discrimination in federally funded education programs.

- **Americans with Disabilities Act (1990).** Protected civil liberties of disabled Americans and mandated "reasonable accommodations" to public facility use.

- **National Voter Registration Act (1993).** Also known as **The Motor Voter Act**, this law allowed people to register to vote when applying for driver's licenses.

- **Patriot Act (2001).** In response to the terrorist attacks of September 11, 2001, Congress granted broad police authority to the federal, state, and local government to interdict, prosecute, and convict suspected terrorists. This law is formally known as the USA-PATRIOT Act, an acronym for "Uniting and Strengthening America by Providing Appropriate Tools Required to Intercept and Obstruct Terrorism."

Government Aid to the People

- **New Deal Legislation (1933–1939).** Legislation that expanded the role of government in the economy and society. Created entities like Social Security, the Securities and Exchange Commission, and the Tennessee Valley Authority. These laws also dramatically expanded the role and size of the federal government.

- **Personal Responsibility and Work Opportunity Reconciliation Act (1996).** The Welfare Reform Act signaled a change in the role of the federal government in the relationship with the states. This law sought to increase the role of personal responsibility in welfare recipients and shifted many responsibilities for welfare provision to state governments.

- **Bipartisan Campaign Reform Act (2002).** Often known as the **McCain-Feingold Bill**, this law banned soft money contributions to national political parties and raised hard money limits to $2,000. In a controversial decision in the case of *Citizens United v. Federal Election Commission* (2010), the Supreme Court struck down several provisions in this law, especially those related to contributions made by corporations to political campaigns.

THE PRESIDENT

Concepts

- How do presidents use their formal and informal powers to get their legislative agenda passed?
- How can Congress curb the foreign policy-making powers of the president?
- How does the president use the appointment power to ensure that policies are carried out?
- What techniques can presidents use to promote their legislative agenda in the face of divided government?
- What impact does the White House staff have on policy making?
- Why would Congress give the president a line-item veto?
- Do executive agreements go against the intent of the framers of the Constitution?

The Formal Powers of the Presidency

The powers delegated by the Constitution to the executive branch are in Article II, Section 2, but they are less specific than the formal powers of Congress. The broadly defined powers were intended to give flexibility but have instead resulted in greatly expanded power.

The president is responsible for enforcing the laws, handling foreign policy, and serving as the ceremonial head of state. He or she is also the administrative head of the government. He or she can force Congress into session, must brief Congress on the "state of the nation," and can veto legislation, as well as grant reprieves and pardons. But regardless of these expansive powers, he or she must cooperate with Congress because the powers of the presidency are intermingled with the powers of the legislature. The president's appointments of federal judges, Supreme Court justices, ambassadors, and department secretaries all require Senate approval. The president negotiates treaties, but they must be ratified by two-thirds of the Senate. Because Senate ratification is sometimes difficult to achieve—a good example is the defeat of the Treaty of Versailles in 1919—the broad powers of the president to initiate foreign policy came to include **executive agreements** (which do not require Senate approval). These are agreements between heads of countries; under international and U.S. law, they are as binding as a treaty. However, executive agreements usually deal with more routine, administrative matters.

The President as Commander in Chief

The president also serves as **commander in chief** of the armed forces. But the framers created a complex institutional situation regarding armed conflict. Only Congress has the power to declare war, but only the president can make war. While the United States has been in numerous wars since that time, no declarations of war have been made.

While the president is the chief strategist and director of the military forces of the United States, he or she is at the mercy of Congress for the money to wage war. However, once the president has committed troops in conflict, it is unlikely that Congress would refuse to fund the weapons needed for the military. For members of Congress, such an action would mean political suicide and probably lead to a constitutional crisis within the U.S. government.

In a national crisis, the other branches of government and the American people look to the president for leadership. Initially, presidents will have strong support for their policies. This helps explain why Congress, in 1964, passed the **Gulf of Tonkin Resolution,** giving the president the broad powers to commit unlimited numbers of troops for an unlimited length of time in the Vietnam conflict. President Johnson was unable to bring that war to a conclusion. Strong criticism of his handling of the war led to a general lack of support for his policies, undermining his ability to govern. The same thing happened to President Carter when he was unable to successfully end the Iranian hostage crisis. As president during the Gulf War, George H. W. Bush's ability to quickly bring the war to a conclusion while suffering relatively few casualties resulted in the second-highest approval rating of any president, at 89%.

Presidential Powers in Wartime
In the post–Vietnam War era, Congress has attempted to place controls on the war-making powers of the president. Congress passed the **War Powers Act** in 1973 in an attempt to force the president to seek congressional approval before making war. The act specifically limits the president to 10,000 troops for 60 days, with 30 additional days to withdraw the troops, unless Congress grants an extension or declares war. The Supreme Court has never ruled on the War Powers Act, and Congress has never invoked it, although whenever the president commits troops overseas, members of Congress have threatened the president with imposition of the War Powers Act.

The Informal Powers

The presidential powers that are not enumerated in the Constitution are referred to as the informal powers, and they are sometimes more important than the formal ones. How well presidents use the informal powers can determine the success of their presidencies.

Presidents are supposed to be morale builders. President Carter's failure to improve the morale of the country contributed to his reelection defeat. President Reagan was a master at morale building, and this characteristic helps explain why he remained popular with the American people.

Presidents serve as legislative leaders and coalition builders. Failure to set and lead the legislative agenda and build coalitions in Congress can doom presidents, particularly when there is divided government (when one or both houses of the legislature are controlled by the opposition party). George H. W. Bush became the "foreign policy president" when he was unable to get his domestic policy agenda passed in a Democrat-controlled Congress. Ronald Reagan and his advisers were experts in building coalitions with Republicans and southern conservative Democrats. This coalition of Republicans and southern Democrats gave Reagan his legislative agenda.

Perhaps the president's most important informal powers are as a policy persuader and communicator to Congress and the American people. Clinton and Reagan were superior communicators. The ability of a president to communicate well with the American people is a very powerful tool for pressuring Congress. Communicating with Congress is also important. Having the congressional leadership down to the White House for lunch and a photo op is another way that presidents try to persuade members of Congress to pass their legislative agenda.

Executive Office of the President

The Executive Office of the President helps carry out the president's administrative responsibilities. It is made up of more than half a dozen agencies involved in the day-to-day operations of the White House and is basically divided into three areas: domestic, foreign, and military affairs. It is staffed by hundreds of personnel located in the White House and the Executive Office Building. All are directly responsible to the president or his designees.

- **The chief of staff** is the top aide to the president. He or she is a person in whom the president has complete trust and is probably a longtime associate and friend. Considered one of the most powerful persons in Washington, the chief of staff is responsible for managing the Executive Office and can control access to the president, thus potentially controlling the information that the president receives. Some presidents, such as Bill Clinton, permitted easy access; others, such as **Richard Nixon**, tended to insulate themselves. Whoever the president chooses as chief of staff can have a tremendous impact on presidential effectiveness. Clinton's first chief of staff, **Thomas McClarty**, a Washington outsider and Clinton friend, ran an undisciplined White House, prone to many errors. He was replaced by a Washington insider, former Congressman **Leon Panetta**, who established order and discipline, emerging as a key policy player in the Clinton administration. In 2009, Panetta became Director of the Central Intelligence Agency. He later resigned from that post to become Secretary of Defense. In 2010, Barack Obama's first chief of staff, former Congressman Rahm Emanuel, left the position to run for mayor of Chicago, an election he won.

- **The National Security Council (NSC)** is headed by the national security advisor, who has direct access to the president in matters relating to military and foreign policy. The NSC has been involved since the late 1940s in the decision-making process during national emergencies. President Kennedy used the NSC during the Cuban missile crisis, President Reagan during the Iran-Contra affair, and President George H. W. Bush during the Gulf War. Unlike the State Department, the NSC is largely free from congressional oversight. For this reason, it has become one of the most favored institutions for many presidents.

- **The Domestic Policy Council** assists the president in formulating policies relating to energy, education, agriculture, natural resources, economic affairs, health and human resources, welfare reform, drug abuse, and crime.

- **The Office of Management and Budget (OMB)** is responsible for preparing the budget of the United States and can be used to control and manage the executive agencies for the president. The OMB has enormous power because of its ability to allocate money to the cabinet departments through the budget process of the executive branch. Increasing or decreasing a department's budget affects how it carries out its responsibilities.

- **The Council of Economic Advisors** is responsible for helping the president make national economic policy. The Council is usually made up of the economists and advises the president on policies that are designed to increase prosperity.

- **The U.S. Trade Representative** is responsible for negotiating complex trade and tariff agreements for the president. Trade agreements such as GATT and NAFTA are negotiated by the Trade Representative on behalf of the president, with the guidance of the White House.

The Cabinet

The **cabinet** is not mentioned in the Constitution but was created through custom and usage. Each cabinet department was instituted by an act of Congress to help administrate the responsibilities of the executive branch.

Each cabinet secretary is appointed by the president and confirmed by the Senate. **Secretaries** can be dismissed at the president's will. Cabinet secretaries are supposed to run their departments and carry out the president's policies.

Those who disagree with presidential policy are expected to resign. Secretaries tend to be lightning rods to be used for deflecting criticism and are responsible for explaining and promoting presidential policies. Over time, secretaries tend to represent their own departments more than the president's policies. They are expected to fight for their department's budget, jurisdiction, and personnel. This creates competition and friction between departments and accounts for why presidents usually do not hold full cabinet meetings. Presidents just don't have the time or inclination to listen to the bickering and arguing between department heads.

Still, despite these institutional shortcomings, cabinet secretaries do rule over vast departmental bureaucracies—each containing numerous powerful government agencies. With the recent addition of the **Department of Homeland Security,** there are now fifteen cabinet departments. After the September 11 attacks, it was felt that a cabinet-level department was necessary to counter possible threats to the United States, and more than twenty-two agencies were consolidated into the new department, making it the third-largest executive branch department. Agencies as disparate as the Bureau of Citizenship and Immigration Services (formerly the INS), the Coast Guard, and the Secret Service were consolidated to shape a coherent agenda to protect the United States against potential attacks. The Department of Homeland Security has four functions: to protect the borders; to support local agencies like police and fire departments; to detect chemical, biological, and nuclear weapons; and to analyze intelligence.

A New Addition

Homeland Security is the first top-level government position created since the Energy Department was formed in 1977 and the first large-scale government reorganization since Harry Truman created the Department of Defense in 1947.

Impeachment

The Constitution gives Congress the power to remove the president from office for "treason, bribery, or other high crimes and misdemeanors." The Constitution does not define high crimes and misdemeanors, leaving those definitions to politicians. The only direction in the Constitution is that the House of Representatives impeaches the president (or brings the charges) by a simple majority vote, and if the impeachment passes, the Senate holds a trial with the Chief Justice of the Supreme Court presiding. Removal of the president requires a two-thirds vote of the Senate. The entire process in Congress has been developed as a result of guesswork, custom, and usage.

Because the definition of an impeachable offense is left to the House, **impeachment** is a highly charged political process. Most constitutional scholars place the standard for impeachment as an act against the government or the Constitution, but there seems to be political disagreement over what standard should be used. Conservatives seem to have one standard, while liberals seem to have another. Every impeachment, or near-impeachment, has divided the Congress along party lines, and some scholars have accused members of Congress of using the process to try to undo the result of an election.

No president of the United States has been removed from office. While the House successfully impeached Andrew Johnson for his violation of the Tenure in Office Act, the Senate fell just one vote short of removing him from office. This act was later invalidated by the Supreme Court. The **Watergate** scandal caused Richard

Nixon to resign before imminent impeachment proceedings could begin. He knew that the Senate would convict if given the opportunity to vote. The impeachment of President Clinton for lying under oath was very political. All parties knew before the trial began that there was little chance of a Senate conviction. Clinton's defenders claimed that while Clinton's behavior had been improper and had brought dishonor to the Office of the President, his conduct had not risen to the level of an impeachable offense.

Federal judges are appointed for life and can be removed only by the impeachment process. Only eight federal judges have ever been removed by the Senate. One of them is **Alcee Hastings**, who was impeached for bribery and perjury, and is now a member of the same House of Representatives who voted for his impeachment.

THE JUDICIARY AND THE LAW

Concepts

- What circumstances are required for a case to be brought before the Supreme Court?
- How do politics enter into Supreme Court decisions?
- Why can it be said that all judicial decisions are activist?
- Why can it be said that a president's strongest legacy is found in the judiciary?
- What control does Congress have over the judiciary?

American Legal Principles

Although the United States plays host to the interlocking systems of state and federal law, a few underlying principles make up the foundation of our legal system. They are **equal justice under the law**, **due process of law**, the **adversarial system,** and **presumption of innocence**.

All who appear in court in the United States must be treated as equals. The founders were very concerned that the new nation avoid the hierarchical legal systems that plagued many other nations and, as a result, enshrined many amendments in the Constitution that establish **equal justice under the law**. For example, whenever jurors hear a criminal case, they are instructed not to privilege the testimony of a police officer over that of a defendant.

Due process can be divided into two types: **substantive due process** and **procedural due process**. Substantive due process law deals with the question of *whether laws are fair*. Fairness is determined by looking at the Constitution, specifically the Bill of Rights and the Fourteenth Amendment. A law that made it illegal for people with blue eyes to ride motorcycles would constitute a violation of substantive due process. Procedural due process law is concerned with the question of *whether laws are fairly applied*. This might seem less important than substantive due process, but procedural issues are actually at the heart of our legal system. If suspects in certain types of crimes were held for ten years before they ever had a trial, this would be a violation of procedural due process, because the law guarantees everyone a speedy trial. Even if a nation has laws that are fair and just, if they are not applied fairly, they are meaningless.

Strange as it may seem to those of us raised in the United States, many nations do not require both sides of legal cases to be represented by advocates. This inquisitorial system, as it is known, is alien to the United States, where we use the **adversarial system**. As you can probably guess from the name, this principle is based on the premise that the best way to work out questions of fact is to have two sides—or adversaries—debate the burden of guilt or liability in a situation. Some critics say that this system creates too many conflicts—particularly in areas such as family law and divorce, and recommend an increased role for mediators who seek rapprochement and can make legally binding decisions.

In his *Commentaries on the Laws of England*, English jurist and professor William Blackstone said, "Better that ten guilty persons escape than that one innocent suffer," and this number became known as the Blackstone ratio. Benjamin Franklin expanded this, writing "that it is better [one hundred] guilty Persons should escape than that one innocent Person should suffer." In both England and America, the idea that the accused are innocent until proven guilty—the **presumption of innocence**—is one of the bedrock principles of the legal system. As a result, the burden of proof is on the prosecutor in criminal cases, and if there is any reasonable doubt as to a person's innocence, juries are instructed to acquit.

Types of Law

In the United States, most legal cases involve either **civil law** or **criminal law**. The distinction between these two types of law is very important, and knowing the differences and similarities can help a great deal when taking the AP exam. The following chart highlights the different processes involved in criminal and civil cases.

Criminal Law vs. Civil Law

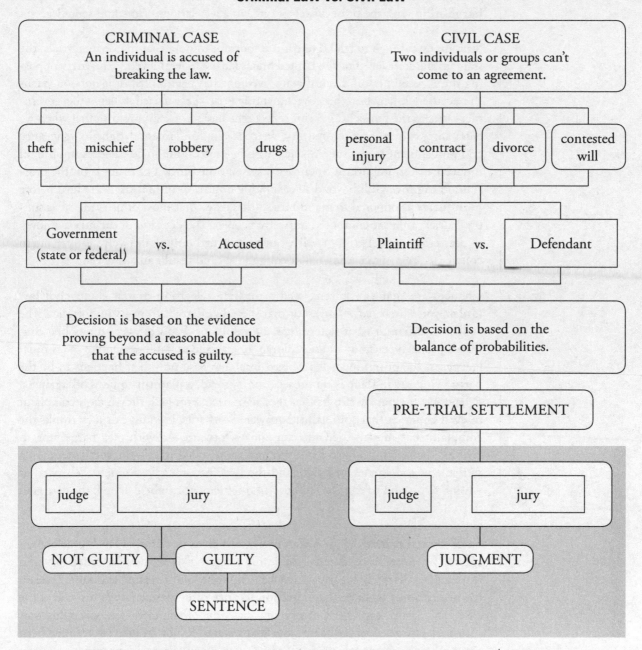

Anyone who watches television police or law dramas has at least some familiarity with the trappings of criminal law. This type of law deals with serious crimes that harm individuals or society. If physical violence is involved, the action will probably end up in the criminal justice system, but fraud and extortion are also crimes. In criminal law, a suspect is arrested and must be indicted. This is done (in most states and at the federal level) by a **grand jury**: a group of 24 to 48 jurors who decide only one thing—whether a trial should commence. Since the grand jury is not deciding guilt or innocence, an accused person does not have many protections at the grand jury level. The prosecution usually has to meet a certain standard of evidence. In fact, defense attorneys are not even allowed to address

Yes, Pleas
Approximately 95% of all criminal cases end in plea bargains.

grand juries. Once the accused is indicted, that person then has the option of **plea bargaining** with the prosecution to agree to a less serious crime and sentence.

Still, many cases go to trial. Here it is important to note that in criminal trials, the state (at the state level) or the United States (at the federal level) is the party opposing the accused person. Even if your loved one has been killed, it is not you versus the accused killer, but the government against the accused killer—the government acts as the prosecution. This reflects the basic Lockean premise that when we enter into a society or community, we cede our fundamental right to vengeance and punishment to the state in exchange for protection. Since the presumption of innocence is so important to our legal system, the burden of proof is on the prosecution to prove guilt beyond a **reasonable doubt**. Criminal trials are held before **petit juries** as opposed to grand juries, (these are what most of us think of as simply "juries" that are composed of twelve people). The decision of the jury is known as the verdict, and a guilty verdict can be returned only if all twelve jurors vote to convict. A split jury is known as a "hung jury" and results in a mistrial.

Chances are that you haven't seen a thrilling television drama about **civil law** (unless you watch *Judge Judy*), but that shouldn't detract from its importance. The civil law system is what determines the results of disputes over things like contracts, property, custody of the children, or an issue of liability. Unlike in criminal law cases, the government is involved in a civil case only if it happens to be the party being sued. There is no prosecution; instead, a plaintiff squares off against a defendant. If a person thinks that they have been wronged, they issue a complaint in **civil court**. If that complaint is answered—that is, if a judge or jury thinks the complaint has merit—then the case moves forward. As with plea bargaining in criminal law, civil law also has a mechanism to avoid trial—the **settlement**. In a settlement, the parties negotiate and the issue becomes how much each party is willing to give up to end the lawsuit. If no settlement can be reached, the case goes to trial.

Since the stakes in civil law are not nearly as high as in criminal law—a defendant cannot be jailed or executed—the burden of proof is lighter. In order to win a case, a plaintiff need not prove that he is right beyond reasonable doubt. Instead, he merely needs to show that a **preponderance of evidence** favors his side of the case. This is the equivalent of proving that 51% of the evidence points his way. Juries are also used in civil cases, but many states do not require twelve members; some allow as few as five or six. Winning can mean either the payment of monetary damages or **equity**, in which the loser may be forced to stop doing something that was annoying or harmful to the winner.

Structure and Jurisdiction

The federal courts are responsible for interpreting and settling disputes arising out of federal law; state courts are responsible for interpreting and settling disputes arising out of state law. It is possible for a citizen to commit a single act that violates both state and federal law—trading in drugs and tax evasion are two examples.

There are three levels of federal courts: the Federal District Courts, which have **original jurisdiction;** the Federal Circuit Courts of Appeals, which hear cases on appeal from the District Courts; and the **Supreme Court**, which hears appeals of cases dealing with constitutional questions from the Circuit Courts and, in rare instances, original suits between states. The Supreme Court also has original jurisdiction in cases involving foreign ministers, which is intended to prevent states from deciding such cases.

The Supreme Court does not have a jury. It is considered a collegial court because its decisions are made by the nine justices. When the Court acts in **appellate jurisdiction,** it can decide only issues of law and never the facts of a case.

There are 94 **Federal District Courts**, created by Congress to fulfill its delegated responsibility of creating courts inferior to the Supreme Court. Federal District Courts decide both civil and criminal cases in original jurisdiction. The trial court that determines guilt or innocence is the court of original jurisdiction. These courts hear evidence and can use juries to decide the verdict. Federal District Courts can also decide liability in civil cases where monetary losses have occurred. Civil cases can also have juries. It is always possible for a defendant to ask a judge to decide a case, but a judge can refuse the request and force the defendant to have a jury trial. (The Constitution guarantees a jury trial but not a trial decided by a judge.)

There are thirteen **Circuit Courts of Appeals**, which hear cases on appeal from the Federal District Courts or from a state Supreme Court. In these cases someone has to claim that a federal constitutional right has been violated. The Circuit Courts decide issues of law and never issues of fact. Circuit courts have no juries. The decisions of these courts are made by panels of appointed judges. In almost every case, the Circuit Court of Appeals is the court of last resort because the Supreme Court rarely agrees to hear cases appealed from the Circuit Courts. Additionally, most Supreme Court judges rise from the Circuit Courts.

The Politics of the Judiciary

All judges in the federal judiciary (only those on the Supreme Court are called justices) are appointed by the president for lifetime terms. Appointees must go through a confirmation process in the Senate. To maintain judicial neutrality and integrity, impeachment is the only method of removal.

The appointment process has become very political. Some presidents have required potential appointees to fill out a judicial questionnaire to determine their political and judicial ideology. Nominees are almost always of the same party as the president. In nomination hearings before the Senate Judiciary Committee, members of both parties try to determine how potential judges would rule in cases dealing with issues such as abortion rights, affirmative action, or school prayer. The American Bar Association is asked to evaluate a nominee's qualifications and interest groups often present their opinions. Senators in a state where an appointee will sit have traditionally exercised **senatorial courtesy**—they submit a list of acceptable names of nominees to the president. Presidents usually choose a nominee from the list submitted. Senatorial courtesy is expected only when the president and senators are of the same party.

Liberals and conservatives often argue over a nominee's judicial philosophy or level of judicial activism. The central point of the argument is whether the nominee is more or less inclined to second-guess a legislative enactment. As the conservatives see it, the courts are the least democratic branch of government (because judges are appointed, not elected), and when they overturn an act of a legislature, they are overruling the will of the people, as expressed in the most democratic branch of government (the legislature). Judges who are reluctant to overturn the acts of a legislature are said to practice **judicial restraint.** Liberals often see judges as constitutional interpreters who should reflect current values. A judge who has no qualms about overturning a legislative action is considered a **judicial activist.** Compromise over these two positions is sometimes very difficult to achieve. The nomination of **Robert Bork** to be a Justice of the Supreme Court was defeated by liberals because of his judicial philosophy. **Clarence Thomas** was confirmed by the closest Senate vote in U.S. history, over concerns related to his conservative judicial philosophy, lack of experience, and the allegation that he sexually harassed an aide.

Process by Which Cases Reach the Supreme Court

The process that the Supreme Court uses to hear cases is not part of the Constitution. The process is a result of custom and usage, time and tradition.

The Supreme Court will not grant an appeal until all opportunities have been exhausted in the lower appellate courts. In the vast majority of cases, the court refuses to hear the appeal because it agrees with the lower court decision. However, the court may choose to review the decisions of lower courts. If four justices agree to this review, the court issues a **writ of *certiorari,*** a legal document used to request the lower court transcripts of a case.

The Supreme Court will rule only in cases that are real and adverse, which means that the case must involve an actual legal dispute. Such cases are said to be **justiciable.** Disputes over political issues cannot be decided by courts—political disputes are not justiciable. The Supreme Court cannot give advisory opinions. It can rule only in an actual legal case involving litigants. In other words, the court will not rule on hypothetical cases.

The Court also places limits on who may bring cases before it. Simply disliking or disagreeing with a law is not sufficient to bring a case. The petitioner (the person who brings the case) must have some vested interest in the outcome of the case. Such petitioners are said to have **standing.**

Judicial Review

The Constitution does not specifically grant the Supreme Court the right to judge the constitutionality of laws. That power was established by the case of *Marbury v. Madison* (1803). This extremely important power is called **judicial review** and was established by John Marshall, the fourth Chief Justice of the Supreme Court (he served from 1800 to 1835). Marshall was a Federalist who worked to increase the powers of the federal government over the states.

Essential Case: *Marbury v. Madison* (1803)

Facts: In the closing hours of his presidency, Thomas Jefferson commissioned William Marbury as a Justice of the Peace in the District of Columbia. Although approved by the Senate, the commission was never formally delivered to Marbury. When President Madison attempted to appoint someone else to the position, Marbury appealed directly to the Supreme Court.

Issue: What was the extent of the Supreme Court's power regarding judicial review as outlined in Article III, Section 2 of the Constitution? Although Marbury filed his suit with the Supreme Court, did it have original jurisdiction over the case?

Holding: In a unanimous decision, the Supreme Court ruled that Marbury was entitled to his position as Justice of the Peace. The ruling also set a precedent that future Courts have followed: when a law comes into conflict with the Constitution, the Supreme Court considers that law unconstitutional. This practice is the foundation of judicial review.

Essential Case: *McCulloch v. Maryland* (1819)

Facts: In 1816, the federal government created the Second Bank of the United States with branches in different states. In 1818, the Maryland legislature passed a law taxing the bank. McCulloch, who managed the bank's Baltimore branch, refused to pay. McCulloch sued first in state court before appealing to the Supreme Court.

Issue: Maryland argued that since the Constitution said nothing about banks, it was legal for the state to impose a tax on a bank run by the federal government. Maryland also argued that a federal banking system was unconstitutional.

Holding: In a unanimous decision, the Supreme Court ruled that the Second Bank of the United States was constitutional and that since states are not truly sovereign over their territory, they cannot impose taxes on government entities or interfere with its operations if they are legal. The case was a victory for those who believed that federal power superseded state power.

You may see the Latin term **stare decisis** on the AP exam. This is simply a synonym for **legal precedent**. Black's Law Dictionary defines "precedent" as a "rule of law established for the first time by a court for a particular type of case and thereafter referred to in deciding similar cases."

Under Marshall, the court made several other rulings concerning the role of the court and the relationship of the federal government to the states. They include the following:

- ***Fletcher v. Peck* (1810).** The first case in which the court overturned a state law on constitutional grounds. *Fletcher* established the court's right to apply judicial review to state laws. Previously, judicial review had been applied only to federal law.

- ***Gibbons v. Ogden* (1824).** The court ruled that the state of New York could not grant a steamship company a monopoly to operate on an interstate waterway, even though that waterway ran through New York. The ruling increased federal power over interstate commerce by implying that anything concerning interstate trade could potentially be regulated by the federal government.

How the Court Hears Cases

Once the Supreme Court decides to take a case, a complicated legal dance swings into motion. Both sides of the case submit summaries of their arguments and legal foundations for them. These summaries are known as **briefs**. At the same time, interest groups affiliated with both sides of the case submit their own briefs to the Supreme Court. These ***amicus curiae*** ("friend of the court") **briefs** constitute an effort to sway the justices to one side or the other and can be quite influential in determining the outcome of the case.

Every year from October to April, the court hears **oral arguments** for the cases it has chosen to take. Usually in oral arguments, lawyers for each party have a half hour each to stand before the nine justices and present their arguments. Often, the federal government will take one side or the other, and in these cases the **solicitor general** gets a portion of that half hour to argue on the government's behalf. The solicitor general is the second-ranking member of the justice department (after the attorney general) and typically makes many appearances before the high court—so much so that the solicitor general is sometimes called the "tenth justice." After the oral arguments, the justices meet for a highly secretive conference. At this point, all the justices cast votes, and opinion-writing duties are handed out.

There are four different types of **opinions**: unanimous, majority, concurring, and dissenting. A **unanimous opinion**, as was the case in *Brown v. Board of Education*, occurs when all of the justices agree—this opinion carries the most force in future legal cases and when legislatures draft new laws. When the justices split, the opinion with the most votes is the **majority opinion**, and it is the opinion that decides the result of the case. Sometimes justices may vote with the majority but take issue with its legal reasoning; these are called **concurring opinions**. Those justices in the minority on an opinion can write a **dissenting opinion**, questioning the reasoning of the winning side. Though these dissents have no immediate significance, if the ideological composition of the court changes, they can sometimes become the legal foundation for future majority opinions.

THE BUREAUCRACY

Concepts

- To what degree is the bureaucracy able to maintain political neutrality?
- How do iron triangles and issue networks foster democratic principles?
- How does Congress control the bureaucracy?
- How does the bureaucracy act to implement the intent of Congress?
- How do regulatory agencies work to protect society?
- How do presidents control their policy preferences through the bureaucracy?

The **bureaucracy** is responsible for ensuring that the policies and programs enacted by Congress and the executive departments are carried out. Because the bureaucracy is responsible for executing the laws, providing for defense, and administering social programs, it is considered part of the executive branch of government. To ensure impartiality, bureaucratic agencies are supposed to function above partisan politics and also ensure that the laws are administered without prejudice.

Bureaucrats are not elected. The 15 cabinet secretaries and the heads of independent agencies are appointed by the president with the consent of the Senate. Most of the hundreds of thousands of civilian employees who work for the government work for one of the 15 executive departments or one of the other "cabinet level" agencies considered by the White House to be part of the cabinet (such as the Director of Management and Budget or the Director of the Drug Control Office). These other cabinet level offices are not actual cabinet departments.

The largest department, the Department of Defense, is administered by the **Secretary of Defense**, who must be a civilian and reports directly to the president. Each of the five military services is headed by a uniformed chief of staff, and the five chiefs work together as the **Joint Chiefs of Staff**, headed by a chairman. The Joint Chiefs and their chairman are responsible for carrying out defense policy and report directly to both the Secretary of Defense and the president. The military is therefore subject to civilian control.

Take a look at the following chart, which shows how the United States bureaucracy is organized.

Bureaucratic Structure of the U.S. Government

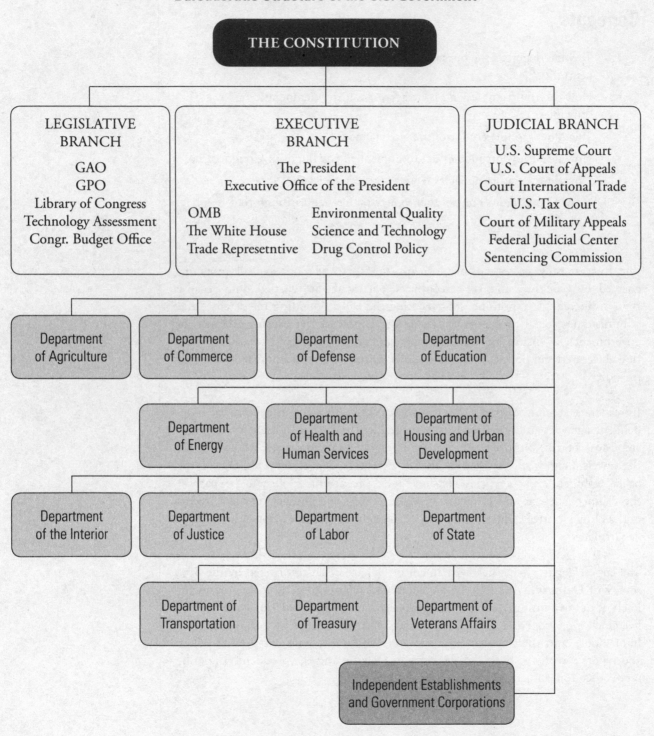

As shown by the chart, the bureaucracy is organized as a hierarchy of 15 pyramids, representing the 15 executive branch departments:

- Department of State
- Department of the Treasury
- Department of Defense
- Department of Justice
- Department of the Interior
- Department of Agriculture
- Department of Commerce
- Department of Labor
- Department of Health and Human Services
- Department of Housing and Urban Development
- Department of Transportation
- Department of Energy
- Department of Education
- Department of Veterans' Affairs
- Department of Homeland Security

At the top of each pyramid is the secretary of the department, who is appointed by the president and confirmed by the Senate. Directly subordinate to the secretary is the undersecretary, who is appointed by the president without Senate confirmation. Because secretaries and undersecretaries are presidential appointments, they are replaced at the end of a president's term. The position of undersecretary attracts young professionals. Because the pay is low compared with private industry, and the position is temporary, undersecretaries often use the appointment to step up to better positions in the private sector.

Below the secretaries are the personnel of the **Senior Executive Service**, including both appointees and non-appointees. Senior Executive Service appointees do not need Senate confirmation. These career officials are supposed to be responsive to the policy goals of the White House and help bureaucrats implement the policy preferences of the chief executive.

Refer to the following chart of the Department of Homeland Security hierarchy as an example.

Departmental Breakdown

Each of the fifteen departments is broken down into smaller units. These smaller units are called bureaus, offices, or services and are responsible for dealing with either a particular clientele or a specific subject. Examples are

- The Bureau of Land Management (Department of the Interior)
- The Federal Bureau of Investigation (Department of Justice)
- The Internal Revenue Service (Department of the Treasury)
- The Federal Aviation Administration (Department of Transportation)

Bureaucratic Structure of the U.S. Department of Homeland Security

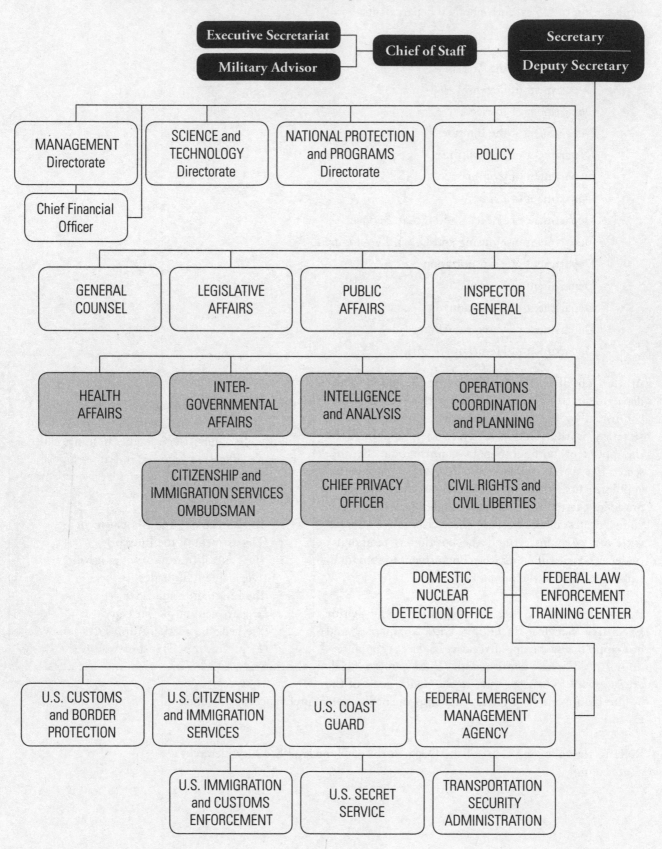

Government Corporations

Government corporations are hybrid organizations. They are a cross between a private business corporation and a government agency. Corporations are supposed to have freedom of action and flexibility and produce at least enough revenue to support themselves. Amtrak, the government corporation created to provide railroad passenger service, is an example. Unfortunately, Amtrak has never made a profit and must ask Congress for subsidies to keep itself from declaring bankruptcy and ending intercity passenger rail service in the United States.

Originally created as a cabinet position, the United States Postal Service has become a government corporation. The intent of Congress was to create a mail delivery system that pays its own way without government assistance. Because of electronic messaging systems and competition from package delivery companies, the post office has had to increase its fees, but it is no longer solvent.

More successful, but at times controversial, is the Corporation for Public Broadcasting, which produces and airs both television and radio programs. Funding for the Public Broadcasting System (PBS) comes from both private and government subsidies. Most of its programming is related to public affairs, news, and culture. The controversy often occurs when groups object to the content of programs. Still others object to the government being involved in any service that could be provided by private sector corporations.

Regulatory Agencies and Commissions

Government entities that are not within the fifteen cabinet departments fall into two categories: the independent agencies and the **regulatory agencies,** sometimes called **independent regulatory commissions.** While independent agencies are generally run-of-the-mill bureaucracies with broad presidential oversight, regulatory commissions are given an extraordinary degree of independence to act as watchdogs over the federal government. Congress and the president are not supposed to become enmeshed in the workings of regulatory commissions. The safety regulations for nuclear power plants or securities exchange should not be regulated by politics.

In contemporary societies, the difficulties and complexities of writing legislation are often beyond the abilities and expertise of lawmakers. The result is that legislation is often written in general terms with many gaps that need to be filled in by the agency with jurisdiction. Independent agencies who have the responsibility for filling in these gaps and writing rules are referred to as **quasi-legislative agencies.** Those responsible for rule enforcement and punishing violators are **quasi-judicial agencies.**

Members of Congress do not have the education to deal with the scientific details that are often required to implement legislation. For example, House and Senate members who sit on committees that deal with environmental issues do not generally have advanced degrees in chemistry. It is the experts who work in the enforcing agencies who have that knowledge. Compounding the problems for Congress are the many competing interests that surround every major issue. Environmentalists have their agenda, while the petroleum industry, electric utilities, and lumber interests have theirs. Even the regulating agency with jurisdiction has its own agenda. These competing interests often delay or prevent legislation. This is the clash of the special interests.

In an age of science and technology, it is the faceless bureaucrat the public knows nothing about who often has the answers for Congress. These bureaucrats, on the one hand, are asked for advice and expertise, and on the other hand, are often ignored because of the pressures from interest groups. Working within the regulatory commissions, they are the people responsible for writing and enforcing rules that regulate the environment, the economy, or industry. If they fail to implement the intent of Congress, they are criticized by Congress and the parties regulated, usually for being too restrictive with their rules and too strict in their enforcement policies.

Examples of regulatory agencies include the following:

- **The Federal Trade Commission** is responsible for preventing fraud in the marketplace by preventing price fixing and deceptive advertising.

- **The Securities and Exchange Commission** protects investors by regulating stock markets and policing corporations to prevent false and misleading claims of profits in an effort to increase stock prices.

- **The Nuclear Regulatory Commission** controls how electric power companies design, build, and operate nuclear reactors.

- **The Federal Communications Commission** is responsible for assigning broadcast frequencies, for licensing radio and television stations, and for regulating the use of wireless communication devices.

- **The Food and Drug Administration** is responsible for ensuring the health of the American people by inspecting the food supply for contaminants and spoilage. The agency is also responsible for regulating the sale of over-the-counter drugs and patent medicines.

- **The Federal Energy Regulatory Commission** is responsible for preventing price fixing and price manipulation in electric utilities, interstate oil and gas pipelines, and natural gas suppliers.

- **The Occupational Safety and Health Administration** is responsible for ensuring workers are employed in a safe work environment. For example, OSHA can regulate the type of ventilation in a factory, as well as the type of clothing worn and tools used.

Case Studies

Considered to be one of the most controversial government bureaucracies, the **Environmental Protection Agency (EPA)** was created in 1970 as an independent body. Its mission is the enforcement of the environmental laws passed by Congress. One of the agency's first responsibilities was to enforce the **1970 Clean Air Act.** The intent of the law was to reduce automobile pollution and increase automobile gasoline mileage. The automobile industry lobbied hard to defeat the bill and claimed that they could not meet the requirements of the law by the time specified. They were granted extensions and eventually complied, although trucks and SUVs are still exempt from the law.

The Clean Air Act was amended in 1990 as a result of scientific evidence indicating that the refrigerants used in air conditioners were instrumental in depleting the ozone layer. The EPA successfully pressured chemical companies and air-conditioning manufacturers to find alternatives to the ozone-destroying chemicals. The EPA has also been successful in reducing the pollutants that cause acid rain.

Clean air is not the EPA's only problem. It is responsible for enforcement of the **Endangered Species Act.** This highly controversial law is intended to protect endangered wildlife habitats from human encroachment. To implement this goal, environmental impact statements are required whenever construction projects are planned. If there is any possibility that an endangered species could be adversely affected, the EPA has the power to prohibit construction. The EPA's ban on lumbering in areas of the Pacific Northwest—the habitat for the spotted owl—and its decision to block the construction of a dam in Tennessee because of the endangered snail darter fish are two examples. In the Tennessee dam case, Congress overruled the decision of the EPA, even though the Supreme Court had sided with the EPA to stop construction. In addition, Congress further weakened the EPA's enforcement powers by amending the Endangered Species Act to permit exemptions in the future.

Another agency that provokes political contention is the **Equal Employment Opportunities Commission (EEOC).** Created by the 1964 Civil Rights Act, the EEOC is responsible for enforcing the antidiscrimination laws of the United States. This commission has been susceptible to political pressure from both Congress and the White House. It is the EEOC's responsibility to implement affirmative action programs for minorities, to bring suits in cases of racial or sexual discrimination, and to enforce the **Americans with Disabilities Act.** The head of the EEOC is a presidential appointment and is supposed to carry out the policies of the president. If the law conflicts with presidential policy, the EEOC has a problem.

The critics of affirmative action claim the policy is a form of reverse discrimination. Feeling pressure from voters, Congress, and the president, the EEOC first promoted affirmative action and then discouraged the policy. The attempts by this agency to implement the will of Congress have been complicated because both Congress and the White House seem to change their mind at will.

Congress and the EPA
The EPA can sometimes become a foe of Congress, which originally gave the EPA its mandate to act.

The Americans with Disabilities Act requires the EEOC to enforce laws against employers who discriminate against disabled employees or job seekers. In addition, part of the Disabilities Act requires that public buildings and large businesses be accessible to the disabled. Critics claim that this attempt at helping the disabled live normal lives has cost taxpayers hundreds of millions of dollars and the cost is too high in relation to the number of persons benefited.

Who Runs Regulatory Agencies?

Independent regulatory agencies are run by panels of administrators called Boards of Commissioners. These commissioners are appointed by the president with the consent of the Senate. The terms of these commissioners usually overlap the term of the appointing president. The staggered term is intended to minimize political pressure from the White House. Depending on the commission, terms can range from 3 to 14 years.

Fede-really!
Janet Yellen, appointed by Barack Obama in 2014, was the first woman to hold this position.

Perhaps the best-known regulatory board is the **Federal Reserve Board** (the Fed) because its policies directly affect the buying power of the public. The Fed accomplishes this by regulating banks, the value and supply of money, and interest rates. Its members serve 14-year terms. Its chairman serves a four-year term.

Because the Fed is an independent agency, its policies can sometimes conflict with the policies of the president. In 1993, in the first weeks of the Clinton administration, Fed Chairman Alan Greenspan told the president that the condition of the economy was worse than the previous Bush administration had told the American people. In addition, the national debt, as bad as it was perceived to be, was actually even greater than anyone realized. Clinton wanted an economic stimulus tax cut to get the economy out of recession. Greenspan told the president a tax cut should not be pursued, and if the White House went forward with the plan, the Fed would raise interest rates. Clinton was forced to break his campaign pledge to lower taxes. Even though the chairman and the president disagreed over economic policy, the president was powerless to do anything about it. In time, the Greenspan policy helped to get the economy out of the recession and into the longest economic boom in American history. Things went so well that Clinton reappointed Greenspan as chairman. Greenspan's legacy would later come into question as a result of the economic collapse of 2008–2009.

Who Controls the Bureaucracy?

Because most boards of commissions and regulatory agencies are appointed by the president with Senate consent, political considerations always play a part in the appointment process. However, presidents come and go with great regularity, as do the appointed governing boards and commissions. It is the rank and file bureaucrats who are permanent, and they do not like political meddling.

While in office, presidents do have the power to promote their supporters and to use the budget to increase or decrease the influence of an agency. Reducing an agency's budget reduces its staff, which reduces its effectiveness. Increasing the agency's budget can have the opposite effect. Presidents can also reorganize an agency.

Congressional power over the bureaucracy is greater than that of the president. The Senate can affirm or reject presidential appointments. Congress can also abolish an agency or change its jurisdiction if it is unhappy with policy implementation. Finally, it is the Congress, through the appropriations process, that has the final say over how much money agencies will receive.

Rule Setting, Alliance Building, and Iron Triangles

The regulatory agencies carry out their responsibilities by setting rules and regulations that industry must follow. Setting regulations is a participatory process in which industry becomes actively involved in determining the rules. Agencies welcome public participation by holding public hearings for testimony and advice. In most instances, the law requires agencies to consult with industry before rules and regulations can go into effect.

The groups that make up an iron triangle work together to formulate and implement policy in their area of interest. Lobbyists representing industries promote their special-interest agendas by claiming each is in the best interest of the American people. For example, drug companies may lobby the Food and Drug Administration to speed up the certification process for a medication because it will benefit the sick faster. Patients and drug companies will pressure Congress, which then pressures the FDA. These are powerful arguments, but speeding up the process can cause the FDA to overlook something dangerous about the medication.

> ### Iron Triangles
> The rule-making process has fostered the creation of **iron triangles.** Typically iron triangles are informal alliances made up of three groups: (1) a particular industry and its lobbyists (for example, weapons manufacturers), (2) the congressional committee dealing with that industry (the Armed Services Committees of the Senate and House), and (3) the agency that actually is affected (in this case, the Pentagon).

Special interests also contribute money to congressional campaigns, and large contributors are never shy about asking for help from congressional representatives, who are asked to help put pressure on regulators, or at a minimum, to listen to the arguments that the special interests put forward for their cause.

Political scientists have recently seen a more complex political process at work. When issues affect many groups, pro and con coalitions of interest groups, members of Congress, and bureaucrats form a close working relationship. This political process is called either an **alliance network** or an **issue network** and is far more complicated than a simple three-part iron triangle.

For example, if a large factory was a polluter but had marginal profits, it would probably fight expensive environmental regulations. Compliance might drive the company into bankruptcy. But more is at stake than just the company. There are jobs involved and secondary industries that supply the raw materials for production at the company. A local government, which relies on the tax revenues from the company, also has something at stake. Environmental groups are going to be involved. This complicated situation would certainly result in the creation of issue networks for the purpose of influencing the regulatory agency's decisions.

After all the opportunities for input and debate have been exhausted, the regulatory agency writes and publishes the rules (this is its **quasi-legislative function**). If the industry still objects to the regulation, it can seek remedies in the courts by suing the regulatory agency. In the above example, if the company is forced to comply with the environmental laws, it could appeal the decision to the courts.

Because regulatory agencies invite so much controversy, there has been a recent trend toward deregulating the marketplace (removing government restrictions and regulations). Those in favor of **deregulation** claim that the competition of the marketplace is all the regulation that is needed. The deregulators say that regulation is too expensive and time-consuming and involves too much unnecessary red tape. They note that over the past 25 years, the **Civil Aeronautics Board**, which was responsible for regulating the airline industry, and the **Interstate Commerce Commission**, which regulated railroads and the trucking industry, were successfully phased out with little negative impact on consumers.

The Civil Service and Maintaining Neutrality

Today, the majority of government jobs are filled through the competitive **civil service system**. This system was established in 1883 with the passage of the Pendleton Act, a law that ended the "**spoils system**," or the practice of handing out government jobs in exchange for political support. The Office of Personnel Management (OPM) acts as the bureaucracy's employment agency. OPM administers the civil service examination, publishes lists of job openings, and hires on the basis of merit. The intent is to create a competent, professional bureaucracy instead of one based on the "spoils system." A Merit Systems Protection Board investigates charges of agency corruption and incompetence and is supposed to protect "whistle blowers."

To ensure bureaucratic neutrality, Congress passed the **Hatch Act** in 1939. This law permitted bureaucrats the right to vote but not the right to actively campaign for political candidates, work for parties, or run for office. The act's revision of 1993 is less restrictive, allowing bureaucrats to join political parties, make campaign contributions, and display political advertising in the form of buttons and bumper stickers. Bureaucrats still cannot run for public office at any level, solicit campaign funds from subordinates, or make political speeches.

KEY TERMS

- Congress
- House of Representatives
- Senate
- census
- congressional district
- redistricting
- House Ways and Means Committee
- bills of attainder
- *ex post facto* laws
- oversight
- sponsor
- House Rules Committee
- poison-pill (or killer) amendment
- filibuster
- cloture
- pork barrels
- earmarks
- conference committee
- standing committee
- joint committee
- select committee
- pocket veto
- line-item veto
- subcommittee
- pigeonhole
- discharge petition
- Speaker of the House
- majority leader
- minority leader
- president *pro tempore*
- Hatch Act
- Freedom of Information Act
- Gramm-Rudman-Hollings Bill
- War Powers Act
- Patriot Act
- executive agreement
- commander in chief
- Gulf of Tonkin Resolution
- chief of staff
- National Security Council
- Office of Management and Budget (OMB)
- cabinet
- secretaries
- impeachment
- Watergate
- Supreme Court
- equal justice under the law
- due process of law (substantive and procedural)
- adversarial system
- presumption of innocence
- civil law
- criminal law
- grand jury
- plea bargaining
- reasonable doubt
- settlement
- civil court
- preponderance of evidence
- original jurisdiction
- appellate jurisdiction
- Federal District Courts
- Circuit Court of Appeals
- senatorial courtesy
- judicial restraint
- judicial activism
- writ of *certiorari*
- justiciable
- standing
- *Marbury v. Madison*
- briefs
- *amicus curiae* briefs
- oral arguments
- unanimous opinion
- majority opinion
- concurring opinion
- dissenting opinion
- bureaucracy
- Joint Chiefs of Staff
- regulatory agency (independent regulatory commission)
- Federal Reserve Board
- iron triangle
- alliance (issue) network
- deregulation
- civil service system
- spoils system

Summary

- Remember that Congress is a bicameral (two-house) legislature, split into the Senate (in which all states receive equal representation) and the House of Representatives (in which representation is proportionate to population).

- The number of House seats a state gets is based on its population as determined by a census. Once the number of seats is determined, the state legislature draws the districts—often using partisan gerrymandering to ensure a majority for one party or the other.

- Congress has numerous powers that range from creation of all law, to funding all executive agencies, to declaring war. It is the first institution defined in the Constitution, and most scholars think that the Founders intended it to be the most powerful of the branches.

- How does a bill become a law? It is introduced to the House or Senate, referred to a committee, amended and debated, reintroduced to the general House and Senate, debated and amended once more, harmonized with its counterpart that has traveled through the other legislative body, voted on again, and signed by the president.

- Given the large size of both houses of Congress, committees do most of the work of legislating. Committees can be standing, select, or joint, and are often further divided into subcommittees.

- The House is led by the speaker, while the Senate has two ceremonial leaders (the vice president and the president *pro tempore*) and one actual power broker—the majority leader.

- This chapter has a ton of laws. Try to remember them by using the four categories: (1) National Growth, Expansion, and Institution Building; (2) Regulation of Government and Industry; (3) Rights and Freedoms; and (4) Government Aid to the People.

- The president is the chief executive of the nation and is responsible for enforcing all laws. Over the years, the power of the presidency has grown dramatically—often at the expense of Congress.

- Even though the Constitution gives Congress the power to declare war, the nature of modern warfare has given the president control of this area. Though Congress does have tools to stop a wartime president, using them would generally be tantamount to political suicide.

o   Being a good president often means going beyond the powers explicitly listed in the Constitution. Mastery of these "informal powers"—like consensus building or boosting the morale of the nation—often determines presidential greatness.

o   The president relies a great deal on the Executive Office of the President (EOP)—his personal staff, which is ensconced within the West Wing of the White House. The EOP is also home to a number of agencies that serve the president and are largely free from congressional oversight.

o   America has fifteen cabinet departments, and each contains a huge array of agencies and bureaucracies designed to help enforce the law of the land. The cabinet secretaries are supposed to advise the president, but due to conflicting loyalties most presidents have kept them out of the loop and relied on the EOP and other informal advisors when making policy decisions.

o   If a president has committed "treason, bribery, or other high crimes and misdemeanors," he can be impeached by a majority vote in the House and then removed from office with a two-thirds vote in the Senate.

o   Remember that America has two legal systems—state and federal—and all people are under the jurisdiction of both. The federal system was created by the Constitution—all federal judges are appointed by the president and approved by the Senate, and the nation is divided into 91 federal districts.

o   The Supreme Court rules on some very divisive social issues, and the battle to appoint new members has gotten more intense. Increasingly, presidents are looking to appoint younger and more ideological candidates who share their political philosophies.

o   The Supreme Court is America's court of last resort and gets most of its cases through appeals from lower courts or by granting writs of certiorari which cause cases to jump straight to their chambers.

o   Though it is not mentioned in the Constitution, the Supreme Court's most important power is judicial review: the ability to strike down any state or federal law that is unconstitutional. This power was established in the case of *Marbury v. Madison* in 1803.

o   Often called "the fourth branch of government," bureaucrats staff the large executive agencies that run the federal government. To get these jobs, applicants must take competitive exams. Bureaucrats play a huge role in creating public policy by making rules that flesh out vague laws passed by Congress.

o   We see four different types of bureaucracy in Washington: cabinet departments, independent agencies, regulatory commissions, and government corporations. Regulatory commissions are largely free of political control and have broad oversight responsibilities, while government corporations like the Postal Service are expected to turn a profit in the free market.

o   Because the issues dealt with by bureaucrats are so technical and often pertain to a small interest group, we see the formation of iron triangles—cooperation between a bureaucracy (like the Department of Defense), a congressional committee (like the Senate Armed Services Committee), and a special interest group (like weapons and aircraft manufacturers).

o   Bureaucrats are supposed to be politically neutral and stable while their political overlords shift due to election results. Still, many suspect that they may take sides, and laws like the Hatch Act were designed to prevent this from happening.

Chapter 8 Drill

See Chapter 11 for answers and explanations.

Questions 1 and 2 refer to the passage below.

Why does a judge swear to discharge his duties agreeably to the Constitution of the United States, if that Constitution forms no rule for his government? If it is closed upon him, and cannot be inspected by him?

If such be the real state of things, this is worse than solemn mockery. To prescribe, or take this oath, becomes equally a crime.

It is also not entirely unworthy of observation that, in declaring what shall be the *supreme* law of the land, the Constitution itself is first mentioned; and not the laws of the United States generally, but those only which shall he made in pursuance of the *Constitution*, have that rank.

Thus, the particular phraseology of the Constitution of the United States confirms and strengthens the principle, supposed to be essential to all written constitutions, that a law repugnant to the Constitution is void; and that *courts*, as well as other departments, are bound by that instrument.

—John Marshall, Chief Justice of the Supreme Court (1801–1835)

1. Which of the following statements best summarizes the whole passage?

   (A) Justices must interpret the Constitution although they do not explicitly have this power.
   (B) There are may questions about why justices have the power to interpret the Constitution.
   (C) Marshall is unsure about how to properly perform his job.
   (D) Justices are loyal to the Constitution because they swear an oath of allegiance.

2. It can be inferred from this passage that Marshall was arguing for which legal doctrine?

   (A) *Ex post facto* laws
   (B) Judicial restraint
   (C) Judicial review
   (D) *Amicus curiae* briefs

3. Which of the following is an accurate comparison of the bureaucratic responsibilities of the Executive and Legislative Branches?

	Legislative Branch	Executive Branch
(A)	Library of Congress	Technology Assessment
(B)	Department of Energy	Government Publishing Office
(C)	Department of Justice	Department of State
(D)	Government Accountability Office	Drug Control Policy

4. Who is the official head of the Senate?

   (A) President of the United States
   (B) Vice president of the United States
   (C) President *pro tempore*
   (D) Chief whip

5. Which of the following is one of the most important legislative powers of Congress?

   (A) The ability to tax and spend
   (B) The power to choose a president
   (C) The ability to propose amendments to the Constitution
   (D) The power to ratify treaties (in the Senate)

6. How do House congressional districts gain their shapes?

   (A) A vote held in the Senate by the majority party
   (B) An executive order of the president
   (C) A census and the various state legislatures
   (D) A nonpartisan commission

7. How are cabinet members chosen?

   (A) By the president and then confirmed by the Senate
   (B) By the president and then confirmed by both houses of Congress
   (C) By the Supreme Court
   (D) By the president alone, without confirmation

REFLECT

Respond to the following questions:

- For which content topics discussed in this chapter do you feel you have achieved sufficient mastery to answer multiple-choice questions correctly?

- For which content topics discussed in this chapter do you feel you have achieved sufficient mastery to discuss effectively in an essay?

- For which content topics discussed in this chapter do you feel you need more work before you can answer multiple-choice questions correctly?

- For which content topics discussed in this chapter do you feel you need more work before you can discuss effectively in an essay?

- What parts of this chapter are you going to re-review?

- Will you seek further help, outside of this book (such as a teacher, tutor, or AP Students), on any of the content in this chapter—and, if so, on what content?

Chapter 9
Public Policy

CONCEPTS

- Why do the poorest people in the United States have the least political power?
- What role does federalism play in the implementation of social welfare policy?
- Why is it so difficult to pass social welfare policy?
- Why are entitlement programs always a threat to the budget-making process?
- Why can it be said that the president is a secondary player when it comes to the economy?
- Why is it so difficult to write a budget for the United States?
- How can the president use the budget-making process to control his policy initiatives?

The process of public policy making consists of first deciding what the problem is and then deciding how to solve it. Policy making can have the following three purposes:

- **solving a social problem,** such as high crime rates, high unemployment, poverty among the aged, or teenage drinking
- **countering threats,** such as terrorism or war
- **pursuing an objective,** such as building a highway, exploring outer space, or finding a cure for cancer

Policy can be achieved by prohibiting certain kinds of behavior, such as polygamy, murder, rape, and robbery. It can also be achieved by protecting certain activities. Granting patents and copyrights to individuals for their intellectual property, protecting the environment, and setting rules for workplace safety are all examples. Policy can promote some social activity; giving tax deductions for donations to charities is an example. Policy can be achieved by providing direct benefits to citizens. These benefits may include building roads, libraries, or hospitals. Benefits can also take the form of individual government subsidies, student loans, and pensions for the elderly.

Policy making can be frustrating because it often depends on public opinion, which can be fickle and unpredictable. The **issue-attention cycle** requires policy makers to act quickly, before the public becomes bored and loses interest. Public complaints over high energy prices can cause a flurry of policy making. But when prices go down, the public forgets about it until the next time.

Policy making often involves trade-offs between competing goods. To find additional energy resources may require access to pristine wildlife reserves. The risks to wildlife and the environment may be too high of a price to pay for the additional energy. Conservation, smaller cars, and alternative energy sources may be better solutions, but each will have its supporters and opponents.

Because policy making can have unforeseen results and can touch off bitter disputes, legislators often use **incrementalism**—the slow, step-by-step approach to making policy—or legislators may decide to use the policy of inaction, because taking no action is one way of making policy. Conflicts over health care reform and Social Security entitlements can result in simply maintaining the status quo (or, not changing a policy).

MAKING POLICY

Policy making has five main steps, and each is influenced by politics.

1. The first involves *defining the role of government* in solving social and economic problems. The political left sees a greater responsibility for government than the right, with the result that governments on the left are larger, more active, and more expensive than on the right.

2. **Agenda setting** identifies social and economic problems, redefines them into political issues, and ranks them in order of importance. A citizen's socioeconomic status can determine which problems seem important and which don't. Poor people may rank job training high on the agenda, while the rich may rank tax cuts higher. When large numbers of people are affected, the concern will be ranked high. However, there are times when it is those with the most money who will have their issues placed high on the agenda. For example, large energy-producing corporations have a great deal of access to policy makers.

Policy can try to address the concerns of opposing sides. Establishing environmental standards for oil exploration and refining tries to address the concerns of two constituencies: the environmentalists and the petroleum producers.

A momentous event, such as a war, an oil embargo, or a collapsing stock market, may set the agenda. Issues such as universal health care, the war on drugs, or environmental concerns can resurface. Scholars can force issues into the agenda through research studies.

3. **Policy formulation and adoption** can be accomplished in a number of ways. Sometimes the most difficult method is the legislative process in Congress, while the easiest may be through the executive branch by the use of executive orders from the president. Rules enacted by regulatory agencies or precedent-setting decisions by the Supreme Court are also sources of policy formulation and adoption. *Brown v. Board of Education* was certainly a policy-making decision.

4. **Policy implementation** puts the policy into effect by enforcement through the appropriate government agency. Timetables and rules for carrying out policies as well as anticipating problems are all part of policy implementation. One of the major concerns of policy making is the unforeseen consequences. The "three-strike rule," intended to get career criminals off the streets, has ended most plea-bargaining arrangements, causing more trials and overloaded courts, judges, and jails. The three-strike rule has turned out to be a much more expensive public policy than anticipated.

5. **Policy evaluation** is the final step. Does a policy work? Have unforeseen consequences caused other policy problems? Evaluation provides feedback to the policy makers, so that modifications can be made to better solve the problems. Evaluation may determine that the problem has been solved and that the policy can be terminated.

Obstacles to Policy Making

The United States is a pluralist democracy, with multiple centers of power for making policy. Those interested in affecting policy making concentrate their efforts at these many centers. Because the United States has a federal system of government, policy can be made at the local, state, and national levels. Separation of powers creates three policy making centers: the executive, the legislative, and the judiciary. There is also the general bureaucracy, with its multiple policy-making centers. Trying to influence legislation, thousands of interest-group lobbyists, like jellyfish in the sea, descend upon these policy-making centers at all levels of government.

In their efforts to prevent tyranny and corruption, the framers created a policy-making nightmare by dispersing the power centers. Getting things done is cumbersome and frustrating. Multiple access points cause **policy fragmentation,** where many pieces of legislation deal with parts of policy problems but never deal with the entire problem. The War on Drugs has at least 75 congressional committees with some type of jurisdiction or oversight; local and state law enforcement agencies are involved, as well as the Army, Navy, Air Force, Coast Guard, Border Patrol, Immigration and Naturalization Service, customs service, DEA, and the FBI.

Because so many agencies of government are involved, the drug war requires policy coordination. Interagency task forces try to iron out policy problems and conflicts between competing agencies, and Congress uses its oversight powers to change agency jurisdiction and give coherence to policy.

ECONOMIC POLICY

Of all the issues that face politicians, the economy is often the most important. Success or failure usually rests with the person the public perceives as responsible for the condition of the economy; and whether it is true, the electorate usually holds the president responsible. In 1992, the economy was in recession and George H. W. Bush was blamed. In 1996, the economy was booming, and Clinton was given credit and reelected.

Because of the importance of the economy in the eyes of the voters, it is in a politician's self-interest to make policies that will increase people's standard of living. The electorate looks to Washington to achieve this objective. For the policy maker, the vexing question is how to achieve it.

Sound economic policy that achieves prosperity is probably the most elusive of all policies. There are many elements to the problem: inflation, deflation, interest rates, the supply of money in circulation, the profitability of corporations, foreign competition, international agreements, and consumer confidence, just to name a few. Complicating the problem are the various economic theories that drive policy decisions, and the various government agencies and institutions that make decisions affecting economic conditions.

Economic Theory

Capitalist free-market systems in which both government and private industry play a role are called **mixed economies.** Mixed free-market systems are characterized by both private and public (government) ownership of the means of production and distribution of goods and services. The price of goods and services is determined by the free-market interplay of supply and demand. The profits after taxes are kept by the owners.

Free-market economic systems are plagued by periods of prosperity followed by periods of economic contraction (decreased activity, economic downturn). Because the United States has a mixed free-market system, the major problem for policy makers is how to maintain prosperity and economic growth while reducing the impact of the inevitable economic contraction. In capitalist systems, the basic question is to what extent the government should intervene.

Laissez-faire economists believe that the government should never become involved in economic issues. They believe that the narrow pursuit of individual profit serves the broader interest of society. Central to laissez-faire economics is the belief that free markets are governed by the laws of nature and government should not interfere with those laws. In vogue with rugged individualists in the 19th century, laissez-faire economics disappeared as a viable government policy option during the Great Depression of the 1930s.

Clinton's Economy
In 1992, Bill Clinton's informal campaign slogan was "It's the economy, stupid!"

Perhaps the most influential economist of the 20th century was John Maynard Keynes, an interventionist. **Keynesian economics**, on which FDR's New Deal was based, holds that the government can smooth out business cycles by influencing the amount of income individuals and businesses can spend on goods and services.

Fiscal Policy

Fiscal policy refers to the government action of either lowering or raising taxes, which results in more or less consumer spending or enacting of government spending programs, such as building highways or hospitals. Keynesians believe that during economic downturns the government should spend money on projects to inject money into the economy. They are less worried about government deficit spending than about keeping the economy prosperous. A prosperous economy means a larger tax base, which will eventually correct deficit spending. In effect, the Keynesian school believes that when the economy is good, surplus taxes (money left over from tax revenues) should be saved to pay for the government spending that must take place during an economic downturn. Using this school of thought, the policy alternatives are obvious, but questions still remain. Should there be tax cuts? If so, how much, and who should get them? How much spending should the government engage in? How much **deficit spending** (funds raised by borrowing rather than taxation) should be allowed? The answers to these questions are extremely difficult, with major political consequences.

In the 1980s, the Reagan-Bush administration became the champion of the **supply-side** school of economic thought. The supply-siders take issue with supporters of Keynesian economics. Inflation is caused by too many dollars chasing too few goods. If the supply of goods is raised, the cost of the goods will decline. According to this theory, supply-siders argue that the government should cut taxes and spending on domestic programs to stimulate greater production.

Going along with supply-side theory, Congress in the 1980s enacted extensive tax cuts and reductions to social welfare programs, a policy later dubbed "Reaganomics." Inflation was brought under control, but huge yearly **budget deficits**, caused in part by a defense buildup, created a four-trillion-dollar debt. In the 1990s, budget surpluses began to shrink the deficit but these gains were reversed as a result of policies enacted during the Bush and Obama administrations, particularly during the Great Recession. Tax cuts followed by rising costs associated with the War on Terrorism, the invasion and occupation of Afghanistan and Iraq, and government stimulus programs have resulted in record budget deficits. The most recent estimates of the Congressional Budget Office (CBO) have warned against increasingly large budget deficits. In 2010, a $1.5 trillion deficit in the federal budget stoked political controversy and contributed to historic Republican gains in both houses of Congress in the 2010 mid-term elections. The next year, congressional Republicans forced a showdown over plans to increase the federal debt ceiling, generating concern over the United States' international credit rating.

Monetary Policy

Monetary policy refers to the process by which the government controls the supply of money in circulation and the supply of credit through the actions of the **Federal Reserve Board** (the Fed). The Fed can increase the amount of money in circulation by lowering interest rates. Rate reductions make borrowing money less expensive because interest on the money is low. This action usually inflates (expands) the economy, resulting in higher prices and wages. If the Fed raises interest rates, the impact on the economy will be deflationary, resulting in either more stable or lower prices or wages.

Monetary policy can be implemented by the Federal Reserve Board in three ways.

- By manipulating the **reserve requirement**, which raises or lowers the amount of money banks are required to keep on hand. Raising the reserve shrinks the amount of money available for borrowing, which raises interest rates. Lowering the reserve will have the opposite effect, lowering interest rates.

- By manipulating the **discount rate**, which raises or lowers the interest banks pay to the Federal Reserve Banks for borrowing money. Lowering the discount rate will lower the interest rates for consumer loans. Raising the discount rate will raise the interest rates for consumer loans. The higher the rate, the less consumers purchase.

- By manipulating **open market operations**, the Federal Reserve buys and sells United States government bonds. People buy bonds because they have a better interest rate than savings accounts. When the Fed sells bonds, people withdraw money from banks to take advantage of the bond's higher interest rate. Because the bank has less to loan, consumer interest rates go up, which slows consumer spending and economic growth. When the Fed buys bonds, money flows back into the banks, which increases the money available for loans. With more money in the bank for consumers to borrow, interest rates are driven down. Lower interest rates means more consumer spending, which increases economic growth.

Some economists believe that government should intervene only to manipulate the money supply, an idea championed by Milton Friedman. These monetarists believe that the money supply should be increased at a constant rate to accommodate economic growth. Monetarists do not believe that interest rate changes and manipulation of tax rates have much of an impact on economic conditions.

In the 1990s, the U.S. economy expanded without tax cuts, creating record employment levels with little inflation. Many gave the credit to the monetary policy of Alan Greenspan and the Federal Reserve.

The Tools of Economic Policy Making

The president receives advice on the state of the economy from the following departments and agencies:

- the Council of Economic Advisors
- the National Economic Council
- the Office of Management and Budget
- the Secretary of the Treasury

The president can influence the fiscal and monetary policies of these departments and agencies through his appointment power and policy **initiatives**. Remember that fiscal policy involves the budget, and monetary policy involves the money supply.

Fiscal Policy Making

The Director of the **Office of Management and Budget (OMB)** is responsible for initiating the budget process. The director meets with the president to discuss his policy initiatives. The state of the economy is discussed, centering on government revenue projections, which is the predicted income from taxes. Based on the president's priorities, some executive departments will receive more money than others. The OMB then writes the president's budget and submits it to Congress. Upon its arrival the budget is sent to three committees. The **House Ways and Means Committee** deals with the taxing aspects of the budget. **Authorization committees** in both houses decide what programs Congress wants to fund. **Appropriations committees** in both houses then decide how much money to spend for those programs that have been authorized.

Shut It Down
Bill Clinton's conflict with congressional Republicans led to government shutdowns over budget issues in 1995 and 1996. A similar impasse occurred in 2013, leading to a shutdown for 16 days in October of that year.

The budget process is complicated, politically divisive, and, in recent years, nearly impossible to conclude. The president's projected revenues and expenditures often conflict with those of Congress. Congress often simply does not trust the president's numbers, and conversely, the president does not trust Congress's. These yearly budget problems forced passage of the **Budget Reform Act of 1974**, which created the **Congressional Budget Office,** with budget committees in both the House and Senate. The congressional committees set their own revenue and spending levels. Negotiations then take place among the White House and the two houses of Congress in an effort to get one budget acceptable to everyone. Failure to achieve a budget by the beginning of the **fiscal year** could mean shutting down the government and sending employees home. When this occurs, budget stop-gap bills are passed to temporarily appropriate money to keep the government operating.

The **Budget Enforcement Act of 1990** was an effort to streamline the budget process and make it easier to arrive at a compromise budget. The law categorizes government expenditures as either mandatory or discretionary spending.

Mandatory spending is required by law, to fund programs such as the **entitlement programs, Social Security, Medicare,** veterans' pensions, and payment on the national debt. **Discretionary spending** programs are not required by law and include defense, education, highways, research grants, and all government operations. Discretionary programs are the primary targets for making cuts to balance the budget.

TRADE POLICY

The United States is by far the richest nation in the world. The output of the economy of the state of California alone ranks among the top ten nations in the world. The economic outputs of each of the three cities of Los Angeles, Chicago, and New York rank among the output of the top twenty nations. For better or for worse, the United States is the largest producer and consumer of products.

Foreign nations depend on the United States as a market for their products, as we depend on them for ours. The ratio of imported products to exported products is called the **balance of trade**. **Trade deficits** occur when imports exceed exports. Trade deficits cause wealth to flow from a nation. When nations face trade deficits, they often place restrictions on imported goods. The nation facing the restrictions can take retaliation by imposing high import taxes or unfair regulations on products, effectively keeping out foreign goods. Trade wars can result, stopping trade between countries. Trade surpluses are the result of more money flowing into a country than out. The oil-producing nations have huge amounts of money flowing into their treasuries and therefore have large trade surpluses when prices are high.

In an effort to promote trade, the United States signed the **General Agreement on Tariffs and Trade (GATT)**, which evolved into the World Trade Organization (WTO). The 125 members of the WTO account for 97% of the world's trade. The organization works to lower tariffs and quotas and reduce unfair trade practices.

In an effort to promote free trade between the United States, Canada, and Mexico, the three nations signed the **North American Free Trade Agreement (NAFTA)** in 1994, effectively removing import tariffs from one another's products. As an economic policy, NAFTA is controversial. It is opposed by U.S. industrial labor unions who fear that jobs will be lost to cheap Mexican labor. Others fear that the industrial capacity of the United States will be damaged because factories will move to Mexico where environmental laws are not strictly enforced. NAFTA supporters claim it will improve the U.S. economy and will also create jobs in Mexico, resulting in less illegal immigration. Supporters also claim that a richer Mexico will purchase more American products. NAFTA has proven to be something of a mixed blessing. Its passage has led to cheaper labor (in Mexico) for many U.S. companies and an increase in trade between the two countries. Nevertheless, many American jobs have undeniably been sent south of the border, and many Mexican farmers are losing their land in a futile attempt to compete with American agribusinesses.

DOMESTIC POLICY

While economic policy is contentious, domestic policy is sometimes even more so because it gets to the very essence of the purposes of government. Liberals believe government has an obligation to provide for social welfare, to help the needy. Conservatives believe **social-welfare programs** are encroachments on individual liberties and responsibilities. They think these programs turn the government into an instrument used to create a permanent class of the underprivileged, dependent upon government handouts. Somewhere in between are the moderates who believe government should provide opportunities and limited help during difficult times.

The 20th century has seen a dramatic change in the way society perceives the role of government in providing for the basic needs of people. Before the Great Depression, there were no government programs to help people who suffered from the hardships of old age, disabilities, unemployment, and poverty. So many people needed help in the 1930s that the government enacted programs to create jobs, provide housing, and feed the hungry. Later on, the **Great Society** programs of the Johnson administration expanded government welfare programs, but because of the expense and questions about their effectiveness, many of the Great Society programs were eliminated or scaled back during and after the Reagan administration.

Today there are two kinds of social-welfare programs.

- **Social insurance programs** are in reality national insurance programs into which employers and employees pay taxes. Because individuals pay into these programs, the benefits derived are considered by the public to have been earned. There seems to be little public debate over a citizen's "right" to Social Security.

- **Public assistance programs**, on the other hand, are not perceived as earned. These programs are a result of condition and a government responsibility to help the needy. Recipients are not required to pay into the system to get something out. Public assistance is considered by some to be a "handout" to the lazy. Because politicians understand this public perception, public policy initiatives from both parties have concentrated on forcing people on public assistance to either seek work or enter work-training programs.

Social Security

Social Security is an entitlement program mandated by law. The government must pay benefits to all people who meet the requirements of the program. Changing the law would require congressional action. Because the largest voting block of the electorate is made up of those nearing or at retirement age, there is little chance of major changes to the system, even though some experts warn that the Social Security trust fund will go bankrupt in the near future. Currently, entitlement programs account for the largest expense in the federal budget.

In its original form Social Security provided benefits only to retired persons beginning at age 65.

The program has now been expanded to include four categories of persons.

- Retired workers and their survivors who are presently age 65 and older receive monthly payments from the Social Security trust fund. To help maintain a recipient's standard of living, recipients are entitled to a **COLA** (cost of living adjustment) if the inflation rate exceeds 3%. COLAs put a strain on the ability of the trust fund to meet its obligations. Changes in the demographic composition of society are also putting a strain on the system. Society is aging, and the ratio of workers to retirees is declining. Because Social Security is a pay-as-you-go system, the money that is now paid into the system pays the present beneficiaries. As the ratio of workers to retirees continues to decline, workers will be faced with higher taxes to maintain the income of those who are retired.

- Insurance for the disabled provides monthly payments to those citizens who are permanently and totally disabled. This category includes the learning disabled and those dependent on drugs and alcohol.

- **Medicare** provides government assistance to people older than 65 for health care. For those retirees who pay an additional tax on their social security benefit, Medicare Part B will pay approximately 80% of their doctor's bills. The high and rising cost of health care has led some to question the solvency of this program, but recent reports note that it is more than able to cover 100% of its costs through at least 2030.

- **Medicaid** provides medical and health-related services for low-income parents, children, seniors, and people with disabilities. It is jointly funded by the states and federal government and is managed and run by the individual states.

- Temporary unemployment insurance for those out of work provides a weekly benefit, for a limited time. Each state government administers its own unemployment insurance program. Both the federal and state governments pay into a trust fund to provide the benefit. While states have traditionally set their own rules on the amount and duration of benefits, Congress has responded at the federal level to the recession that began in 2009 by helping states offer up to 99 weeks of benefits to the unemployed, significantly more than the previous standard of 26 weeks. In 2012, however, Congress imposed additional restrictions on those extended federal benefits, including a measure to gradually decrease the limit to 73 weeks. With the unemployment rate below 5% at the beginning of 2018, the extension of benefits continues to decrease.

Social Welfare

No matter how well intentioned the government has been, and no matter how much money has been spent, poverty has remained a perpetual problem for policy makers at both the state and federal levels. The first federal welfare programs were established by the Social Security Act in the 1930s. The largest and most controversial became known as Aid to Families with Dependent Children (AFDC).

All social welfare programs are designed to help targeted groups. Public assistance programs, known as welfare, target families whose total income falls below the federally determined minimum amount required to provide for the basic needs of a family. The present amount is approximately $17,000 for a family of four. The larger the family, the more income is required and the more money is paid out. Critics claimed that welfare was an incentive for families to have more children. Further complicating matters were complaints from recipients about a system that was degrading because investigators, looking for welfare cheaters, were invading their privacy.

In addition to AFDC, the federal government has established **supplemental public assistance programs** (known as SSI) to help the disabled and the aged who are living at or near the poverty level. To improve the diet and increase the buying power of the poor, the federal government also provides **food stamps**. Recipients use government-provided debit cards to help pay for food. Both SSI and the food-stamp program are federal programs administered through local and state agencies.

In an effort to reduce the number of people living on public assistance, the **Welfare Reform Act** was passed in 1996. Under the law, social welfare programs are funded by both the state and federal governments, with the federal government contributing the greatest share in the form of block grants. Block grants are important because they allow states to experiment with new types of programs designed to get people off welfare and into work programs. The administration of programs (the distribution of cash payments) and the incentives for finding work and providing job training are left to the states. The intent of the law is to reduce the welfare rolls and force people to find work. This is accomplished by

- abolishing Aid to Families with Dependent Children (AFDC), which has affected 22% of the families in the United States with children and replacing it with Temporary Assistance for Needy Families (TANF)

- requiring adults to find work within two years or be cut off

- placing a lifetime limit of five years for welfare eligibility, although it is possible to get a waiver if a recipient is actively seeking work

- prohibiting undocumented immigrants from receiving assistance

The political debate over public assistance centers on two issues: who pays how much, and what is the fair standard to be used for the recipient? Both Democrats and Republicans have tried to reduce these programs. Cutting them, however, places more people at risk, reducing food stamp programs and school lunch programs, causing increased hunger.

Health Care

One of the most vexing problems for policy makers is what to do about the high cost of health care. Americans spend more than 17% of the nation's **gross domestic product**, or **GDP** (the total of goods and services produced in a year), on health care. The United States has the most expensive health care system in the world and is the only fully industrialized nation without a national health care program. High costs have not guaranteed any longer life expectancy, nor better treatment than that found in other industrialized nations. Instead of a national program run by the government, most Americans have relied on various types of insurance programs to pay for health care costs. The premiums for these health care programs are paid by workers and employers. For many reasons, but primarily because of cost, 15.4% of the population was without health insurance in 2010.

High Costs
The average cost for these insurance programs is at least $5,000 per person per year and is rising faster than the cost of living.

As with other government programs, the electorate is divided on how to solve the two issues of universal health care and the burden of health care costs. Voters seem to want increased coverage but there is little evidence to indicate they are willing to pay for it. The only taxes the American electorate seems willing to pay are the so-called "sin taxes"—still fairly unpopular in some circles—on alcohol and tobacco products, which will not generate enough revenues to provide increased coverage. Proposals for "anti-obesity" taxes on sugary drinks and sodas have been met with mixed reactions from the public. Another basic issue for which there is no consensus is whether health benefits should be a government or privately administered program. With little public consensus, over the past two decades, reform has been extremely contentious.

An ill-fated attempt at health care reform was made in the first Clinton administration. The proposed policy called for universal coverage and strict cost controls. The policy would have required increased taxes coupled with cost-cutting limits on the types of medical procedures allowable. The lack of public consensus killed the proposal within a year.

The debate over health care continued during the 2000 presidential election. Both candidates agreed that something had to be done about both escalating costs and the increasing numbers of uninsured. The Democrats promoted a policy of a government-paid prescription drug program for senior citizens. The Republicans promoted a prescription-drug program run by insurance providers, but again there was no consensus.

The most significant health-care legislation in American history was signed into law by President Obama on March 23, 2010. The **Patient Protection and Affordable Health Care Act**, popularly known as Obamacare, was passed over the course of several months and it generated significant political debate and controversy. The law was celebrated by most Democrats, who touted it as the much-needed solution to the long-term flaws in the American health-care system. Republicans and some independent voters criticized the law, claiming it was an expensive intrusion of the federal government into the public sector. The debate lasted until the midterm elections in November of 2010, when Republicans gained a large number of congressional seats partly as a result of voter discontent with the law.

The most important of the law's provisions allowed the federal government, beginning in 2014, to fine individuals who do not participate in an insurance program. This policy, known as the "individual mandate," has been the basis of many Republican criticisms of the law. The attorneys general of twenty-eight states challenged this provision in the law in federal court, claiming that the Constitution prohibits Congress from taxing individuals for not purchasing a product (say, health insurance). However, the Supreme Court ruled that the individual mandate is constitutional in the 2012 case *National Federation of Independent Business v. Sebelius.*

KEY TERMS

- issue-attention cycle
- incrementalism
- agenda setting
- policy implementation
- policy fragmentation
- mixed economy
- laissez-faire
- Keynesian economics
- fiscal policy
- deficit spending
- supply-side economics
- budget deficit
- monetary policy
- Federal Reserve Board
- reserve requirement
- discount rate
- open market operations
- initiative
- Office of Management and Budget (OMB)
- House Ways and Means Committee
- authorization committees
- appropriation committees
- Budget Reform Act of 1974
- Congressional Budget Office
- fiscal year
- Budget Enforcement Act of 1990
- mandatory spending
- entitlement programs
- discretionary spending
- balance of trade
- trade deficit
- General Agreement on Tariffs and Trade (GATT)
- North American Free Trade Agreement (NAFTA)
- social welfare programs
- Great Society
- Social Security
- COLA
- Medicare
- Medicaid
- supplemental public assistance programs
- food stamps
- Welfare Reform Act
- gross domestic product (GDP)
- Patient Protection and Affordable Health Care Act

Summary

o Public policy is made when the government decides to take action to solve a societal problem, and consists of five steps.

   1. Defining the role of government
   2. Agenda setting
   3. Policy formulation
   4. Policy implementation
   5. Policy evaluation

o Economic policy has been one of the most important areas of public policy in American history. Policy makers have oscillated between supporting laissez-faire free market principles and redistributionist, interventionist policies.

o The United States has joined international trade organizations like the World Trade Organization (WTO) and the North American Free Trade Agreement (NAFTA) in order to boost our commerce with the rest of the world. Nevertheless, we still use tariffs and subsidies to protect large swathes of our industry and agriculture.

o Before FDR, the federal government did not engage in much domestic policy making, but since that era we have seen the rise of programs like Social Security, Welfare (through the Aid to Families with Dependent Children and new state-based systems), and Medicaid.

Chapter 9 Drill

See Chapter 11 for answers and explanations.

Questions 1 and 2 refer to the graph below.

ACCUMULATED MONTHS OF PARTICIPATION IN A GOVERNMENT ASSISTANCE PROGRAM
(Percentage of non-institutionalized civilian population receiving Medicare, welfare, food stamps, housing assistance and/or Social Security Insurance for 1 or more months)

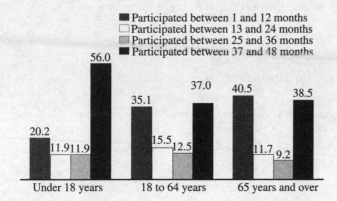

- ■ Participated between 1 and 12 months
- □ Participated between 13 and 24 months
- ▨ Participated between 25 and 36 months
- ■ Participated between 37 and 48 months

Source: U.S. Census.

1. Which of the following statements best summarizes a trend in the graph above?

   (A) Americans 18 to 64 years are better at getting off government assistance programs than Americans 65 years and older.
   (B) Americans 18 to 64 years use government assistance for 1-12 months at a higher rate than other Americans.
   (C) Americans 65 years and over are more likely to use government assistance for 13–36 months than the other age groups.
   (D) Americans under 18 years remain on government assistance programs for the longest amount of time.

2. Which of the following arguments does the data in the graph support?

   (A) The government isn't doing enough to help Americans living in poverty.
   (B) Americans who receive public assistance often become reliant on it.
   (C) Government spending is out of control due to assistance programs.
   (D) Public insurance programs should take precedence over public assistance programs.

3. Which of the following is an accurate comparison between laissez-faire economics and supply-side economics?

	Laissez-faire Economics	Supply-Side Economics
(A)	Pursue individual profit	The government should influence wages and prices
(B)	Fell out of favor during the Great Depression	Influenced by beliefs of rugged individualists
(C)	Massive deficit spending	Meant to bring inflation under control
(D)	No government interference	Tax cuts to encourage economic growth

4. Which of the following describes the responsibilities of the Office of Management and Budget (OMB)?

   (A) Assessing the nation's economic health
   (B) Writing the national budget
   (C) Planning out the national budget for the president
   (D) Providing long-term and highly theoretical economic advice

5. Which of the following people would receive money from Social Security?

   (A) A worker retiring after 40 years
   (B) A foreign tourist injured on U.S. soil
   (C) A veteran working as a security guard
   (D) A family that is chronically poor

6. Which of the following terms describes a time when a nation's imports exceed its exports?

   (A) Trade deficit
   (B) Trade surplus
   (C) In default
   (D) Bankrupt

7. Which of the following programs is categorized as discretionary spending under the Budget Enforcement Act of 1990?

   (A) National debt payments
   (B) Social Security
   (C) Medicare
   (D) Education

REFLECT

Respond to the following questions:

- For which content topics discussed in this chapter do you feel you have achieved sufficient mastery to answer multiple-choice questions correctly?

- For which content topics discussed in this chapter do you feel you have achieved sufficient mastery to discuss effectively in an essay?

- For which content topics discussed in this chapter do you feel you need more work before you can answer multiple-choice questions correctly?

- For which content topics discussed in this chapter do you feel you need more work before you can discuss effectively in an essay?

- What parts of this chapter are you going to re-review?

- Will you seek further help, outside of this book (such as a teacher, tutor, or AP Students), on any of the content in this chapter—and, if so, on what content?

Chapter 10
Civil Rights and
Civil Liberties

CONCEPTS

- Why would Justice Thurgood Marshall blame the Supreme Court for the racial policies practiced in the United States before the *Brown* decision?

- Why did the Supreme Court allow the use of affirmative action programs?

- Why is it said that the Warren Court took the handcuffs off the criminals and put them on the police?

- What mechanism did the Supreme Court use to ensure the rights of defendants in state criminal prosecutions?

- What impact has the interpretation of speech as a preferred right had on the government's power to censure?

- How does the Supreme Court interpret the right to privacy on matters dealing with human reproduction?

- How has the Supreme Court changed its reasoning in dealing with religious activities in schools financed by the public?

How to Discuss a Court Case

First, an important tip: in responding to an essay question involving Supreme Court decisions, do not take more than one sentence per case to explain the relevant background. Explain the essential questions and answers of cases, as well as the reasoning the court used in the decision. The most important aspect of a case, for political science purposes, is its impact on government or society. When asked about a case, make sure the consequences of the decision are discussed. For example, the most important consequence of *Marbury v. Madison* is the establishment of judicial review, which is arguably the most important principle ever enshrined by the court. The consequence of *Heart of Atlanta Motel v. United States* is the affirmation of the power of Congress, through the use of the commerce clause, to end segregation by law in the United States.

The term **civil liberties** generally applies to those protections (enjoyed by all Americans) from the abuse of government power. The term **civil rights** is used specifically to describe protections from discrimination based on race, gender, or other minority status. Often, the term is used to refer specifically to the struggles of African Americans for equal status (for example, the Civil Rights Movement).

The Extension of Civil Liberties Through American History

In *Barron v. Baltimore* (1833), the Supreme Court determined that the Bill of Rights restricted the national government but not the state governments. It was not until 1925 that the court overturned this ruling, citing Fourteenth Amendment restrictions on the states ("no state shall…deprive any person of life, liberty, or property, without due process of law; nor deny to any person within its jurisdiction the equal protection of the laws"). That case, *Gitlow v. New York*, concerned freedom of speech and freedom of the press. The court ruled that state limits on speech and the press could not exceed the limits allowed the national government.

Since then, the court has applied the Bill of Rights to state law on a case-by-case basis. This process is called **selective incorporation.** Currently, the following rights have NOT been incorporated and may thus be restricted by the states:

- the Third Amendment protection against forced quartering of troops in private homes
- the Fifth Amendment right to **indictment** by a grand jury
- the Seventh Amendment right to a jury trial in civil cases
- the Eighth Amendment protection against excessive bail and fines

All other provisions of the Bill of Rights, however, apply equally to the states and the national government. In defining individual rights, the court has consistently weighed the rights of individuals against the needs of society at large. Therefore, none of the rights guaranteed in the Bill of Rights is absolute.

FIRST AMENDMENT RIGHTS AND RESTRICTIONS

The **First Amendment** guarantees **freedom of speech, freedom of the press, freedom of petitioning the government, freedom of assembly,** and **freedom of religion.** None of these important rights, however, is absolute. Throughout the nation's history, the Supreme Court has ruled that these rights may be limited in the interest of the greater public good. It has also ruled, however, that such restrictions must be well justified, well defined, and limited only to those few instances in which the public welfare is genuinely threatened.

Freedom of Speech

The most famous limit on free speech is the **clear and present danger test.** In the case of *Schenck v. United States* (1919), Justice Oliver Wendell Holmes argued that a person may not falsely scream "fire!" in a crowded theater, because doing so would likely result in panic. The court has also ruled that there is no constitutional protection for false defamatory speech (called **slander** when it is spoken and **libel** when it is in a more permanent form, such as print), **obscenity**, or speech intended to incite violence.

Since the 1940s, the court has followed the **preferred position doctrine** in determining the limits of free speech. The doctrine reflects the court's belief that freedom of speech is fundamental to liberty; therefore, any limits on free speech must address severe, imminent threats to the nation. They must also be limited to constraining those threats; any restriction that fails to meet this test would probably be overturned by the Supreme Court. The court continues to protect offensive but nonthreatening speech such as flag burning (usually undertaken by protesters, who burn the flag as a symbolic indication that the country has failed to protect American values such as democracy and freedom for all).

Essential Case: *Schenck v. United States* (1919)

Facts: During the First World War, the United States prosecuted thousands of dissenters. Near the end of the war, Charles Schenck, a Socialist, was arrested in Philadelphia for handing out leaflets calling on men not to enlist. Schneck was arrested and convicted of violating the Espionage Act of 1917. He appealed to the Supreme Court.

Issue: Schneck's attorney argued that the Espionage Act of 1917 violated the First Amendment.

Holding: In a unanimous decision, the Supreme Court ruled that Schneck's conviction was constitutional and that his speech posed "a clear and present danger" to the United States.

Although *Schenck* has never been formally overturned, the Court loosened its stance on what defined a clear and present danger in *Brandenburg v. Ohio* (1969). It ruled that for speech to be "a clear and present danger," the speaker must be making a specific threat, and not just advocating violence in general.

Essential Case: *Tinker v. Des Moines* (1969)

Facts: The mid-1960s saw the beginnings of anti-Vietnam War protests throughout the United States. In 1965, teenager John Tinker wore a black armband to school as a form of silent anti-war protest. After multiple warnings, Tinker was suspended for his actions. The ACLU helped the Tinker family take their case to the Supreme Court.

Issue: In *West Virginia State Board of Education v. Barnette* (1943), the Supreme Court had ruled that the First Amendment protects minors at school under certain circumstances. However, the Court needed to consider whether the First Amendment and *West Virginia State Board of Education* applied to Tinker's protest.

Holding: In a 7-2 decision, the Supreme Court ruled that children in public schools were protected fully by the First Amendment as long as their speech did not violate specific, constitutional regulations. The dissenting justices argued that although the speech was constitutional, specific locations, such as schools, were not an appropriate venue for anti-war protests.

Essential Case: *Citizens United v. Federal Election Commission* (2010)

Facts: The Campaign Reform Act of 2002 (McCain-Feingold Act) prohibited corporations from spending money on political advertising less than sixty days from the date of a presidential election. Citizens United, a special-interest group, sued the FCC for allowing corporations to advertise politically charged films within sixty days of the 2004 presidential election.

Issue: Where is it appropriate to draw the line of what constitutes political speech by corporations?

Holding: In a 5-4 decision, the Supreme Court ruled that restricting political spending by corporations violated those corporations' First Amendment rights. The dissenting justices argued that the ruling would weaken democratic institutions, as corporations could now spend as much as they pleased to influence elections.

Important Cases

Gitlow v. New York (1925). This case created the "Bad Tendency Doctrine," which held that speech could be restricted even if it has only a tendency to lead to illegal action. Though this element of the decision was quite restrictive, Gitlow also selectively incorporated freedom of speech to state governments.

Bethel School District v. Fraser (1986). This case gave public school officials the authority to suspend students for speech considered to be lewd or indecent.

Hustler Magazine v. Falwell (1988). In this much-publicized case, the court held that intentional infliction of emotional distress was permissible First Amendment speech—so long as such speech was about a public figure and could not reasonably be construed to state actual facts about its subject. In other words, parody is not an actionable offense.

Texas v. Johnson (1989). *Johnson* established that burning the American flag is an example of permissible free speech, and struck down numerous anti-flag burning laws.

Morse v. Frederick (2007). This case was known as the "Bong Hits 4 Jesus" case, in which the Supreme Court limited students' free speech rights. The justices ruled that Frederick's free speech rights were not violated by his suspension over what the majority's written opinion called a "sophomoric" banner.

Freedom of the Press

On occasion the government has tried to control the press, usually claiming national security interests. This occurred during the 1990 Persian Gulf War, when the Pentagon limited media access to the war zone and censored outgoing news reports. The media objected to these limitations. Such conflicts usually end up in the courts, where judges are forced to weigh conflicting national interests: the need to be informed versus security concerns.

An even more contentious issue involves the media's responsibility to reveal the sources of their information. The Supreme Court has ruled that reporters are not exempt from testifying in court cases and that they can be asked to name their sources. Reporters who refuse to do so, as many have, can be jailed. A number of states have enacted **shield laws** to protect reporters in state cases, but in other states and in federal cases reporters have no such protection.

The Pentagon Papers

A previous similar case involved the Pentagon Papers (1971), a secret report on American involvement in Vietnam. The report was leaked to *The New York Times*, which published excerpts from the report. The government tried to halt further publication, claiming that national security was at stake. In that case, the court rejected the government's efforts to prevent publication (called **prior restraint**), ruling that the public's need to be well informed outweighed the national security issues raised. The Pentagon Papers case demonstrates the preferred position doctrine.

As mentioned above, libel and obscenity are not protected by the First Amendment. In the case of *Miller v. California* (1973), the court established a **three-part obscenity test.**

- Would the average person, applying community standards, judge the work as appealing primarily to people's baser sexual instincts?
- Does the work lack other value, or is it also of literary, artistic, political, or scientific interest?
- Does the work depict sexual behavior in an offensive manner?

Essential Case: *New York Times v. United States* (1971)

Facts: In 1971, Daniel Ellsberg leaked The Pentagon Papers, a top-secret report on the country's role in Vietnam, to *The New York Times*. When the *Times* began summarizing the finding of the report in a series of articles, the government sued and sought a restraining order. When *The Washington Post* began publishing The Pentagon Papers, the government filed a lawsuit that went to the Supreme Court.

Issue: The government claimed that the release of the Pentagon Papers violated the Espionage Act of 1917 and that it had the right to use prior restraint—the suppression of harmful information.

Holding: In a 6-3 decision, the Supreme Court ruled that the newspapers could publish the Pentagon Papers, as the government had not met the burden of proof necessary to enact prior restraint. Dissenting justices noted that the Court did not have enough time to adequately research information relevant to the case, as the Pentagon Papers spanned over 7,000 pages.

Important Cases

Near v. Minnesota (1931). *Near* established that state injunctions to prevent
>publication violate the free press provision of the First Amendment
>and are unconstitutional. This case is important in that it selectively
>incorporates freedom of the press and prevents prior restraint.

New York Times v. Sullivan (1964). If a newspaper prints an article that turns
>out to be false but that the newspaper thought was true at the time of
>publication, has the newspaper committed libel? This case said no.

Hazelwood School v. Kuhlmeier (1988). In *Hazelwood,* the court held that
>school officials have sweeping authority to regulate free speech in
>student-run newspapers.

Freedom of Assembly and Association

The First Amendment protects the right of people to assemble peacefully. That right does not extend to violent groups or to demonstrations that would incite violence. Furthermore, the government may place reasonable restrictions on crowd gatherings, provided such restrictions are applied equally to all groups. Demonstrators have no constitutional right, for example, to march on and thereby close down a highway. They may not block the doorways of buildings. In short, crowd gatherings must not unnecessarily disrupt day-to-day life. That is why groups must apply for licenses to hold a parade or street fair.

The court has also ruled that the combined rights of freedom of speech and freedom of assembly imply a **freedom of association**. This means that the government may not restrict the number or type of groups or organizations people belong to, provided those groups do not threaten national security.

When Assembly Was Persecuted: Martin Luther King Jr.'s "Letter from a Birmingham Jail"

In April 1963, Martin Luther King, Jr., was arrested in Birmingham, Alabama, for his role in helping to organize a series of marches and sit-ins to protest racial segregation. From his jail cell, King wrote an open letter to the city's African American religious leaders. This letter outlined many of his key ideas regarding the importance of nonviolent resistance in the form of peaceful assembly. His letter convinced many, and African Americans and their supporters continued to use nonviolent resistance to dismantle legal segregation throughout the South.

You can read "Letter from a Birmingham Jail" in full at http://web.cn.edu/kwheeler/documents/Letter_Birmingham_Jail.pdf.

Important Cases

Thornhill v. Alabama (1940). Labor unions have been controversial since the dawn of the industrial revolution—did their strikes constitute a form of unlawful assembly? In *Thornhill*, the court held that strikes by unions were not unlawful.

Cox v. New Hampshire (1941). When a group of Jehovah's Witnesses were arrested for marching in New Hampshire without a permit, they claimed that permits themselves were an unconstitutional abridgment of their First Amendment freedoms. In *Cox*, the court held that cities and towns could legitimately require parade permits in the interest of public order.

Lloyd Corporation v. Tanner (1972). This case allowed the owners of a shopping mall to throw out people protesting the Vietnam War. The key element here is that malls are private spaces, not public. As a result, protesters have substantially fewer assembly rights in malls and other private establishments.

Boy Scouts of America v. Dale (2000). Private organizations' First Amendment right of expressive association allows them to choose their own membership and expel members based on their sexual orientation even if such discrimination would otherwise be prohibited by antidiscrimination legislation designed to protect minorities in public accommodations. As a result of this case, the Boy Scouts of America were allowed to expel any member who was discovered to be homosexual.

Update:
The Boy Scouts removed the ban for youth effective January of 2014, and for adults in July of 2015.

Freedom of Religion

The Constitution guarantees the right to the free exercise of religion, meaning that the government may not prevent individuals from practicing their faiths. This right is not absolute, however. Human sacrifice, to give an extreme example, is not allowed. The courts have ruled that polygamy is not protected by the Constitution, nor is the denial of medical treatment to a child, regardless of individual religious beliefs. However, the court has ruled that Jehovah's Witnesses cannot be required to salute the American flag and that Amish children may stop attending school after the eighth grade. In all cases, the court weighs individual rights to free religious exercise against society's needs.

The Constitution also prevents the government from establishing a state religion (the establishment clause). The establishment clause has been used to prevent school prayer, government-sponsored displays of the Christmas nativity, and state bans on the teaching of evolution (because such bans were religiously motivated). However, the wall between church and state is not rock solid. The court has allowed government subsidies to provide some aspects of parochial education (such as lunches, textbooks, and buses). It has also allowed for tax credits for non-public school costs. In deciding whether a law violates the establishment clause, the court uses a three-part test, called the **Lemon test** after the case *Lemon v. Kurtzman* (1971).

- Does the law have a secular, rather than a religious, purpose?

- Does the law neither promote nor discourage religion?
- Does the law avoid "excessive entanglement" of the government and religious institutions?

Essential Case: *Engel v. Vitale* (1962)

Facts: In the early 1960s, a group of Jewish families in New York brought suit against their children's school district for imposing prayer in the classroom. The New York Court of Appeals upheld school prayer before the families took the case to the Supreme Court.

Issue: The families argued the school prayer violated the First Amendment's establishment clause.

Holding: In a 6-1 decision (One justice was ill and another recused himself based on the fact he was not a member of the Court during oral arguments.), the Court ruled that school prayer violated the First Amendment's establishment clause. The lone dissenting justice argued that forbidding prayer in school denied children the nation's "spiritual heritage."

Essential Case: *Wisconsin v. Yoder* (1972)

Facts: The Amish faith discouraged higher education so as to preserve the Amish way of life. In the early 1970s, Wisconsin fined three Amish families $5 for taking their children out of school after the 8th grade. The Amish families appealed the case, and after the state Supreme Court ruled in the families' favor, the state took the case to the Supreme Court.

Issue: In a conflict between the free expression of religious belief and state laws regarding compulsory education, who wins?

Holding: In an 8-1 decision, the Supreme Court ruled that Amish families taking their children out of school after the 8th grade was protected by the First Amendment's free exercise clause. The single dissenting justice argued that allowing parents to take their children out of school sets a dangerous precedent.

Important Cases

Abington School Dist. v. Schempp (1963). Given the court's ruling in *Engel*, it's not surprising that in *Abington* they decided that the establishment clause of the First Amendment forbids state-mandated reading of the Bible, or recitation of the Lord's Prayer in public schools.

Epperson v. Arkansas (1968). In line with the establishment clause, *Epperson* prohibited states from banning the teaching of evolution in public schools.

Lemon v. Kurtzman (1971). This case dealt with state laws intending to give money to religious schools or causes. The court held that in order to be consistent with the establishment clause, the money had to meet three qualifications: (1) it must have a legitimate secular purpose, (2) it must not have the primary effect of either advancing or inhibiting religion, and (3) it must not result in an excessive entanglement of government and religion. These qualifications are known as the "Lemon test."

Employment Division v. Smith (1990). This case determined that the state could deny unemployment benefits to a person fired for violating a state prohibition on the use of peyote, even though the use of the drug was part of a religious ritual. In short, states may accommodate otherwise illegal acts done in pursuit of religious beliefs, but they are not required to do so.

THE SECOND AMENDMENT GOES TO COURT

Essential Case: *McDonald v. Chicago* (2010)

Facts: In 2008, Otis McDonald, a Chicago resident, wanted to purchase a handgun for self-defense. However, he could not buy one due to the city's laws restricting new handgun registrations. McDonald and a group of other Chicago residents sued the city.

Issue: Lawyers representing McDonald argued that Chicago's laws violated the Fourteenth Amendment's due process clause. As McDonald had not committed a crime, the city had no right to deny him the right to own a handgun.

Holding: In a 5-4 decision, the Supreme Court used the Fourteenth Amendment to incorporate the Second Amendment to the states, striking down gun control laws in Chicago and other cities. Dissenting justices argued that the case was the not the right vehicle for incorporation, as self-defense is not mentioned in the Second Amendment.

Essential Case: *United States v. Lopez* (1995)

Facts: In 1992, high school senior Alfonso Lopez was arrested for bringing a gun to school. He was tried and convicted for violating the Gun-Free School Zones Act of 1990. He appealed the decision to the Supreme Court.

Issue: Lopez argued that the Gun-Free School Zones Act of 1990 violated the Constitution, as the federal government did not have the power to regulate public schools. The federal government argued that the law was constitutional based on the commerce clause—firearms were interstate commerce.

Holding: In a 5-4 decision, the Supreme Court struck down the Gun-Free School Zones Act of 1990. The majority argued that merely carrying a gun did not qualify as commerce. The dissenting justices argued that school shootings violently disrupt children's education, education being a crucial component for financial success later in life. In this way, guns in schools interrupted interstate commerce.

THE RIGHTS OF THE ACCUSED

Rights granted to the accused are a fundamental protection against governmental abuse of power. Many of these rights are found in the Fifth Amendment. Without them, the government could imprison its political opponents without trial or could guarantee conviction through numerous unfair prosecutorial tactics. However, these rights are also controversial. Anticrime organizations and politicians frequently decry these protections when arguing that it is too difficult to capture, try, and imprison criminals. These accusations have grown louder and more frequent since the 1960s, when the **Warren Court** (the Supreme Court under Chief Justice Earl Warren) greatly expanded those protections that are granted to criminal defendants.

Essential Case: *Gideon v. Wainwright* (1963)

Facts: In 1961, Earl Gideon was accused of breaking-and-entering, destruction of property, and theft. During the trial, the judge did not appoint him an attorney, as the crimes Florida charged him with were non-capital offenses. A jury convicted Gideon of the crime. From prison, Gideon studied constitutional law and drafted a handwritten appeal to the Supreme Court.

Issue: Gideon argued that Florida had violated his Sixth Amendment right to an attorney.

Holding: The Supreme Court unanimously ruled that Florida had violated Gideon's right to an attorney. This ruling had the effect of incorporating the Sixth Amendment to the states. Since Gideon, all defendants in jury trials must have the option of having an attorney represent them.

Important Cases

Weeks v. United States (1914). Though the Constitution is unequivocal when it forbids unlawful search and seizure, such ill-gotten evidence was still commonly used to prosecute defendants. Weeks established the exclusionary rule, which held that illegally obtained evidence could not be used in federal court.

Powell v. Alabama (1932). The Constitution is clear in the Sixth Amendment when it guarantees all those accused of a federal crime the right to have a lawyer. But what about those accused of state crimes? Should they get a lawyer if they can't afford one? In *Powell*, the court ruled that state governments must provide counsel in cases involving the death penalty to those who can't afford it.

Betts v. Brady (1942). The Betts case established that state governments did not have to provide lawyers to indigent defendants in capital cases.

Mapp v. Ohio (1961). By 1961, the exclusionary rule meant that any unlawfully gathered evidence could not be introduced in federal court, but such evidence was introduced all the time in state courts. The *Mapp* case extended the exclusionary rule to the states, increasing the protections for defendents.

Escobedo v. Illinois (1964). *Escobedo* is another important Warren Court decision. Here, the court held that any defendant who asked for a lawyer had to have one granted to him—or any confession garnered after that point would be inadmissible in court.

Miranda v. Arizona (1966). *Miranda* is the most dramatic and well-known of the Warren Court decisions. The court found that all defendants must be informed of all their legal rights before they are arrested. It is thanks to *Miranda* that we all know the phrase "You have the right to remain silent…" and you can't get through an episode of *Law & Order* without hearing it at least once.

Protection from Self-Incrimination

The Constitution protects individuals from **self-incrimination.** A defendant cannot be forced to testify at trial, and the jury is not supposed to infer guilt when a defendant chooses to not testify. Furthermore, a defendant must be notified of his or her right to remain silent, his or her right to a lawyer, and his or her protection against self-incrimination at the time of his arrest.

For years, the courts rarely admitted into evidence confessions from arrestees who had not been properly "Mirandized." In recent years, however, the Supreme Court has defined some situations in which such confessions are admissible. In 1991, the court ruled that a coerced confession does not automatically invalidate a conviction. Rather, an appeals court may consider all evidence entered at trial. If the court decides that a conviction was probable even without the confession, it may let the guilty verdict stand.

Miranda Rights

This precedent was established in the 1966 Supreme Court case **Miranda v. Arizona.** Ernesto Miranda had been arrested for kidnapping and rape, and within two hours of his arrest, he had confessed to his crimes. His lawyer appealed the case on the grounds that Miranda had not been advised of his constitutional rights (for example, the protection against self-incrimination and the right to legal counsel). In *Miranda*, the Supreme Court decided that the police had deprived Miranda of his Fourteenth Amendment right to due process. Those rights have since come to be known as Miranda rights.

Protection from Unreasonable Search and Seizure

The **Fourth Amendment** limits the power of the government to search for evidence of criminal activity. When the police want to search private property, in most circumstances they must first go before a judge and justify the search. If the judge is convinced that the search is likely to uncover evidence of illegality—called **probable cause**—the judge issues a **search warrant**, which limits where the police may search and what they may take as evidence. Evidence found by police who disregard this procedure may not be admitted as evidence in trial. This is called the **exclusionary rule.** The Supreme Court applied the exclusionary rule to federal trials in 1911.

As with all constitutional rights, however, there are exceptions to this rule. In 1984, the Supreme Court established the **objective good faith** exception, which allows for convictions in cases in which a search was not technically legal (either because it violated the warrant or because the warrant itself was faulty) but was conducted under the assumption that it was legal. The court has also determined that illegally seized evidence that would eventually have been found legally is also admissible in court. This principle is known as the **inevitable discovery rule.**

There are also circumstances under which the police may conduct a search without a warrant. Police may conduct an immediate search following a legal arrest, for example. Police may also conduct an immediate search of private property if the owner consents to that search. Evidence found in plain view may be seized immediately; if, for example, a person is growing marijuana on his or her front lawn, the police may seize that evidence without first acquiring a search warrant. Finally, police may conduct an immediate search if they have probable cause to believe they will find evidence of criminal activity, especially when there are **exigent circumstances**, or reason to believe evidence would disappear by the time they received a warrant and returned. The police would later have to demonstrate that they had probable cause in court.

Rights to an Attorney and a Speedy Trial

The **Sixth Amendment** guarantees criminal defendants the **right to an attorney in federal cases.** In 1932, the Supreme Court used the Fourteenth Amendment to incorporate this right in capital cases ("the Scottsboro boys" case). In the 1963 case *Gideon v. Wainwright*, the court ruled that all criminal defendants in state courts were entitled to legal counsel. In both cases, the court ruled that the state must provide a lawyer to defendants too poor to hire a lawyer. The court has since extended this protection to misdemeanor cases, provided those cases could result in jail time for the defendant. However, the court has held that states are not required to provide a lawyer to litigants in civil cases.

The Sixth Amendment also guarantees defendants **the right to a speedy trial.** The courts have become so overburdened with cases that the Supreme Court recently imposed a 100-day limit between the time of arrest and the start of a trial. The limit has had little practical effect, however, because both prosecutors and defense attorneys can request an extension to prepare their cases. Courts have generally granted such extensions. As a result, it is not unusual for a defendant to wait a year or more between his or her arrest date and a trial.

Mapp v. Ohio
In the 1961 case *Mapp v. Ohio*, the court incorporated the exclusionary rule, thus making it applicable to state trials as well.

Protection from Excessive Bail and "Cruel and Unusual Punishment"

The **Eighth Amendment** states that "excessive bail shall not be required, nor excessive fines imposed, nor cruel and unusual punishments inflicted." The government is not required, however, to offer bail to all defendants. In 1984, Congress passed the Bail Reform Act to allow federal judges to deny bail to defendants considered either dangerous or likely to flee the country. The protection from excessive bail has *not* been incorporated, and states are therefore free to set bail as high as state law permits.

The **cruel and unusual punishment** clause of the Constitution lies at the heart of the debate over the death penalty. The court has placed limits on when the death penalty can be applied; however, it has upheld the constitutionality of the death penalty when properly applied. Critics point to statistics that those convicted of killing black people are far less likely to receive the death penalty than those convicted of killing white people. The court has rejected this argument. In recent years, the court has moved to make it easier for states to carry out the death penalty by limiting the number and nature of appeals allowed by convicted murderers on death row. Recently too, however, some states have enacted moratoriums on the death penalty for reasons including methodology problems, flawed trial processes, and ethical objections.

Important Cases

Furman v. Georgia (1972). Here, the court looked at the patchwork quilt of nationwide capital punishment decisions and found that its imposition was often racist and arbitrary. In *Furman*, the Court ordered a halt to all death penalty punishments in the nation until a less arbitrary method of sentencing was found.

Woodson v. North Carolina (1976). North Carolina tried to satisfy the court's requirement that the imposition of the death penalty not be arbitrary—so they made it a mandatory punishment for certain crimes. The Court rejected this approach and ruled mandatory death penalty sentences as unconstitutional.

Gregg v. Georgia (1976). Georgia was finally able to convince the Court that it had come up with a careful and fair system for trying capital offenses. As a result, the Court ruled that under adequate guidelines the death penalty did not, in fact, constitute cruel and unusual punishment. Thus *Gregg* allowed the resumption of the death penalty in America.

Atkins v. Virginia (2002). Here, the United States lined up with most other nations in the world by forbidding the execution of defendants who are mentally handicapped.

Roper v. Simmons (2005). Building on *Atkins*, the Court declared the death penalty unconstitutional for defendants whose crimes were committed as minors, even if they were charged as adults.

THE RIGHT OF ALL AMERICANS TO PRIVACY

The right to privacy is not specifically mentioned in the Constitution. However, in the 1965 Supreme Court case of *Griswold v. Connecticut,* the Court ruled that the Bill of Rights contained an **implied right to privacy.** The Court ruled that the combination of the First, Third, Fourth, Fifth, Ninth, and Fourteenth Amendments added up to a guarantee of privacy. The *Griswold* case concerned a state law banning the use of contraception; the Supreme Court decision overturned that law. *Griswold* also laid the foundation for the landmark *Roe v. Wade* case of 1973, which legalized abortion.

Essential Case: *Roe v. Wade* (1973)

Facts: 'Roe' was the alias of Norma McCorvey, a young Texas mother of two. In 1969, she unsuccessfully tried to have an abortion in Texas, a state that forbid the practice except in the cases of incest and rape. After having the child, McCorvey sued Dallas County.

Issue: The Supreme Court faced two issues when deciding the case. Was abortion a medical procedure, and was the practice covered by the right to privacy established in *Griswold v. Connecticut*?

Holding: In a 7-2 decision, the court ruled that abortion was protected by the right to privacy established in *Griswold,* supported by the Ninth and Fourteenth Amendments. The dissenting justices claimed that the majority opinion created constitutional rights out of thin air.

Important Cases

Griswold v. Connecticut (1965). The Constitution never explicitly grants
Americans a right to privacy, but the court discovers one in this
landmark and controversial case. Writing for the majority, Justice
William O. Douglas noted that amendments like the Third, Fourth,
and Ninth all cast "penumbras and emanations" which showed that
the Founders really had intended for a right to privacy all along.
Webster v. Reproductive Health Services (1989). This case did not overturn
Roe v. Wade, but it did give states more power to regulate abortion.
Planned Parenthood v. Casey (1992). A Pennsylvania law that would have
required a woman to notify her husband before getting an abortion
was thrown out, but laws calling for parental consent and the
imposition of a 24-hour waiting period were upheld. All in all, the
message was that states *can* regulate abortion but not with regulations
that impose an "undue burden" upon women.
Lawrence v. Texas (2003). With this ruling, the Supreme Court struck
down a sodomy law that had criminalized homosexual sex in Texas.
The court had previously addressed the same issue in *Bowers v.
Hardwick* (1986), where it did not find constitutional protection
of sexual privacy. *Lawrence* explicitly overruled *Bowers* saying that
consensual sexual conduct was part of the liberty protected under
the Fourteenth Amendment.

CIVIL RIGHTS

The AP U.S. Government and Politics Exam occasionally tests your knowledge of key civil rights legislation. Here is what you need to know about civil rights for the test.

Civil Rights and African Americans

Prior to the Civil War, most of the African American population in the United States consisted of slaves who were denied virtually any legal rights whatsoever. Free blacks were also denied basic civil rights such as the right to vote and the right to equal protection under the law. Because the Supreme Court had ruled in 1833 that the Bill of Rights applied to the federal government only, states were free to enact discriminatory and segregationist laws. Many did so to ensure the oppression of African Americans.

The Civil War began the long, slow development toward equality of the races before the law. Here is a list of key events in that process.

- **The Civil War (1861–1865).** The Civil War began, at least in part, over the issue of slavery (the debate over the relative powers of the federal and state governments was also a major cause of the war). The war was more clearly defined as a war about slavery in 1863, when President Lincoln issued the **Emancipation Proclamation,** which declared the liberation of slaves in the rebel states. The Civil War also influenced the civil rights process in a less direct and less immediate way, as it resulted in an increase in the power of the federal government. One hundred years later, the increased power vested in the federal government would be the means of imposing and enforcing equal rights laws in the states.

- **Thirteenth Amendment (1865).** The Thirteenth Amendment, ratified after the Civil War, made slavery illegal.

- **Fourteenth Amendment (1868).** The Fourteenth Amendment, ratified during Reconstruction, was designed to prevent states in the South from depriving newly freed blacks of their rights. Its clauses guaranteeing **due process** and **equal protection** were later used by the Supreme Court to apply most of the Bill of Rights to state law. However, in the 1880s the Supreme Court interpreted the amendment narrowly, allowing the states to enact segregationist laws. The Fourteenth Amendment also made African Americans citizens of the nation and of their home states, overruling the ***Dred Scott* case** (1857), which had ruled that slaves and their descendants were not citizens.

- **Fifteenth Amendment (1870).** The Fifteenth Amendment banned laws that would prevent African Americans from voting on the basis of their race or the fact that they previously were slaves.

- **Civil Rights Act of 1875.** The Civil Rights Act of 1875 banned discrimination in hotels, restaurants, and railroad cars, as well as in selection for jury duty. The Supreme Court declared the Act unconstitutional in 1883.

- **Jim Crow laws and voting restrictions.** As the federal government exerted less influence over the South, states, towns, and cities passed numerous discriminatory and segregationist laws. The Supreme Court supported the states by ruling that the Fourteenth Amendment did not protect blacks from discriminatory state laws, and that blacks would have to seek equal protection from the states, not from the federal government. In 1883, the court also reversed the Civil Rights Act of 1875, thus opening the door to legal segregation. These segregationist laws are known collectively as **Jim Crow laws.** The states also moved to deprive blacks of their voting rights by imposing **poll taxes** (a tax that must be paid in order to vote) and literacy tests. To allow poor, illiterate whites to vote, some states passed **grandfather clauses** that exempted from these restrictions anyone whose grandfather had voted. Grandfather clauses effectively excluded blacks whose grandparents had been slaves and therefore could not have voted.

- **Equal Pay Act of 1963.** This federal law made it illegal to base an employee's pay on race, gender, religion, or national origin. The Equal Pay Act was also important to the women's movement and to the civil rights struggles of other minorities.

- **Twenty-fourth Amendment (1964)**. This outlawed poll taxes, which had been used to prevent blacks and poor whites from voting.

- **Civil Rights Act of 1964.** The Civil Rights Act of 1964 was a landmark piece of legislation. It not only increased the rights of blacks and other minorities, but also gave the federal government greater means of enforcing the law. The law banned discrimination in public accommodations (public transportation, offices, and so on) and in all federally funded programs. It also prohibited discrimination in hiring based on color and gender. Finally, it required the government to cut off funding from any program that did not comply with the law, and it gave the federal government the power to initiate lawsuits in cases of school segregation. States that had previously ignored federal civil rights mandates now faced serious consequences for doing so.

- **Voting Rights Act of 1965.** The Voting Rights Act was designed to counteract voting discrimination in the South. It allowed the federal government to step into any state or county in which less than 50% of the population was registered to vote, or in areas that used literacy tests to prevent voting. In those areas, the federal government could register voters (which is normally a function of the states).

- **Civil Rights Act, Title VIII (1968).** This banned racial discrimination in housing.

- **Civil Rights Act of 1991.** This law was designed to address a number of problems that had arisen in civil rights law during the previous decade. Several Supreme Court decisions had limited the abilities of job applicants and employees to bring suit against employers with discriminatory hiring practices; the 1991 act eased those restrictions.

Essential Case: *Brown v. Board of Education* (1954)

Facts: In 1951, twenty families from Topeka, Kansas, filed suit against the city's board of education for enforcing school segregation. A District Court upheld school segregation as it did not violate *Plessy v. Ferguson* (1896). The families appealed the case to the Supreme Court where the case was heard alongside four other school segregation cases.

Issue: Did the Fourteenth Amendment's equal protection clause apply to school segregation?

Holding: In a unanimous decision, the Supreme Court struck down school segregation nationwide. In fact, many justices had made up their minds long before hearing the case, as racial segregation was tarnishing America's image abroad. The ruling overturned the precedent set by *Plessy*.

Important Cases

Plessy v. Ferguson (1896). This case famously allowed southern states to twist the equal protection clause of the Fourteenth Amendment by allowing "separate but equal" facilities based on race.

Brown v. Board II (1955). One year later, the Warren Court saw that segregation was still ubiquitous. So in Brown II, they ordered schools to desegregate "with all due and deliberate speed."

Heart of Atlanta Motel, Inc. v. United States (1964). Did the Federal Civil Rights Act of 1964 mandate that places of public accommodation are prohibited from discrimination against African Americans? Yes, said the court.

Katzenbach v. McClung (1964). The Civil Rights Act of 1964 prohibited discrimination in public places, but what about in private businesses? The *Katzenbach* case established that the power of Congress to regulate interstate commerce extends to state discrimination statutes. This ruling made the Civil Rights Act of 1964 apply to virtually all businesses.

Regents of the University of California v. Bakke (1978). Alan Bakke was a white applicant who was rejected from medical school because of an affirmative action plan to boost the number of black students. The court ruled that Bakke had been unfairly excluded and that quotas requiring a certain percentage of minorities violated the Fourteenth

Amendment. But the court also held that race-based affirmative action *was* permissible so long as it was in the service of creating greater diversity.

Grutter v. Bollinger (2003) and *Gratz v. Bollinger* (2003). These cases involved the University of Michigan Law School and the University of Michigan undergraduate school. Both used affirmative action, but the undergraduate school did so by giving minority applicants a large boost in the score used by officers deciding on admission. The court threw out the undergraduate system of selection, but generally upheld *Bakke.*

Shelby v. Holder (2013). The Supreme Court struck down Section 4 of the Voting Rights Act, which required federal pre-clearance of voting law changes for states with a history of voter discrimination. The ruling spurred fear among minorities, as concern about voter suppression rose.

Although the number of major new civil rights laws has decreased in the past decades, the fight for civil rights for African Americans and other minority groups is far from over. Although legally enforced segregation of public facilities no longer exists, racial segregation remains a national concern. Most public school systems remain essentially segregated because the neighborhoods that feed them are segregated. The impact of this *de facto* **segregation** (as opposed to *de jure* **segregation,** which is segregation by law) is increased by the disparity in average incomes between white people and black people. Because many local school systems are supported by property taxes, lower-income neighborhoods end up with poorly funded, overcrowded schools.

> **Attempts at Integration**
> In the 1970s, the Supreme Court ruled that the government could bus children to different school districts to achieve the goal of integration, provided the affected districts had been intentionally segregated. Busing plans failed, however, due to public protest and the abandonment of cities by whites.

Furthermore, discrimination continues in employment, housing, and higher education. Because such discrimination is subtler—few employers tell job applicants, "I won't hire you because you're black"—it is more difficult to enforce antidiscrimination laws and punish offenders in these areas. **Affirmative action** programs, which seek to create special employment opportunities for minorities, women, and other victims of discrimination, address these questions but have become increasingly controversial and politically unpopular in recent years. In *Regents of the University of California v. Bakke* (1978), the Supreme Court ruled that affirmative action programs could not use quotas to meet civil rights goals; however, it did say that gender and race could be considered among other factors by schools and businesses practicing affirmative action. Opponents of affirmative action programs argue that such programs penalize whites and thus constitute **reverse discrimination,** which is illegal under the Civil Rights Act of 1964.

Civil Rights and Women

The granting of equal rights for women in the United States is a relatively recent phenomenon. Women were not given the right to vote in all 50 states until 1920. Employment discrimination based on gender was not outlawed until 1964. As recently as the early 1990s, women were not guaranteed 12 weeks of unpaid leave from work after giving birth (this finally changed with the **Family and Medical Leave Act of 1993,** which gives this right to both mothers and fathers). Those who fought for the failed **Equal Rights Amendment** to the Constitution (1972–1982) continue to argue that women do not yet have a full guarantee of equality under the law from the federal government.

Here is a list of events of the women's rights movement that the AP U.S. Government and Politics Exam sometimes tests.

- **Nineteenth Amendment (1920).** Granted women the right to vote.

- **Equal Pay Act of 1963.** This federal law made it illegal to base an employee's pay on race, gender, religion, or national origin. Prior to this bill, many businesses and organizations maintained different pay and raise schedules for their male and female employees. In fact, many continued to do so after the bill passed. Federal enforcement of the law, however, has helped narrow the gap between the salaries and wages of the genders.

- **Civil Rights Act of 1964.** The provision pertaining to gender discrimination was included in the Civil Rights Act of 1964 by an opponent of the bill. Representative Howard Smith of Virginia believed his proposal was ridiculous and would therefore weaken support for the bill. Much to his surprise, the bill passed with the gender provision—prohibiting employment discrimination based on gender—included. The Ledbetter Fair Pay Act of 2009 enhanced those protections.

- **Title IX, Higher Education Act (1972).** This law prohibits gender discrimination by institutions of higher education that receive federal funds. Title IX has been used to force increased funding of women-only programs, such as women's sports. The **Civil Rights Restoration Act of 1988** increased its potency by allowing the government to cut off all funding to schools that violate the law (and not just to the specific program or office found in violation). As a result of these laws mandating equity in college athletics spending, colleges have eliminated many less popular men's sports, resulting in a backlash against Title IX and the Civil Rights Restoration Act.

- **Lilly Ledbetter Fair Pay Act of 2009.** This law closed a loophole that limited suits on discriminatory pay based on the timing of the issuance of the first discriminatory paycheck. The Ledbetter Act expanded those limits to allow suits based on any discriminatory paycheck, an important adjustment for employees who learn of inequities in wages or salary only after they have persisted for some time.

As women have entered the workplace in greater numbers, the issue of sexual harassment at work has gained prominence. **Sexual harassment** is defined as any sexist or sexual behavior—physical or verbal—that creates a hostile work environment. It can range from suggestive remarks to attempts to coerce sex from a subordinate. Like other forms of discrimination, it is difficult to prove legally. Efforts to combat it range from public-awareness programs to sensitivity training to increased legal penalties for harassers.

Abortion has remained a controversial and prominent political issue since the Supreme Court affirmed a woman's right to an abortion in *Roe v. Wade* (1973). In that case, the court ruled that a woman's right to an abortion could not be limited during the first three months of pregnancy (increased limits are allowed as the development of the fetus progresses). Opponents of abortion, who call themselves *pro-life*, argue that the procedure is murder and should be criminalized. Those who support women's right to abortions (dubbed the *pro-choice* movement) argue that women should ultimately decide the ambiguous moral issues for themselves. Because of the very personal, life-and-death issues involved in the abortion debate, advocates on both sides of the issue feel very strongly, and as a result abortion is a major political issue. The decision in *Roe v. Wade* has influenced every election and Supreme Court nomination since; as a result of this case, candidates' opinions about the abortion issue are often the first thing the public learns about them. In most European countries, abortion rights were established legislatively (by laws). Many legal scholars believe that the judicial solution (left up to the courts) applied by the United States has opened the door to ideologues.

Other Major Civil Rights Advances

- **Age Discrimination Act of 1967.** As its name states, this law prohibits employment discrimination on the basis of age. The law makes an exception for jobs in which age is essential to job performance. An amendment to this law banned some mandatory retirement ages and increased others to 70.

- **Twenty-sixth Amendment (1971).** Extended the right to vote to 18-year-olds.

- **Individuals with Disabilities Education Act (1975).** Ensured that children with disabilities have the opportunity to receive a free, appropriate public education, just like other children.

- **Voting Rights Act of 1982.** This law requires states to create congressional districts with minority majorities in order to increase minority representation in the House of Representatives. The law has resulted in the creation of numerous strangely shaped districts, such as one in North Carolina that was 160 miles long and, at points, only several hundred yards wide. The Supreme Court nullified the district just described, leaving it unclear how the government may both achieve the goals of the Voting Rights Act and maintain the regional integrity of congressional districts.

- **Americans with Disabilities Act of 1990.** This law requires businesses with more than twenty-four employees to make their offices accessible to the disabled. It also requires public transportation, new offices, hotels, and restaurants to be wheelchair-accessible whenever feasible. Finally, it mandated the development of wider telephone services for the hearing-impaired.

Essential Case: *Baker v. Carr* (1962)

Facts: In 1960, Tennessee had not redrawn its legislative districts since the turn of the century. Charles Baker sued the state as his county's population had grown considerably in that time without benefiting from increased representation in the state legislature. The defendant in the case was Tennessee's secretary of state.

Issue: Did Tennessee's refusal to redistrict violate the Fourteenth Amendment's guarantee of "equal protection of the law"? Lawyers representing Tennessee argued that redistricting was a state issue.

Holding: After nearly a year of deliberations, the Supreme Court ruled in a 6-2 decision that the federal government can force states to redistrict every ten years after the national census. Dissenting justices claimed that the ruling imperiled the separation of powers between the legislative and judicial branches.

Other Important Cases

Federalism

Marbury v. Madison (1803). This most important of all decisions established **judicial review**—the Supreme Court's power to strike down acts of United States Congress which conflict with the Constitution.

McCulloch v. Maryland (1819). This case is important because it established a precedent of federal courts using judicial review to strike down congressional legislation.

Gitlow v. New York (1925). *Gitlow* began the process of selective incorporation—the practice of transferring protections that Americans had from the federal government and applying them to state governments.

South Dakota v. Dole (1987). The federal government mandated the 21-year-old drinking age by threatening to withhold federal highway funds from all states that did not comply. In this case, such withholding was held to be constitutional.

Executive Power

Korematsu v. United States (1944). This case was not the Supreme Court's finest hour, as it ruled that American citizens of Japanese descent could be interned and deprived of basic constitutional rights due to executive order.

United States v. Nixon (1974). In this case, Congress claimed that there was no such thing as **executive privilege** as it went after tapes that President Nixon had made of all his conversations in the Oval Office. The court disagreed and allowed for executive privilege. But they forbid its usage in criminal cases, which meant that Nixon ultimately did have to turn over the tapes.

Clinton v. New York (1998). This case banned the presidential use of a line-item veto as a violation of legislative powers.

KEY TERMS

- civil liberties
- civil rights
- selective incorporation
- indictment
- First Amendment
- freedom of speech
- clear and present danger test
- slander
- libel
- obscenity
- preferred position doctrine
- *Schenck v. United States*
- freedom of the press
- prior restraint
- shield laws
- three-part obscenity test
- freedom of assembly
- freedom of association
- freedom of religion
- Lemon test
- rights of the accused
- Warren Court
- *Gideon v. Wainwright*
- self-incrimination
- *Miranda v. Arizona*
- Fourth Amendment
- probable cause
- search warrant
- exclusionary rule
- objective good faith
- inevitable discovery rule
- Sixth Amendment
- Eighth Amendment
- cruel and unusual punishment
- implied right to privacy
- *Griswold v. Connecticut*
- *Roe v. Wade*
- Thirteenth Amendment
- Fourteenth Amendment
- due process
- equal protection
- Fifteenth Amendment
- Jim Crow laws
- poll tax
- grandfather clause
- Twenty-fourth Amendment
- Civil Rights Act of 1964
- Voting Rights Act of 1965
- *Plessy v. Ferguson*
- *Brown v. Board of Education*
- *de facto* segregation
- *de jure* segregation
- affirmative action
- reverse discrimination
- Family and Medical Leave Act of 1993
- Equal Rights Amendment
- Nineteenth Amendment
- Lilly Ledbetter Fair Pay Act of 2009
- sexual harassment
- abortion
- Twenty-sixth Amendment
- executive privilege

Summary

o It is very important to remember that the Bill of Rights protects Americans only from the federal government. It wasn't until the passage of the Fourteenth Amendment and the advocacy of the 20th-century Supreme Court that these freedoms were selectively incorporated to the states.

o Know about freedom of speech, clear and present danger, and the preferred position doctrine.

o Freedom of the press is protected by the ban on prior restraint, but has limits (as in the case of slander or libel).

o The rights of the people to assemble generally can't be limited, though there are some exceptions to this rule.

o The Constitution forbids the creation of an official religion through the establishment clause, but also prevents the government from infringing on religious freedom through the free exercise clause.

o We have seen a steady expansion of the rights of the accused, particularly since the decisions of the Warren Court.

o Rising from the disgrace of slavery and Jim Crow laws, the court has acted in the latter half of the 20th century to protect racial minorities from discrimination. Today, most controversy swirls around the issue of affirmative action and whether it constitutes a form of reverse racism and thus constitutes a violation of the Fourteenth Amendment.

Chapter 10 Drill

See Chapter 11 for answers and explanations.

Questions 1 and 2 refer to the passage below.

We should never forget that everything Adolf Hitler did in Germany was "legal" and everything the Hungarian freedom fighters did in Hungary was "illegal." It was "illegal" to aid and comfort a Jew in Hitler's Germany. Even so, I am sure that, had I lived in Germany at the time, I would have aided and comforted my Jewish brothers. If today I lived in a Communist country where certain principles dear to the Christian faith are suppressed, I would openly advocate disobeying that country's antireligious laws.

—Martin Luther King, Jr., "Letter from a Birmingham Jail"

1. Which of the following statements best reflects King's message in this passage?

    (A) Nazi Germany and the suppression of Hungarian freedom fighters were both cruel events.
    (B) All laws are corrupt.
    (C) A law does not automatically mean that something is right or wrong.
    (D) The law can be a dangerous tool when used by dictators.

2. Which of the following statements best explains why King included this passage in "Letter from a Birmingham Jail"?

    (A) To claim that the United States was as bad as Nazi Germany and Communist Hungary
    (B) To show how segregationist laws were no different than unjust laws in oppressive states
    (C) To promote himself as an activist who would work under the harshest conditions
    (D) To educate readers on the horrors of Nazi Germany and Communist Hungary

3. Which of the following is an accurate comparison between civil liberties and civil rights?

	Civil Liberties	Civil Rights
(A)	Enshrined in the Bill of Rights	The equal application of the law to all Americans
(B)	Have never been restricted	Supreme Court has always ruled to expand civil rights
(C)	Supreme Court has changed the scope of Americans' civil liberties	Only applies to African Americans
(D)	Can be amended at the state level	Legislation, Supreme Court decisions, and constitutional amendments have expanded civil rights

4. Which Supreme Court case established the right to always have counsel present in court cases?

    (A) *Powell v. Alabama*
    (B) *Betts v. Brady*
    (C) *Gideon v. Wainwright*
    (D) *Miranda v. Arizona*

5. The "right to privacy" established by *Griswold v. Connecticut* was further enhanced by which Supreme Court case?

    (A) *Roe v. Wade*
    (B) *Citizens United v. Federal Elections Commission*
    (C) *McDonald v. Chicago*
    (D) *New York Times Co. v. United States*

6. Which of the following issues did the Supreme Court consider when deciding *Engel v. Vitale?*

    (A) Students' ability to protest in school
    (B) Students' freedom of speech in school
    (C) State-sponsored prayer in school
    (D) State-sponsored funding of religious schools

7. *Wisconsin v. Yoder* addressed which of the following provisions of the First Amendment?

    (A) Freedom of Press
    (B) Freedom of Speech
    (C) Freedom of Assembly
    (D) Freedom of Religion

REFLECT

Respond to the following questions:

- For which content topics discussed in this chapter do you feel you have achieved sufficient mastery to answer multiple-choice questions correctly?

- For which content topics discussed in this chapter do you feel you have achieved sufficient mastery to discuss effectively in an essay?

- For which content topics discussed in this chapter do you feel you need more work before you can answer multiple-choice questions correctly?

- For which content topics discussed in this chapter do you feel you need more work before you can discuss effectively in an essay?

- What parts of this chapter are you going to re-review?

- Will you seek further help, outside of this book (such as a teacher, tutor, or AP Students), on any of the content in this chapter—and, if so, on what content?

Chapter 11
Chapter Drills:
Answers and
Explanations

CHAPTER 4 DRILL

1. **D**   Choice (A) is incorrect as the excerpt does not describe the relationship between the national government and the states. Choice (B) is incorrect as the text clearly states that only Congress can declare war. Choice (C) is incorrect as the excerpt does not refer to Congress as being the sole governing body. Therefore, (D) is correct as the final sentence states that a majority of states must agree to major decisions.

2. **C**   Choices (A) and (B) can be eliminated as the Articles gave more power to the states. Choice (D) can be eliminated as many of the powers of Congress in the Articles are identical to those granted to Congress by the Constitution. As a result, (C) is correct as the Articles created an inefficient government that could not meet the challenges facing the new nation.

3. **B**   Choices (A) and (C) are incorrect as each one attributes elements of the New Jersey Plan to the Virginia Plan, and vice-versa. Choice (D) is incorrect as the Virginia Plan first suggested the Electoral College as a method to elect the president. Therefore, (B) is correct as the Virginia Plan called for a bicameral legislature, while the New Jersey Plan called for a unicameral legislature.

4. **A**   Choices (B) and (C) can be eliminated as these terms refer to powers shared within the federal government. Choice (D) can be eliminated as "limited government" only refers to the federal government. As a result, (A) is correct as federalism refers to the concurrent, or shared, powers between the state and national governments.

5. **C**   Choice (A) can be eliminated as free speech refers to the First Amendment. Choice (B) can be eliminated as searches and seizures refer to the Fourth Amendment. Choice (D) can be eliminated as cruel and unusual government refers to the Eighth Amendment. Therefore, (C) is correct as one of Americans' Fifth Amendment rights is protection against double jeopardy—being tried for the same crime more than once.

6. **B**   Choice (A) is incorrect as the Revolutionary War led to the overthrow of British rule. Choice (C) is incorrect as slavery had existed in the Americas for centuries before the founding of the United States. Choice (D) can be eliminated because Shay's Rebellion took place in Massachusetts. As a result, (B) is correct as after the national government put down the rebellion, elites realized a new national government was necessary to prevent future rebellions.

7. **A**   Choice (B) can be eliminated as the Connecticut Compromise refers to how states would be represented in Congress, not whether their slaves would count toward representation. Choice (C) can be eliminated as this compromise put a moratorium on the international slave trade. Choice (D) can be eliminated as the Bill of Rights does not mention slavery or congressional representation. Therefore, (A) is correct as the Three-Fifths Compromise counted each slave as 3/5 of a person when determining a state's congressional representation.

CHAPTER 5 DRILL

1. **B** Choice (A) is incorrect as the U.S. adult population rose between 1990 and 2008. Choice (C) is incorrect as "Other response" fell between 2001 and 2008. Choice (D) is incorrect as the number of Christians rose between 1990 and 2001. As a result, (B) is correct, as the number of Americans who do not follow a religion more than doubled between 1990 and 2008.

2. **B** Choice (A) can be eliminated as "Other Religions" is still a small group compared to Christians and non-believers. Choice (C) can be eliminated as the chart does not indicate anything about the future of political socialization as a whole. Choice (D) can be eliminated as the chart does not compare the impact of religion versus other means of political socialization. Therefore, (B) is correct: as more Americans become non-religious, they will experience political socialization in different ways.

3. **D** Remember that both sides of a comparison question must be correct, so if either is wrong, rule out that entire choice. For instance, conservatives are actually the largest voting block, so eliminate (A). Moderates often change their mind on political issues, so delete (B). Conservatives do not support affirmative action, so eliminate (C). Conservatives do oppose government regulation and moderates do view themselves as pragmatists, which makes (D) the correct answer.

4. **D** Remember that "intensity" refers to the strength of a feeling Americans, as a whole, have about an issue or topic. Although some Americans have strong opinions about (A), (B), and (C), they are incorrect as (D), Social Security, is an issue that the majority of Americans strongly support.

5. **B** Remember that many factors influence someone's ideological behavior. Choices (A) and (C) can be eliminated as they have no effect on ideological behavior. Choice (D) can be eliminated as someone's ideological beliefs rarely change over time. As a result, (C) is correct, as men and women typically have differences of opinion regarding political ideology.

6. **B** It is possible for a politician to change his or her view, but whether that is seen as positive depends largely on how the public feels about the issue in question. The timing matters, too; during a campaign, changing positions can lead to attacks from one's opponent. For these reasons, eliminate (A). Many Americans do not approve of divorce, so you can also eliminate (C). As for soliciting political donations from foreign governments—this is illegal, and unlikely to generate anything positive, so eliminate (D). This leaves (B), which is a fit, as appearing in photographs with military veterans suggests that the candidate is patriotic and supports veterans.

7. **A** Choices (B), (C), and (D) are incorrect: public opinion regarding incumbent U.S. House members, Social Security benefits, and the U.S. Supreme Court rarely go up or down except in the case of extreme circumstances. As a result, (A) is correct. Presidential public opinion often changes as a result of the president's decisions while in office.

CHAPTER 6 DRILL

1. **D** Look to the passage, as you may be able to find answers to some of your questions there. Choice (A) can be eliminated as Washington does not approve of political parties. Choice (B) can be eliminated as Washington states that that political parties sometimes work toward "popular ends." Choice (C) can be eliminated as Washington calls the men who run political parties "unprincipled." Washington warns that political parties will destroy the system which gave them power so that no one else can take power from them, which means that (D) is the correct answer.

2. **C** It may help to reassert Washington's message—which was the answer to the previous question—before trying to find the choice that matches it. Washington warned that political parties would take power, which should allow you to eliminate (A), (B), and (D), since those measures attempted to regulate the influence of interest groups and the political parties they represent. By contrast, *Citizens United v. Federal Election Commission* dramatically increased the amount of money spent on elections, a decision many would argue gives political parties/interest groups more political power than voters. This makes (C) the correct answer.

3. **C** Remember that on comparison questions, you only need to rule out one of the two options for each choice. Interest groups do not undergo realignment every few decades, so you can eliminate (A). You can get rid of both (B) and (D) because they are flipped. Political parties do nominate candidates for office, and interest groups do endorse candidates they prefer to win, so (C) is the correct answer.

4. **D** A splinter party is a small group that has broken off from a larger group with which it still shares some ideas. Choices (A), (B), and (C) are larger, ideological groups that are not today thought of as "splinter" parties. The Reform Party "splintered" away from the Republican Party, and so (D) is correct. (The Tea Party is another example of a splinter party.)

5. **D** Assess each set of views in sequence. Cuban Americans disapprove of the Democrats' stance on Cuba, which makes (A) incorrect. The Republican Party embraced the evangelical movement in the 1980s, and that relationship still holds today, so eliminate (B). The relationship between white Southerners and Republicans has also still largely held since the 1980s, so you can also eliminate (C). Mexican Americans tend to support Democrats' stance on immigration, which makes (D) the correct answer.

6. **B** Choice (A) can be eliminated, as PACs do not run their own candidates for office. Choice (C) can be eliminated, as PACs do not have a formal voice in government. Choice (D) can be eliminated as PACs often oppose one another. Therefore, (B) is correct: PACs allow unions and corporations to funnel unlimited sums of money toward political activities not directly affiliated with a candidate.

7. **B** Major historical events often cause party realignments, points at which political power dramatically shifts from one party to another. Choices (A), (C), and (D) are incorrect as these historical events did not cause the American people to switch their political allegiance. As a result, (B) is correct as Americans blamed the Great Depression on the Republican Party.

CHAPTER 7 DRILL

1. **A**   For the first of two quantitative analysis questions, the answer is mostly found in the data itself, so start there and use Process of Elimination. Even if you don't recognize that Ross Perot is a third-party candidate, the fact that there are three candidates, and that the lowest among them still won nearly 19% of the popular vote, should indicate that (B) is not true and can therefore be eliminated. You can eliminate (C) because it talks about information that has not been provided: the table does not identify how Perot voters would have voted if Perot had not run for president. You can also eliminate (D) by looking at the Electoral Vote column; even if you don't remember that it takes 270 votes to win, you can see that Clinton had over 200 votes more than Bush. This also points to (A) as the correct answer: if Clinton won, then Bush could not have won, and therefore must have lost.

2. **B**   For the second of two quantitative analysis questions, you may have to apply some outside knowledge of political scenarios, but you should still primarily rely upon the given data when eliminating choices. Choices (A) and (C) can be eliminated because the table neither describes the three candidates' positions nor offers evidence supporting or refuting the simplicity of a presidential election. There is also no evidence for (D) in the table, especially since it claims that the winning candidate ran a poor campaign. This leaves (B) as the correct answer, which is supported by the fact that despite receiving nearly 20,000,000 votes, Perot did not gain a single electoral vote.

3. **B**   Remember: if you can eliminate either option for a choice, you can eliminate the entire choice. For (A), neither option seems true—they're reversed. During a primary, a candidate runs against other members of his or her own party, and those are the opponents whose policies they must criticize. Eliminate (A). Choice (C) is also a reversal, and one that might be hinted at by the term "general" election: candidates move from a specific campaign to their base during the primary to a more general campaign to all of America during the general. While it is true that a convention is planned during the primary, you can eliminate (D) because that convention is where the superdelegates vote—there is no need to cultivate them during the general election. This leaves (B) as the correct answer. During the primary, candidates focus on winning convention delegates. During the general election, they focus on the electoral map to ensure an Electoral College victory in November.

4. **D**   Pay close attention to the modifiers for a given scenario. You aren't being asked about any primary, or even any Republican primary—you're looking at an *open* Republican primary. These modifiers can help you to eliminate choices. Both (A) and (B) describe closed primaries, not open ones, so eliminate them. An open primary is one in which *any* registered voter can participate—not just Republicans or Democrats—and so (C) can also be eliminated. Only (D) correctly identifies that any registered voter can vote, so this is the correct answer.

5. **A**   Choices (B) and (C) are incorrect as these committees do not deal with a party's positions. The Credentials Committee decides if a delegate has voting privileges. The Rules Committee decides the all-important process of how delegates may vote during the primary (for example, whether they can change their vote after the first round of voting). Choice (D) is incorrect as there is no Ideology

Committee. Choice (A) is correct, as the Platform Committee decides the positions the party will take over the next four years.

6.   **B**   Choices (A), (C), and (D) can be eliminated as the older and more educated someone becomes, the more likely it is that they will vote in the general election. As a result, (B) is the correct answer, as this person is the oldest and has the highest level of education.

7.   **C**   Choice (A) is incorrect as states award delegates based on the proportion of the vote a candidate won. Choice (B) is incorrect as this describes a caucus. Choice (D) is incorrect as this also describes a caucus. As a result, (C) is correct as the majority of states use the primary system to choose presidential candidates.

CHAPTER 8 DRILL

1.   **A**   Choice (B) is incorrect as nothing in the paragraph suggests a question concerning the reasons judges interpret the Constitution. Choice (C) is incorrect as Marshall is not asking how to do his job. Choice (D) is incorrect as the paragraph says nothing about judges taking office. Therefore, (A) is correct as "no rule for his government" suggests that the Constitution does not specifically describe the responsibilities of the Supreme Court.

2.   **C**   Choice (A) can be eliminated as *ex post facto* laws refer to applying a law to an action that took place before the law was written. Choice (B) can be eliminated as judicial restraint refers to justices not injecting personal opinion or the national mood into their decisions. Choice (D) can be eliminated as *amicus curiae* briefs refer to letters written to the court by an interested party not directly involved with a case. As a result, (C) is correct. The passage, especially the final paragraph, affirms the principle of judicial review, the Supreme Court's ability to strike down unconstitutional laws.

3.   **D**   Don't be tricked because one of the two options for a choice is correct. Both have to match. So for (A), it's true that the Legislative Branch handles the Library of Congress, but it's not true that the Executive Branch handles technology assessment (that, too, is handled by the Legislative). Eliminate (A). Choice (B) is incorrect as the Executive Branch oversees the Department of Energy and the Legislative Branch oversees the Government Publishing Office. Choice (C) is incorrect as both departments fall under the control of the Executive Branch. Therefore, (D) is correct. The Legislative Branch oversees the GAO and the Executive Branch oversees Drug Control Policy.

4.   **B**   Choice (A) can be eliminated given that the president is the head of the Executive Branch and the checks-and-balances of the government would prevent him or her from also being the head of a Legislative branch. Choice (C) can be eliminated as the president *pro tempore* is just below the official head of the Senate. Choice (D) can be eliminated because the chief whip is the *functional* head of the Senate, not the official head. This leaves the correct answer, (B), which is that the vice president is the official head of the Senate, also known as the president of the Senate.

5. **A** Consider the modifying word here, "legislative." "Legislative" refers to Congress's power to pass laws. Choices (B), (C), and (D) are all powers of Congress, but they are not legislative. Therefore, (A) is correct as the power to tax and spend through legislation such as spending bills is one of the most important legislative powers possessed by Congress.

6. **C** Congressional districts are, as the question suggests, determined by the states, which should help you to eliminate both (A) and (B), given that it would be a violation of the Tenth Amendment for the federal government to determine districts for the House. Likewise, (D), which would take power away from the state and give it to a vague "commission" can also be ruled out. The correct answer, (C), describes the actual process, which is that after a national census, the state legislatures draw congressional maps.

7. **A** Choice (C) is incorrect, as the Supreme Court has no say in the nomination or appointment of cabinet members. Choices (A), (B), and (D) all involve the president, which is correct, as the president nominates all cabinet members. Choice (D) can be eliminated as all cabinet members require confirmation. So can (B), as the House has no say in the appointment of cabinet members. Therefore, (A) is correct, as the president nominates cabinet members. The Senate interviews each candidate before voting.

CHAPTER 9 DRILL

1. **D** Choice (A) is incorrect as more Americans 65 and older remain on government assistance programs for 3–4 years compared to Americans over 65. Choice (B) is incorrect as Americans over 65 use government assistance for 1-12 months more than any other group. Choice (C) is incorrect as Americans 18–64 are more likely to participate for only 13–36 months. Therefore, (D) is correct as 56% of all children who start using government assistance programs stay on those programs for at least three years, exceeding all other groups.

2. **B** Choice (A) can be eliminated as the graph does not provide information on the effectiveness of government assistance programs. Choice (C) can be eliminated as the graph does not provide information on the cost of government assistance programs. Choice (D) can be eliminated as the graph does not provide information on the relationship between public insurance programs and public assistance programs. In the first two groups, the largest percentage of those who use public assistance programs have done so for more than three years, and in the third group, this is *almost* the largest percentage. This does seem to support that after a certain amount of time, citizens may become reliant on these services. This means that (B) is correct.

3. **D** If a description doesn't directly apply to the option it's listed under, then that choice can and should be eliminated. "The government should influence wages and prices" refers to Keynesian economics, which isn't even being compared here, so eliminate (A). This is true also of "Massive deficit spending," so get rid of (C). Choice (B) may at first seem good, but *both* options are describing laissez-faire economics, not just the first one, so delete (B) as well. This leaves (D), which

correctly explains that laissez-faire economics is based upon having no government interference in the economy and that supply-side economics revolves around using tax cuts to encourage economic growth.

4. **C**   Even if you can't remember exactly what the OMB does, you may be able to eliminate choices that you can connect with different organizations. For instance, the National Economic Council is responsible for the items in (A) and (D), and so these two can be eliminated. Congress writes the national budget, so eliminate (B). This leaves (C), which is correct: the OMB plans the national budget for the president.

5. **A**   Social security is a financial safety net for many Americans. Choice (B) is incorrect as foreign tourists do not qualify for Social Security benefits; foreigners who are permanent residents do qualify. Choice (C) is incorrect as although veterans receive many benefits from the government, a veteran who is employed does not qualify for Social Security benefits. Choice (D) is incorrect as chronic poverty does not qualify a family for Social Security. However, the family may qualify for other federal and state government benefits.

6. **A**   Imports and exports have to do with trade, whereas defaults and bankruptcy have to do with not being able to pay debts and/or being broke, so eliminate (C) and (D). Between the two remaining choices, consider that a deficit means a loss and a surplus represents a gain. If a situation imports—buys—more than it exports—sells—does it have *more* (surplus) or *less* (deficit)? Eliminate (B); the correct answer is (A).

7. **D**   Discretionary spending is something that doesn't have a fixed amount that needs to be spent on it. Whether you remember the specifics of the Budget Enforcement Act or not, you should be able to identify the national debt, social security, and Medicare as mandatory, fixed payments; eliminate (A), (B) and (C). This means that (D) is the correct answer: education programs fall under discretionary spending.

CHAPTER 10 DRILL

1. **C**   For a Qualitative Analysis question, be very careful with choices that may be historically true or morally sound, but which do not match the passage itself. This applies even to implications; (A) and (D) can therefore be eliminated. Choice (B) is incorrect, as King does not make this claim. The correct answer, (C), matches what King says, which is that the legality or illegality of something does not make that thing inherently right or wrong.

2. **B**   Choice (A) is more than a little extreme, and unsupported by the text; there's nothing to say that America was as bad as the other two nations mentioned. The focus of the passage is on the righteousness of certain laws. Martin Luther King, Jr., isn't promoting himself, but is instead talking

about the importance of nonviolent protest, so eliminate (C). King isn't trying to educate readers about Germany or Hungary; he's using them to make a point about his actions in America, so eliminate (D). This point about unjust laws is what is expressed in (B), so that is the correct answer.

3. **A** On a comparison question, you can look to eliminate options that use extreme language, because if you can find even one instance to the contrary, that means the choice is incorrect. That's certainly true for (B), as there are many cases in which the Supreme Court has ruled to restrict civil rights (e.g., *Plessy, Korematsu*). You can also eliminate (C), because civil rights are not limited to only one minority group. Finally, eliminate (D) because civil liberties cannot be amended at the state level. This leaves (A), which is correct: the Bill of Rights enshrines Americans' civil liberties and the equal application of the law to all Americans is the foundation of civil rights.

4. **C** Choice (A) can be eliminated as although *Powell* expanded defendants' right to legal representation, this right did not extend to all court cases. Choice (B) can be eliminated as *Betts* denied the right to counsel in certain circumstances. Choice (D) is incorrect as *Miranda* concerned informing defendants of their rights at the time of arrest. Therefore, (C) is correct as after *Gideon*, all defendants were allowed an attorney no matter the crime.

5. **A** In *Griswold,* the Supreme Court ruled that women have a Fourteenth Amendment "right to privacy" with their physicians, which legalized birth control throughout the United States. Choice (B) is incorrect as *Citizens United* dealt with federal election law. Choice (C) is incorrect as *McDonald* expanded Americans' right to bear arms. Choice (D) is incorrect as *New York Times* expanded newspapers' First Amendment rights. As a result, (A) is correct; with *Roe v. Wade,* the Court used *Griswold* as a precedent to legalize abortion nationwide.

6. **C** During the 20th century, the Supreme Court took on many cases that affected students attending public schools. Choice (A) can be eliminated as *Tinker v. Des Moines* centered on the issue of student protest. Choice (B) can be eliminated as *Hazelwood School District v. Kuhlmeier* decided that schools can regulate students' speech in school. Choice (D) can be eliminated as *Lemon v. Kurtzman* decided that states cannot directly fund religious schools. Therefore, (C) is correct as *Engel v. Vitale* barred the practice of state-sponsored prayer in school.

7. **D** *Wisconsin v. Yoder* pitted the state's Amish community against Wisconsin's compulsory education laws. Although the First Amendment was central to the case, (A), (B), and (C) were at issue. As a result, (D) is correct as the Amish community successfully argued that their religious beliefs prompted them to remove their children from school after the 8th grade.

Part VI
Practice Test 2

Practice Test 2

Completely darken bubbles with a No. 2 pencil. If you make a mistake, be sure to erase mark completely. Erase all stray marks.

1. YOUR NAME:
(Print)
Last   First   M.I.

SIGNATURE: _____   DATE: _____ / _____ / _____

HOME ADDRESS: _____
(Print)
Number and Street

_____
City   State   Zip Code

PHONE NO. : _____
(Print)

IMPORTANT: Please fill in these boxes exactly as shown on the back cover of your test book.

2. TEST FORM

3. TEST CODE

4. REGISTRATION NUMBER

0	A	0	0	0	0	0	0	0	0	0	0
1	B	1	1	1	1	1	1	1	1	1	1
2	C	2	2	2	2	2	2	2	2	2	2
3	D	3	3	3	3	3	3	3	3	3	3
4	E	4	4	4	4	4	4	4	4	4	4
5	F	5	5	5	5	5	5	5	5	5	5
6	G	6	6	6	6	6	6	6	6	6	6
7		7	7	7	7	7	7	7	7	7	7
8		8	8	8	8	8	8	8	8	8	8
9		9	9	9	9	9	9	9	9	9	9

6. DATE OF BIRTH

Month	Day		Year	
JAN				
FEB				
MAR	0	0	0	0
APR	1	1	1	1
MAY	2	2	2	2
JUN	3	3	3	3
JUL		4	4	4
AUG		5	5	5
SEP		6	6	6
OCT		7	7	7
NOV		8	8	8
DEC		9	9	9

7. SEX
MALE
FEMALE

5. YOUR NAME

First 4 letters of last name				FIRST INIT	MID INIT
A	A	A	A	A	A
B	B	B	B	B	B
C	C	C	C	C	C
D	D	D	D	D	D
E	E	E	E	E	E
F	F	F	F	F	F
G	G	G	G	G	G
H	H	H	H	H	H
I	I	I	I	I	I
J	J	J	J	J	J
K	K	K	K	K	K
L	L	L	L	L	L
M	M	M	M	M	M
N	N	N	N	N	N
O	O	O	O	O	O
P	P	P	P	P	P
Q	Q	Q	Q	Q	Q
R	R	R	R	R	R
S	S	S	S	S	S
T	T	T	T	T	T
U	U	U	U	U	U
V	V	V	V	V	V
W	W	W	W	W	W
X	X	X	X	X	X
Y	Y	Y	Y	Y	Y
Z	Z	Z	Z	Z	Z

The Princeton Review®

© The Princeton Review, Inc.

FORM NO. 00001-PR

Section ① Start with number 1 for each new section.
If a section has fewer questions than answer spaces, leave the extra answer spaces blank.

1. A B C D
2. A B C D
3. A B C D
4. A B C D
5. A B C D
6. A B C D
7. A B C D
8. A B C D
9. A B C D
10. A B C D
11. A B C D
12. A B C D
13. A B C D
14. A B C D
15. A B C D

16. A B C D
17. A B C D
18. A B C D
19. A B C D
20. A B C D
21. A B C D
22. A B C D
23. A B C D
24. A B C D
25. A B C D
26. A B C D
27. A B C D
28. A B C D
29. A B C D
30. A B C D

31. A B C D
32. A B C D
33. A B C D
34. A B C D
35. A B C D
36. A B C D
37. A B C D
38. A B C D
39. A B C D
40. A B C D
41. A B C D
42. A B C D
43. A B C D
44. A B C D
45. A B C D

46. A B C D
47. A B C D
48. A B C D
49. A B C D
50. A B C D
51. A B C D
52. A B C D
53. A B C D
54. A B C D
55. A B C D

The Exam

AP® U.S. Government and Politics Exam

SECTION I: Multiple-Choice Questions

DO NOT OPEN THIS BOOKLET UNTIL YOU ARE TOLD TO DO SO.

At a Glance

Total Time
80 minutes
Number of Questions
55
Percent of Total Grade
50%
Writing Instrument
Pencil required

Instructions

Section I of this examination contains 55 multiple-choice questions. Fill in only the ovals for numbers 1 through 55 on your answer sheet.

Indicate all of your answers to the multiple-choice questions on the answer sheet. No credit will be given for anything written in this exam booklet, but you may use the booklet for notes or scratch work. After you have decided which of the suggested answers is best, completely fill in the corresponding oval on the answer sheet. Give only one answer to each question. If you change an answer, be sure that the previous mark is erased completely. Here is a sample question and answer.

Sample Question   Sample Answer

Chicago is a   Ⓐ ● Ⓒ Ⓓ
(A) state
(B) city
(C) country
(D) continent

Use your time effectively, working as quickly as you can without losing accuracy. Do not spend too much time on any one question. Go on to other questions and come back to the ones you have not answered if you have time. It is not expected that everyone will know the answers to all the multiple-choice questions.

About Guessing

Many candidates wonder whether or not to guess the answers to questions about which they are not certain. Multiple-choice scores are based on the number of questions answered correctly. Points are not deducted for incorrect answers, and no points are awarded for unanswered questions. Because points are not deducted for incorrect answers, you are encouraged to answer all multiple-choice questions. On any questions you do not know the answer to, you should eliminate as many choices as you can, and then select the best answer among the remaining choices.

GO ON TO THE NEXT PAGE.

UNITED STATES GOVERNMENT AND POLITICS

Section I

Time—80 minutes

55 Questions

Directions: Each of the questions or incomplete statements below is followed by five suggested answers or completions. Select the one that is best in each case and then fill in the corresponding oval on the answer sheet.

Questions 1 and 2 refer to the graph.

Congressional Job Approval Ratings

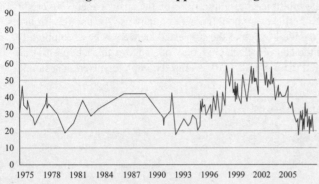

1. Which of the following best describes a trend in the line graph above?

   (A) The approval rating of Congress was higher in the early 1990s than in the late 1990s.
   (B) Congress was more popular in the mid-1990s than in the late 1980s.
   (C) Americans are usually displeased with the performance of Congress.
   (D) A majority of Americans disapproved of the performance of Congress immediately after September 11, 2001.

2. Which of the following has been a direct consequence of the trend illustrated in the line graph?

   (A) Since the 2000s, a greater number of congressional candidates have run as independents rather than as members of political parties.
   (B) Elected officials and candidates running for congressional office are increasingly using social media to reach out to voters and constituents.
   (C) Internet websites with political content have become less popular with younger people.
   (D) Increased political polarization in the general public and the decline in congressional job approval ratings continue to the present time.

Questions 3 and 4 refer to the table.

Latino Participation in Presidential Elections, 1988–2012
(in millions)

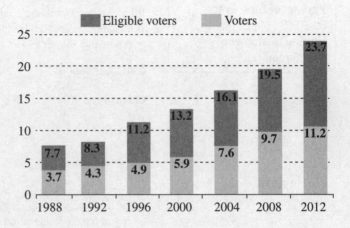

3. Which of the following statements is reflected in the data in the table?

   (A) No more than half of eligible Latino voters have ever participated in presidential elections.
   (B) The number of registered voters always increases between elections.
   (C) Latino voters were more dissatisfied with their electoral choices in the 1990s than they were during the 2000s.
   (D) As measured by the percentage of eligible voters, voter turnout for Latinos declined from 1988 to 2008.

GO ON TO THE NEXT PAGE.

4. Which of the following is an accurate conclusion based on the data in the table above and your knowledge of voter behavior?

(A) A minority of Latinos vote in presidential elections because fewer citizens register to vote in presidential election years than in midterm election years.

(B) Latinos vote in presidential elections in larger numbers than in midterm elections in part because there is more media coverage in those years.

(C) More Latinos vote in midterm elections because they understand the greater importance of Congress in the legislative process.

(D) More Latinos vote in midterm elections than in presidential elections because congressional candidates devote more money and resources to their campaigns in midterm years.

Questions 5 and 6 refer to the graphics below.

Percentage of Voters for Democratic Candidates in Presidential Elections (1972–2012)

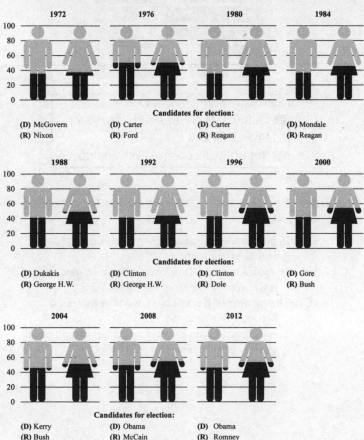

5. Which of the following accurately describes the information presented in the graphs?

(A) If only men had voted in the 1980 election, Jimmy Carter would have won.

(B) There is little difference in the level of support that the Republican Party receives from men and women.

(C) The gender gap was more prominent in the 1980s and 1990s than it was in the 1970s.

(D) In order for a Republican candidate to win, he or she must receive more votes from women than from men.

6. Which of the following could best explain the gender differences in the number of people who voted for Dole and Clinton in 1996?

(A) Clinton had previously won the Election of 1992 with a majority of male voters.

(B) Dole's campaign received the majority of its funding from corporations, while Clinton's funding was largely from smaller donors and grassroots organizations.

(C) Dole primarily focused on traditional Republican issues such as fiscal discipline, whereas Clinton attracted female voters of both parties by staking out moderate positions on a host of issues including crime, drugs, and education funding.

(D) Since married women are more likely to vote for Democrat candidates, Clinton appealed to new voters in this demographic by focusing on domestic policy issues such as education, health care, and social welfare programs.

GO ON TO THE NEXT PAGE.

Questions 7 and 8 refer to the table below.

Dissemination of Medicare Benefits by Region
(Millions of $)

	2000	2004	2008	2012
North	12.4	13.2	14.0	16.4
Northeast	8.2	9.0	9.6	10.1
Midwest	12.0	13.2	14.2	15.0
West	14.8	16.2	15.8	17.0
East	9.8	10.4	10.4	11.0
South	11.8	13.6	16.2	18.4

7. Which of the following is an accurate statement about the information in the line graph?

   (A) The dissemination of Medicare funding has continually increased across all regions between 2000–2012.
   (B) The West received the most Medicare funding in 2012.
   (C) In 2008, the Northeast received approximately one and a half times the amount of Medicare funding as the North.
   (D) The South experienced the greatest increase in Medicare funding from 2000–2012.

8. Based on the information in the table, which of the following is the most likely implication of Medicare spending as a portion of the federal budget?

   (A) Increases in Medicare spending put pressure on discretionary spending.
   (B) Medicare spending levels are set by law and cannot be changed.
   (C) Since states control entitlement spending, congressional budget committees do not control Medicare spending.
   (D) Democrats and Republicans throughout the country generally agree on increases to entitlement spending.

Questions 9 and 10 refer to the table below.

Partisan Composition of State Legislatures

Years			
'78	31	8	11
'80	28	7	15
'82	34	6	10
'84	28	12	10
'86	27	14	9
'88	29	13	8
'90	29	15	6
'92	26	17	7
'94	22	13	15
'96	20	13	17
'98	20	13	17
'00	16	16	18
'02	16	13	21
'04	19	11	20
'06	23	11	16
'08	27	9	14
'10	27	9	14
'12	15	8	27
'14	19	4	27

Number of state legislatures
■ Democrats control both chambers
□ Split D/R Control
▨ Republicans control both chambers

9. Which of the following statements is reflected in the data in the chart?

   (A) In most states, registered Democrats outnumber registered Republicans.
   (B) Democrats outnumbered Republicans in state legislatures throughout the early 1990s.
   (C) The number of Republican governors increased between 1990 and 1996.
   (D) The Democrats and Republicans controlled an equal number of state legislatures in 1996.

GO ON TO THE NEXT PAGE.

10. Which of the following was the most likely consequence of the trend illustrated in the bar chart?

(A) After 1996, more candidates for state legislatures ran as independents rather than as members of political parties.

(B) In the late 1990s, Democrats running for state office were more likely than Republicans to use social media to reach out to voters and constituents.

(C) In the late 1990s, Democrats in state legislatures were more likely to seek bipartisan support for their initiatives, especially on controversial policy issues.

(D) The shift in party power in state legislatures in the 1990s led to increased political polarization in the general public.

Questions 11–14 refer to the passage below.

"It is in the context of the present world struggle between freedom and tyranny that the problem of racial discrimination must be viewed. The United States is trying to prove to the people of the world, of every nationality, race, and color, that a free democracy is the most civilized and most secure form of government yet devised by man. We must set an example for others by showing firm determination to remove existing flaws in our democracy.... The existence of discrimination against minority groups in the United States has an adverse effect upon our relations with other countries. Racial discrimination furnishes grist for the Communist propaganda mills."

– Attorney General James P. McGranery, December 1952

11. Which of the following conclusions can be drawn based on McGranery's argument?

(A) Since the civil rights of racial minorities are protected by the Bill of Rights, there is no need to enact additional legislation in these areas.

(B) Civil rights legislation may have positive effects on foreign policy goals.

(C) The protection of civil rights is essential for a functioning democracy.

(D) Positive relationships with other countries are necessary to protect civil rights at home.

12. McGranery's statements were most likely made during the Supreme Court ruling on which of the following cases?

(A) *Gideon v. Wainwright*
(B) *Marbury v. Madison*
(C) *Plessy v. Ferguson*
(D) *Brown v. Board of Education*

13. Which of the following constitutional provisions enables the power of the federal government in enacting legislation regarding the issues raised in McGranery's argument?

(A) Equal protection clause of the Fourteenth Amendment
(B) Faithful execution of the laws in Article II
(C) Judicial review in Article III
(D) Establishment clause in the First Amendment

14. Based on the text, with which of the following statements would McGranery most likely agree?

(A) The United States Constitution explicitly prohibits racial segregation in schools.
(B) Without civil rights legislation, many people in foreign countries would be confused about the meaning of the United States Constitution.
(C) Domestic policy can impact foreign policy.
(D) Institutions which perpetuate racial discrimination ought to be held accountable for the spread of Communism in foreign lands.

GO ON TO THE NEXT PAGE.

Questions 15–17 refer to the passages below.

"The [Tenth] Amendment states but a truism that all is retained which has not been surrendered. There is nothing in the history of its adoption to suggest that it was more than declaratory of the relationship between the national and state governments as it had been established by the Constitution before the amendment or that its purpose was other than to allay fears that the new national government might seek to exercise powers not granted, and that the states might not be able to exercise fully their reserved powers."

—*United States v. Darby Lumber Co* (1941)

15. The Tenth Amendment most often comes into conflict with which section of the Constitution?

    (A) The "full faith and credit" clause
    (B) The "necessary and proper" clause
    (C) The provisions for the impeachment of a president
    (D) The clause prohibiting states from coining money and entering into treaties

16. People who interpret the Tenth Amendment as greatly restricting the powers of the national government are often referred to as

    (A) Federalists
    (B) isolationists
    (C) loose constructionists
    (D) states' righters

17. Which of the following actions would be justified by the Tenth Amendment?

    (A) A city government asserts exemption from a federal environmental regulation.
    (B) A state asserts its right to waive federal minimum wage laws for part-time workers in a struggling industry.
    (C) The federal government provides financial incentives for state governments to expand Medicaid spending.
    (D) State police refuse to allow federal agents to enforce drug laws within state boundaries.

Questions 18 and 19 refer to the map below.

The Evolution of North Carolina's Congressional District

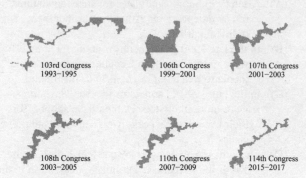

Credit: Professor Alasdair Rae and the USGS.gov website.

18. The map shows how the borders of a congressional district have changed between 1993 and 2015. Which of the following statements, if true, could best explain the reasons for these changes?

    (A) Due to an economic recession in 1999, moderate voters in North Carolina migrated to areas with greater opportunity in the inland portions of the state. After 2001, the migration ended and the district was restored to its prior boundaries.
    (B) Democrats and Republicans have negotiated cooperatively since 1993 to create a district with fair representation for all.
    (C) The boundaries of the district have been gerrymandered to create highly competitive elections.
    (D) The boundaries of the district have been drawn and redrawn over time to maintain a district with a majority of voters who are registered with the same party.

19. Which of the following has most likely been a consequence of the way the district is drawn on the map?

    (A) It has led to less competitive elections.
    (B) It has led to highly competitive elections.
    (C) It has been beneficial to independent and third-party candidates.
    (D) It has led to high voter turnout in most elections.

GO ON TO THE NEXT PAGE.

Questions 20 and 21 refer to the cartoon below.

Credit: Rick McKee, PoliticalCartoons.com

20. Which of the following best describes the message in the political cartoon?

   (A) Although voters may claim to want change in Congress, then often wind up reelecting their local senators and representatives in primary elections.
   (B) Incumbents often win, despite the efforts of their local constituency to vote them out of office.
   (C) Incumbents often lose primary elections, though they tend to win in general elections.
   (D) Although voters wish to vote their local representatives out of office, they are apathetic about the overall makeup of the U.S. Congress.

21. Which of the following general trends in political elections most aligns with the message of the cartoon?

   (A) Senate incumbents are more likely to maintain their congressional seats than are incumbents in the House of Representatives.
   (B) Incumbents have a large advantage over their challengers, both in party support and campaign finance.
   (C) Since incumbents spend much of their time in Washington, D.C., voters are often unsuccessful in their attempts to communicate with their congressional leadership.
   (D) When voters become disgruntled with Congress, they often react by voting incumbents out of office.

Questions 22 and 23 refer to the graph below.

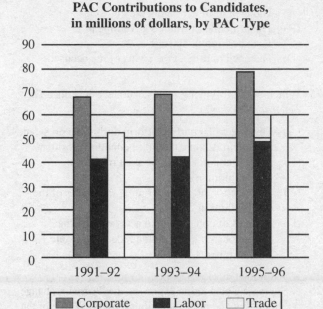

PAC Contributions to Candidates, in millions of dollars, by PAC Type

22. Which of the following conclusions is supported by the graph?

   (A) Corporations have more political influence than do labor unions.
   (B) Trade PACs are the fastest-growing sector of political activism in the United States.
   (C) Corporate PACs are more likely to donate to Republican candidates than to Democratic candidates.
   (D) In the first half of the 1990s, PACs consistently contributed more than $150 million to different candidates.

23. Based on the graph, which of the following claims would an opponent of PAC campaign contributions most likely make?

   (A) Corporations wield undue influence in politics by contributing a disproportionate share of money to PACs.
   (B) Voter turnout will continue to be poor as long as PACs contribute more money to campaigns than individuals do.
   (C) The continued presence of PAC money in political campaigns will likely lead to election fraud.
   (D) PACs can more effectively influence politics by diverting their money into lobbying efforts rather than contributing to campaigns.

GO ON TO THE NEXT PAGE.

24. Which of the following concepts did the ratification of the Constitution in 1788 most clearly commit to?

    (A) The idea of direct democracy
    (B) The principle of limited government
    (C) The abolition of slavery
    (D) The need to protect the rights of the accused

25. Which of the following most accurately describes *The Federalist Papers*?

    (A) The Federalist party platform during the presidency of John Adams, the first Federalist president
    (B) A popular anti-British booklet of the pre-Revolutionary era
    (C) A collection of essays arguing the merits of the Constitution
    (D) A series of congressional acts defining the relationship between the federal and state governments

26. A Supreme Court judge expresses the desire to change public policy and alter judicial precedent. Which of the following terms describes this action?

    (A) judicial activism
    (B) due process
    (C) judicial restraint
    (D) *ex post facto* lawmaking

27. Which of the following statements about Congress is true?

    (A) Congress cannot override a presidential veto.
    (B) A proposed constitutional amendment must be approved by two-thirds of the delegates in both houses of Congress.
    (C) Congress can establish an official church of the United States.
    (D) Congressional power over the bureaucracy is less than that of the president.

28. Which of the following demonstrates why The House Rules Committee is considered one of the most powerful groups in the House of Representatives?

    (A) It supervises the ethical conduct of House members.
    (B) It oversees the selection of federal judges.
    (C) It determines the number of subcommittees that a standing committee may establish at any given time.
    (D) It determines the scheduling of votes and the conditions under which bills are debated and amended.

29. Which of the following is the primary function of a political action committee (PAC) ?

    (A) To contribute money to candidates for election
    (B) To coordinate local get-out-the-vote campaigns
    (C) To promote the defeat of incumbents in the federal and state legislatures
    (D) To organize protest demonstrations and other acts of civil disobedience

30. Voters who rely exclusively on television network news coverage of national elections are most likely to be aware of which of the following?

    (A) Which special interest groups have endorsed which candidates
    (B) The relative strength of each candidate's support, as indicated by public opinion polls
    (C) Candidates' positions on international issues
    (D) Candidates' positions on domestic issues

31. Which of the following rights does the First Amendment protect?

    (A) Due process of the law in any criminal case
    (B) Retention of personal property unless justly compensated by the government
    (C) Not being subjected to excessive fines or unusual punishment
    (D) Petitioning the government for a redress of grievances

32. Which of the following cases focused on the right to privacy for all American citizens?

    (A) *Near v. Minnesota* and *New York Times v. Sullivan*
    (B) *Texas v. Johnson* and *Morse v. Frederick*
    (C) *Thornhill v. Alabama* and *Cox v. New Hampshire*
    (D) *Griswold v. Connecticut* and *Roe v. Wade*

33. Which of the following is American federalism most clearly exemplified by?

    (A) A system of checks and balances among the three branches of the national government
    (B) A process by which international treaties are completed
    (C) The special constitutional status of Washington, D.C.
    (D) The Tenth Amendment to the Constitution

GO ON TO THE NEXT PAGE.

34. Which of the following is specifically mentioned in the U.S. Constitution?

    (A) Judicial review
    (B) The national census
    (C) Recall elections
    (D) The right to public education

35. The president wishes to influence the legislative process. Which of the following actions can he legally perform?

    (A) call special sessions of Congress
    (B) introduce bills to the floor of Congress
    (C) address Congress during its debate on bills
    (D) vote on acts of Congress

36. Which of the following presidential powers is shared with the Senate?

    (A) Deploying troops
    (B) Drafting appropriations bills
    (C) Negotiating treaties
    (D) Forcing Congress into session

37. Which of the following best describes why Republican presidential candidates who are successful in the primaries tend to be more conservative than rank-and-file Republicans?

    (A) Moderate Republicans are less likely than conservative Republicans to gain widespread support in the general election.
    (B) Most moderate Republicans have approved of the Democratic presidential candidate.
    (C) Most rank-and-file Republicans do not care whether their party's nominee shares their political views.
    (D) Party activists, whose political participation is disproportionate to their numbers, tend to be very conservative.

38. What is the primary reason that the committees in the House of Representatives are more influential than they are in the Senate?

    (A) The difference in size between the two chambers means that more work is done on the floor in the Senate and more work is done in committees in the House.
    (B) The Senate as a whole has confirmation powers that the House does not have.
    (C) Members are appointed to the committee in the House but are elected to committees in the Senate.
    (D) A member of any party can serve a committee in the House, but only major party members can serve on committees in the Senate.

39. Which of the following accounts for the fact that the power and prestige of the presidency have grown since 1932?

    (A) America's decreased role in international affairs
    (B) Increasing public confidence in the federal government
    (C) Decreased spending on entitlement programs
    (D) The president's increased visibility, due to the development of mass media

40. Which of the following generally results when the Senate and House of Representatives pass different versions of the same bill?

    (A) The president signs the version he prefers.
    (B) The bill goes back to each house's committee and restarts the legislative process.
    (C) All amendments to the bill are invalidated, and the original version of the bill is sent to the president to sign.
    (D) The two legislative bodies form a conference committee.

41. Which of the following statements concerning the likelihood that a person will vote is true?

    (A) When there is a strong front-runner in a state, people in that state are more likely to vote.
    (B) White-collar workers are more likely to vote than are blue-collar workers, with the exception of blue-collar workers who belong to unions.
    (C) Voters who are registered as independent are more likely to vote than those who are registered Democrats or Republicans.
    (D) There is no difference in the likelihood of voting among those with undergraduate degrees and those with postgraduate degrees.

42. A member of which of the following demographic groups is most likely to support a Republican presidential candidate?

    (A) Married white male
    (B) Unmarried white female
    (C) African American, male or female
    (D) Youths under the age of 25, male or female

GO ON TO THE NEXT PAGE.

43. Which of the following is an accurate comparison of the two court cases?

	United States v. Lopez (1995)	*McDonald v. Chicago* (2010)
(A)	Declared an act of Congress unconstitutional	Found that the personal right to own firearms is protected by the due process clause of the Fourteenth Amendment
(B)	Set limits to Congress' power under the commerce clause	Recognized the importance of state sovereignty and local control
(C)	Allowed for the possession of firearms on public school property	Ruled that state laws were supreme to national laws
(D)	Resolved uncertainty left in the wake of *District of Columbia v. Heller* as to the scope of gun rights in the states	Declared the Gun-Free School Zones Act unconstitutional

44. Which of the following is an accurate comparison of federal and state judiciaries?

	Federal Judiciaries	**State Judiciaries**
(A)	May overturn state decisions on any grounds	Higher than federal courts
(B)	Does not hear cases which originated in state courts	Is entirely autonomous
(C)	May rule on the constitutionality of state court decisions	Are largely autonomous
(D)	Are appeal courts	Are trial courts

45. Which of the following is an accurate comparison between a pardon and a reprieve?

	Pardon	**Reprieve**
(A)	Lasts ten years	Lasts one year
(B)	Postpones legal punishment	Grants a release from legal punishment
(C)	Grants a release from legal punishment	Postpones legal punishment
(D)	Can only be granted by presidents	Can only be granted by governors

46. Which of the following is an accurate comparison of Republican and Democrat views on government?

	Republicans	**Democrats**
(A)	Tend to be liberal	Tend to be conservative
(B)	Favor more governmental regulation of the marketplace	Favor personal privacy
(C)	Favor a national religion	Favor private education
(D)	Favor fewer regulations	Favor more governmental regulation of the marketplace

47. Which of the following is an accurate comparison of the First and Fourth Amendments to the Constitution?

	First Amendment	**Fourth Amendment**
(A)	Contains the establishment and free exercise clauses	Was clarified by the ruling in *Wisconsin v. Yoder*
(B)	Guarantees the right to an attorney, as stipulated by *Gideon v. Wainwright*	Protects citizens against unlawful searches and seizures
(C)	Protects freedom of religion	Requires that evidence illegally seized by law enforcement cannot be used in criminal prosecutions
(D)	Protects freedom of speech	Was used to justify the decision in *Roe v. Wade*

GO ON TO THE NEXT PAGE.

48. The Civil Rights Act of 1964 was passed to reinforce the

    (A) presidential veto
    (B) system of checks and balances
    (C) states' power to challenge federal regulation
    (D) Fourteenth Amendment

49. According to *The Federalist Papers*, federalism has which of the following effects on political factions?

    (A) It provides a structured environment in which factions may flourish.
    (B) It limits the dangers of factionalism by diluting political power.
    (C) It allows factions to dominate on the national level while limiting their influence on state governments.
    (D) It eliminates any opportunity for factions to form.

50. The Constitution, as originally ratified, addressed which of the following weaknesses of the Articles of Confederation?

    (A) inclusion of a chief executive office
    (B) national government's inability to levy taxes effectively
    (C) imposition of a central authority to regulate interstate trade
    (D) omission of a universal suffrage clause

51. Congress's power to determine national policy

    (A) usually increases as a president's popularity decreases, and vice versa
    (B) has declined steadily since the ratification of the Constitution
    (C) is severely limited by the "elastic clause" of the Constitution
    (D) increases during times of war

52. Which of the following statements about cabinet departments is true?

    (A) They are established by the judicial branch.
    (B) Their members sometimes do not share the president's goals.
    (C) They cannot all be run by leaders who belong to the same political party the president does.
    (D) Every federal agency is a cabinet department.

53. Which of the following statements about the Electoral College is correct?

    (A) Each state must split its electoral votes among all the candidates that receive votes.
    (B) Each state is equally represented in the Electoral College.
    (C) The Electoral College was created by an amendment to the Constitution.
    (D) The results of Electoral College voting tend to distort the winner's margin of victory when compared with the popular vote.

54. Before serving in the House of Representatives or Senate, the greatest number of federal legislators

    (A) work in cabinet positions
    (B) teach political science at the college level
    (C) work as journalists
    (D) earn law degrees

55. Which of the following would best represent a conservative view concerning social policy?

    (A) The federal government should have a strong role in regulating public education.
    (B) Gun-owners should be permitted to openly carry firearms in public.
    (C) Racial and gender considerations should be taken into account in state university admissions decisions.
    (D) Individuals should rely on government aid for their economic well-being.

STOP
END OF SECTION I

IF YOU FINISH BEFORE TIME IS CALLED, YOU MAY CHECK YOUR WORK ON THIS SECTION.
DO NOT GO ON TO SECTION II UNTIL YOU ARE TOLD TO DO SO.

UNITED STATES GOVERNMENT AND POLITICS

Section II

Time—1 hour and 40 minutes

Directions: It is suggested that you take a few minutes to plan and outline each answer. It is suggested that you spend approximately 20 minutes each on questions 1, 2, and 3 and 40 minutes on question 4. Unless directions indicate otherwise, respond to all parts of all four questions. In your response use substantive examples where appropriate.

1. "Think back to the Bush vs. Kerry election of 2004. There was hardly any social media…. During that election, candidates didn't speak directly to the public via social channels, and everyday people didn't have as many outlets to share and debate their political views. Today, social media gives candidates a direct line of communication to the American people. That's a positive change. But on the flip side, social media is an uncontrolled, democratized soap box where individuals can spread opinions that are not substantiated, which can change the public's view of a candidate overnight."

—Entrepreneur, July 16, 2015

After reading the scenario, respond to (a), (b), and (c) below:

    (a)   Identify ONE way that candidates for public office are using social media in their campaigns.

    (a)   For the method identified in Part A, explain the advantages to the candidates of using social media in this way.

    (c)   Identify and explain one way that social media can harm a candidate's campaign.

GO ON TO THE NEXT PAGE.

Defense budgets, fiscal years 1948–2018

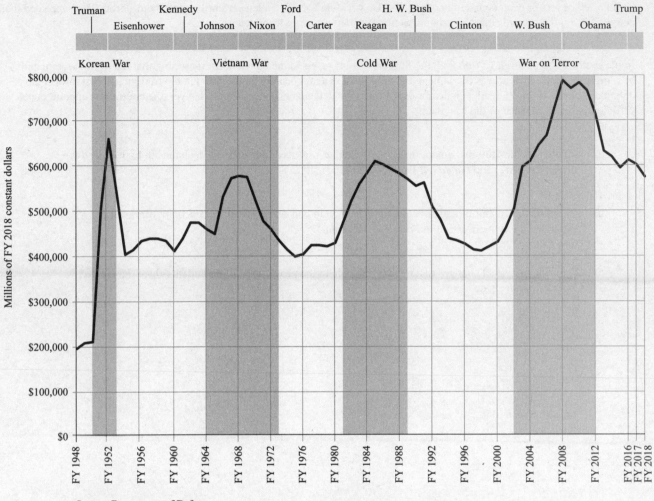

Source: Department of Defense

2. Use the information graphic to answer the questions.

(a) Which two presidents were responsible for the greatest increases of defense spending since 1953?

(b) Describe a trend in the data and draw a conclusion about the defense spending habits of Republican and Democratic presidents.

(c) Explain how the defense spending as shown in the graph relates to iron triangles within the federal government.

GO ON TO THE NEXT PAGE.

3. In March 1931, nine black men from Alabama were accused of raping two young white women. Less than a week later, after a series of one-day trials, most of the defendants were sentenced to death. Prior to the trials, the defendants were not told they could hire lawyers or even contact their families. They had no access to a lawyer until shortly before trial. They appealed their convictions on the grounds that the group was not provided adequate legal counsel.

In the ensuing case, *Powell v. Alabama*, the Supreme Court reversed the convictions, reasoning that the right to retain and be represented by a lawyer was fundamental to a fair trial in death penalty cases, and that the trial judge must inform the defendant of this right. In death penalty cases in which the defendant cannot afford a lawyer, the court must appoint one sufficiently far in advance of the trial date.

    (a)   Identify a constitutional amendment or clause that was used to justify the decisions in both *Powell* v. *Alabama* (1932) and *Gideon* v. *Wainwright* (1963).

    (b)   Based on the constitutional amendment identified in part A, explain how *Gideon v. Wainwright* expanded upon the decision in *Powell* v. *Alabama*.

    (c)   Describe historical changes that have been made to the prosecution of defendants since the *Gideon* v. *Wainwright* decision.

GO ON TO THE NEXT PAGE.

4. Develop an argument that explains whether increased power vested to the federal government or increased power vested to the States best achieves the founders' intent for American democracy in terms of ensuring a stable government run by the people.

In your essay, you must:

- Articulate a defensible claim or thesis that responds to the prompt and establishes a line of reasoning

- Support your claim with at least TWO pieces of accurate and relevant information:
  - At least ONE piece of evidence must be from one of the following foundational documents:
    - Brutus 1
    - Articles of Confederation
    - Federalist No. 10
    - U.S. Constitution
  - Use a second piece of evidence from another foundation document from the list or your study of the electoral process

- Use reasoning to explain why your evidence supports your claim/thesis

- Respond to an opposing or alternative perspective using refutation, concession, or rebuttal

GO ON TO THE NEXT PAGE.

Practice Test 2:
Answers and
Explanations

PRACTICE TEST 2 SCORING WORKSHEET

Section I: Multiple-Choice

_____ × 1.0000 = _____
Number of Correct   Weighted
(out of 55)   Section I Score
                  (Do not round)

Section II: Free Response

Question 1   _____ × 3.000 = _____
              (out of 3)   (Do not round)

Question 2   _____ × 4.000 = _____
              (out of 3)   (Do not round)

Question 3   _____ × 4.000 = _____
              (out of 3)   (Do not round)

Question 4   _____ × 5.500 = _____
              (out of 4)   (Do not round)

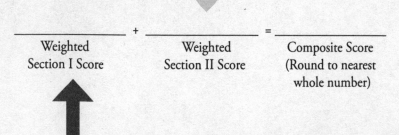

Sum   = _____
             Weighted Section II
             Score (Do not round)

The following conversion chart provides only a rough estimate, as the new 2019 Exam has not yet been scored and may have a different range.

AP Score Conversion Chart U.S. Government and Politics

Composite Score Range	AP Score
83–110	5
72–82	4
56–71	3
38–55	2
0–37	1

Composite Score

_____ + _____ = _____
Weighted   Weighted   Composite Score
Section I Score   Section II Score   (Round to nearest
                                      whole number)

PRACTICE TEST 2 ANSWER KEY

1.	C	21.	B	41.	B
2.	D	22.	D	42.	A
3.	D	23.	A	43.	A
4.	B	24.	B	44.	C
5.	C	25.	C	45.	C
6.	C	26.	A	46.	D
7.	D	27.	B	47.	C
8.	A	28.	D	48.	D
9.	B	29.	A	49.	B
10.	C	30.	B	50.	B
11.	B	31.	D	51.	A
12.	D	32.	D	52.	B
13.	A	33.	D	53.	D
14.	C	34.	B	54.	D
15.	B	35.	A	55.	B
16.	D	36.	C		
17.	C	37.	D		
18.	D	38.	A		
19.	A	39.	D		
20.	A	40.	D		

MULTIPLE-CHOICE SECTION: ANSWERS AND EXPLANATIONS

1. **C** Upon quick scan of the graph, a simple deduction is that Congress is usually "flunking" in the eyes of the American people. There's a burst in approval just after the attacks of September 11, 2001, but don't be misled by that answer choice—it is saying the opposite of what the graph is showing. Choice (A) is incorrect because the approval rating of Congress was in the 20–40% range in the early 1990s and in the 30–50% range in the late 1990s. Choice (B) is incorrect because the approval rating of Congress was in the 25–35% range in the mid–1990s and between 35% and approximately 43% in the late 1980s. Choice (D) is incorrect because approximately 85% of Americans approved of Congress's performance immediately following September 11, 2001, and (D) says that Americans "disapproved" of Congress during that era. The correct answer is (C), since a majority of Americans (that is, more than 50%) approved of Congress's performance only from the late 1990s until about 2004; that's less than 10 years, and the graph shows data for more than 30.

2. **D** Use Process of Elimination. Choice (A) is incorrect, since it has always been extremely rare for congressional candidates to run as independents. Choice (B) may be true, but has no obvious connection to congressional job approval ratings. Choice (C) is probably untrue, and likewise has no obvious connection to congressional job approval ratings. This leaves (D), which is correct because the general trend over the past twenty years has been toward congressional job approval ratings that are consistently smaller than 20%.

3. **D** Use Process of Elimination. More than half of all eligible Latino voters participated in the elections of 1992, so (A) is contradicted right off the bat. (Additionally, this chart doesn't show any results prior to 1988, so avoid answers that draw conclusions about years prior to that.) Choice (B) is unsupported by the data, since we aren't given the number of *registered* voters. Choice (C) is incorrect, since the chart provides no information about "satisfaction" and may well be untrue, since the number of voters increased every year. Choice (D) is correct; the chart shows a widening gap between the number of eligible voters and those who actually voted, so the *percentage* of voter turnout has been declining.

4. **B** There is a consistently higher voter turnout in presidential years (years divisible by 4), than in midterm election years. Choices (A), (C), and (D) contradict this known trend, so choose (B), which accurately suggests that the higher national media coverage of a presidential candidate brings more focus to those elections.

5. **C** The chart shows little difference between the presidential votes of men and women in both the 1972 and the 1976 elections. Starting with the 1980 election, however, a clear gender gap can be seen, with women consistently giving greater support to the Democratic candidate than the men do. Choice (A) is incorrect, since the chart shows that, had only men voted, Ronald Reagan would have won the 1980 election by a greater margin than he actually did. Choice (B) is unsupported, since the chart is measuring Democrat voters, not Republicans, and actually suggests that

from 1980 forward a smaller percentage of women than men voted for the Republican presidential candidate. Because the chart illustrates only the percentage of votes from each gender, it is impossible to draw a conclusion about the number of votes that the candidates received from men and women, so (D) must be incorrect.

6. **C** Some knowledge of the Dole/Clinton election may help here, but is not necessary. Use Process of Elimination. Choice (A) may look correct based on the data supplied in the graph, but it is not certain that the election of 1992 would have bearing on the results of the election of 1996. Choice (B) is incorrect, since both of the major parties tend to receive funding from corporations and trade unions. Also, it is unclear how funding would affect the gender voting gap. That leaves us with (C) and (D), the only answers which directly address the issue of gender. Choice (C) is the best, since Clinton would have successfully captured votes from both Democrat women and moderate Republican women by appealing to domestic issues of concern to them. Dole was unsuccessful by appealing solely to his party's base. Choice (D) is incorrect, since married women do not swing Democrat in most elections.

7. **D** To eliminate (A), you'd have to find at least one instance in which Medicare funding does not increase; that's in the West between 2004 and 2008. To eliminate (B), see if there are any regions that got more than the West's 17,000,000 in funding; that would be the South, with 18,400,000. In 2008, the North (14.0) received approximately one and a half times the amount of Medicare funding as the Northeast (9.6). Accordingly, the correct answer is (D) because the South experienced the greatest increase in Medicare funding from 2000–2012, having increased by $6.6 million over the 12-year period.

8. **A** Medicare is a federal entitlement program that provides health insurance to senior citizens and certain disabled people. Since the spending on entitlement programs can vary from year to year, Congress must often debate where to get the funding for such programs; eliminate (B). Although states do have some control over the disbursement of entitlements, federal budget committees do have the final say on how much federal money is allotted to such programs, which rules out (C). Democrats and Republicans often disagree on spending of all kinds, which also eliminates (D). This leaves (A) as the best answer, since spending on entitlement programs will often put pressure on budget committees to cut discretionary spending.

9. **B** Compare each of the four "Democratic" bars (on the bottom) with the corresponding "Republican" bars on the top and then run through the choices, eliminating those that don't match. Choice (A) is incorrect because the chart does not include information about registered voters. Choice (C) is incorrect because the chart does not include information about governors. Choice (D) is likewise wrong because the chart does not include information about party representation in individual state legislatures. (Remember that graph questions on the AP U.S. Government and Politics Exam ask only that you identify indisputable conclusions. Do not try to "read between the lines" and interpret the data—you will only get into trouble that way.) Only (B), the correct answer, reflects that Democrats controlled more seats through the early '90s before that trend began to reverse itself in 2000.

10. **C** According to the bar graph, throughout the 1990s and early 2000s, Republicans generally gained more seats in state legislatures, while Democrats generally lost seats. Therefore, the trend is toward a more equal balance of power. Choice (A) is incorrect, since there is no reason to conclude that more Republican victories would encourage third-party activity. Choice (B) is incorrect, since social media was virtually nonexistent in the 1990s and would not have been favored by either party in particular. Choice (D) is tempting, but we do not know if the shift in party dominance was a cause or effect of political polarization; either is equally plausible. Only (C) matches the data, which is that despite having a majority in many legislatures, Democrats would have needed the support of at least a few Republicans for controversial pieces of legislation, so as to offset any Democrat legislators who might not vote in harmony with the majority of the party.

11. **B** Choice (A) would contradict McGranery's belief that resolving civil rights questions would be in the best interests of the United States overall. Choice (C) may look tempting, but is worded much more broadly than the thesis McGranery puts forward. Choice (D) is close, but actually reverses McGranery's argument: he thinks that "removing flaws in our democracy" promotes better relationships with other countries, not vice versa. The correct answer must be (B), which aptly summarizes the message in McGranery's remarks.

12. **D** Use Process of Elimination. Choices (A) and (B) have no connection to racial civil rights, which is the topic of McGranery's quote. *Brown v. Board of Education* effectively reversed the "separate but equal" doctrine that had stood under *Plessy v. Ferguson*, thus (D) is our best choice.

13. **A** McGranery dealt with the legal issues of providing African Americans around the country with "equal protection" from undue discrimination and with the unlawfulness of school segregation. Choices (B) and (C) are largely procedural in nature, and don't encompass the scope of this legislation. The establishment clause, (D), is bigger, but largely pertains to religious freedom cases, which are another category altogether. Choice (A) is correct because the Supreme Court has used the equal protection clause of the Fourteenth Amendment to provide justification for federal laws over state laws.

14. **C** This question is asking you to summarize McGranery's argument. Choice (A) is untrue, since the Civil Rights Act of 1964 was necessary to bring an end to discrimination laws in the South. Choice (B) may seem close, but there is no mention of "confusion" in McGranery's quote, nor would foreign nations necessarily concern themselves with our Constitution. Choice (D) is too strong and is not supported by McGranery's statements. Since McGranery believes that U.S. domestic policy regarding civil rights can affect our relationships with other countries around the world (foreign policy), (C) is the best choice.

15. **B** Recall that the Tenth Amendment clarifies whether the federal or state government has authority in any given situation. The "full faith and credit" clause requires states to honor one another's laws, licenses, and so on. It does not, however, deal with infringements on state governments by the

national government, and so you can eliminate (A). The provisions for the impeachment of a president pertain only to the national government, so (C) can also be eliminated. The clause prohibiting states from coining money and entering into treaties appears in the body of the Constitution, which means that there is no conflict with the amendment, and (D) can be eliminated as well. Only the "necessary and proper" clause, often referred to as the elastic clause, creates an issue with the Tenth Amendment, as it allows Congress to pass new laws that would expand its authority over states' rights; this means that (B) is the correct answer.

16. **D** The term Federalist, (A), refers either to those who support the federal system or to members of the Federalist Party, which existed from the late 1700s until the late 1810s. Either way, it describes a person who supports a strong central government, so eliminate it. The term isolationist, (B), refers to a person who believes that the government should avoid involvement with foreign governments and nations. Choice (B) can be eliminated. The term loose constructionist, (C), refers to a person who believes the national government should use the elastic clause to expand its powers. Loose constructionists argue that the national government may do anything not expressly forbidden by the Constitution. They do not see the Tenth Amendment as a significant limitation of federal power, and for this reason, (C) can be elimianted. States' Righters, (D), believe that the Constitution limits the national government to its specifically enumerated powers. They also believe that the vast majority of governance should be left entirely to the states. This makes (D) the correct answer.

17. **C** Although the Tenth Amendment grants that states often have discretion in how they govern their own affairs, they do not have the legal right to circumvent federal law. Attempts by state and local governments to assert actions such as those described in (A), (B), and (D) have consistently failed in federal courts. Choice (C) is an attempt by the federal government to influence the states, while not unduly coercing them, and so would be harmonious with the Tenth Amendment.

18. **D** Since the boundaries of the district are oddly shaped and have changed over time, this is a classic example of gerrymandering. Gerrymandering is a practice of designing districts with non-geographical considerations in mind, which rules out (A). Although racial gerrymandering is illegal, in some parts of the country parties routinely create districts with irregular boundaries in order to deliberately include (or exclude) certain cities or counties that have historically voted for one party or another. This is the opposite of what (B) and (C) suggests, so you can also eliminate those. Choice (D) is the best description of gerrymandering.

19. **A** Gerrymandered congressional districts such as the one in this map are designed to group together voters of a single party, hoping that the results of an election in that district will be easily predicted. This leads to less competitive elections (A), not more competitive ones (B). There is no benefit to third-party candidates (C), nor is gerrymandering linked to high voter turnout (D). If anything, voters in the minority party may become less likely to participate, believing that their votes have less influence.

20. **A** The first frame of the cartoon humorously depicts an angry voter holding up a newspaper indicating that it is congressional primary season. The voter says, "Throw the bums out!," a common

refrain among citizens who have a low opinion of members of Congress generally. In the second frame, we see the headline "Entrenched Incumbents Win" and a smiling voter. We can infer that voters, no matter how upset they may be with Congress in general, tend to be loyal to their local senators and representatives. Thus, the make-up of Congress does not change dramatically from one election to another, despite its generally low approval ratings. Choice (B) is not supported by the second frame, which depicts the voter expressing happiness that his "entrenched incumbent" has won. Choice (C) is incorrect, since the cartoon is about primary elections. (Also, it would be impossible to win general elections without winning primaries first.) Choice (D) is backward: according to the cartoon, voters are angry about Congress in general, but tend to reelect their local representatives. Choice (A) is the best match.

21. **B**   Since the cartoon depicts incumbents winning elections, we are looking for a choice which is close to that. Choice (A) is not always true, and the cartoon does not distinguish between the two houses of Congress. Choice (C) is incorrect, since the cartoon is about voting, not communication. Choice (D) is going in the opposite direction. Choice (B) is true; incumbents do generally enjoy a tremendous advantage over their challengers.

22. **D**   Compare each choice to what's shown in the graph and use Process of Elimination. Choice (A) can be ruled out immediately, as the graph measures money, not political influence. Choice (B) can be likewise dismissed, since we have no evidence that it is the "fastest-growing." Be careful with (C). Though it may be true, this graph does not break down contributions by political party. For (D), add the totals of all PAC contributions in each of the listed elections from the early 1990s. In each election, the sum is greater than $150 million, which means that (D) is the correct answer. (Remember that this is only the tip of the iceberg: candidates raise money from private donors and many other sources as well.)

23. **A**   This question asks what an opponent of PAC contributions might claim, which means you're looking for a valid concern about PAC money. Voter turnout and election fraud are not clearly linked to PAC contributions, so rule out (B) and (C). Choice (D) is too vague, because opponents of PACs fear their influence in all aspects of politics, including lobbying. This leaves (A), which is a valid concern about how a politician might end up beholden to a few corporate sources, as opposed to having to represent many individual sources.

24. **B**   A constitution specifies what a government is allowed to do, and also what it may not do. Eliminate any choice that does not match with the framers' intentions for the Constitution. Choice (A) describes a form of democratic government in which all citizens vote on all issues, but the Constitution established a representative democracy, in which citizens vote for representatives who, in turn, act on their behalf and assume the nation's legislative and executive duties. Eliminate (A). Choice (C) is also incorrect, as the abolition of slavery was not committed to until the ratification of the Thirteenth Amendment in 1865. You can eliminate (D) for a similar reason; the Bill of Rights, which would protect the rights of the accused, was not ratified until 1791. This leaves (B) as the correct answer, and it is true that by setting limits on the government with the constitution, the framers hoped to prevent the government from seizing power, as the British monarchy had done.

25. **C** If you don't recall what *The Federalist Papers* were, use Process of Elimination to find wrong answers. You can eliminate (A) because the Federalist party did not have a platform; platforms are the product of political conventions, which were not a part of American politics until after the Federalist Party. You may be able to eliminate (B) if you can recall that *The Federalist Papers* were neither anti-British nor, as they were written in 1787, pre-Revolutionary. Choice (D) can also be ruled out, as this is describing a portion of the U.S. Constitution. This leaves (C), which correctly identifies the collective essays of Alexander Hamilton, James Madison, and John Jay published in support of ratification of the Constitution.

26. **A** Consider whether each choice fits with the notion of changing public policy or altering precedent. The due process clause of the Fourteenth Amendment prohibits the states from depriving citizens of life, liberty, or property without a fair and impartial hearing; this has nothing to do with changing policy, so eliminate (B). Judicial restraint suggests an unwillingness to break with precedent or to overturn legislative and executive acts, which is the opposite of what the question is looking for, so you can also eliminate (C). An *ex post facto* law allows a government to prosecute citizens for acts that were legal at the time they occurred, but were later deemed illegal. Not only doesn't this match the question, but this form of lawmaking is explicitly prohibited by the Constitution, so throw out (D) as well. Judicial activism refers to the actions of a court that frequently strikes down or alters the acts of the executive and/or legislative branches, which perfectly describes the given scenario. Choice (A) is the correct answer.

27. **B** Use Process of Elimination. Congress can override a presidential veto, so eliminate (A). The First Amendment prohibits the establishment of a national religion, which rules out (C). And when it comes to control of the bureaucracy, Congress often has more power than the president, given that it can affirm or reject presidential appointments, abolish agencies, determine the funding an agency receives, and change agency jurisdiction if unsatisfied with policy implementation. Eliminate (D). Choice (B) is the correct answer.

28. **D** The House Rules Committee is in charge, as you might expect from the name, of setting certain rules. The House Ethics Committee is in charge of investigating ethics charges against House members, so eliminate (A). The Senate, not the House, provides "advice and consent" to the president on judicial nominees, so rule out (B). The number of subcommittees is limited by budget and staffing considerations, not by a separate committee, so eliminate (C) as well. This leaves (D) as the correct answer: the Rules Committee controls the terms of debate and the scheduling of floor votes, which makes them quite powerful.

29. **A** Political action committees (PACs) want to see that those who represent their point of view are elected. Choice (B) wouldn't necessarily have this effect, as a get-out-the-vote campaign might lead voters to choose a different candidate. Choice (C) is also not specific enough; a PAC might try defeat an incumbent, but would do so only if that incumbent failed to represent their point of view or actively worked against them. Choice (D) can be outright eliminated; a PACs primary function is not to organize protests or civil disobedience, which would be very indirect ways of influencing

an election. Choice (A) is correct because a PAC largely exists to raise political funds for electoral campaigns and distribute them to candidates.

30. **B** Network news programs—which are separate from debates and long-form interviews—tend to favor information that changes regularly and can be communicated quickly. The endorsement of a special interest group is generally stable, and is likely to be reported on only once; eliminate (A). The same goes for candidates' positions on issues, which are not only complex and difficult to capture in sound bites or TV-friendly phrases and clips, but unlikely to change. As a result, you can eliminate (C) and (D) as well. The correct answer is (B), because public opinion is constantly shifting and is most likely to be repeated on a regular basis.

31. **D** This question is testing one of the less-discussed facets of the First Amendment. Be careful on questions like these, as the wrong answers—which appear in other amendments—will sound familiar. Choices (A) and (B) can be eliminated because they have to do with the Fifth Amendment, whereas (C) is from the Eighth Amendment. Choice (D) is the correct answer, as the First Amendment, which deals with different types of freedom of speech, states that "Congress shall make no law...abridging...the right of the people...to petition the Government for a redress of grievances."

32. **D** Use Process of Elimination. You don't need to recognize both cases in an answer choice; if one of them doesn't apply, then the whole choice can be eliminated. You can eliminate (A) because *Near v. Minnesota* and *New York Times v. Sullivan* focused on freedom of the press, not privacy. You can cross off (B) because *Texas v. Johnson* and *Morse v. Frederick* were rulings regarding freedom of speech. Throw out (C) because *Thornhill v. Alabama* and *Cox v. New Hampshire* were related to the freedom of assembly and association. While the right to privacy is not explicitly mentioned in the Constitution, in *Griswold v. Connecticut* the Warren Court ruled that the Bill of Rights contained an implied right to privacy. In *Roe v. Wade*, the Court established national abortion guidelines by extending the inferred right of privacy from *Griswold v. Connecticut*.

33. **D** Federalism is a system under which the federal government shares power with the states. The system of checks and balances among the three branches of the federal government concerns the national government only, and not the states, eliminate (A). International treaties are the sole responsibility of the federal government, and do not relate to the states in any way, so (B) can also be eliminated. Washington, D.C., does have special constitutional status as the nation's capital, and is governed by the federal government. However, it is not represented in Congress at the state level, so (C) doesn't really pertain to American federalism. Choice (D) must be the correct answer: the Tenth Amendment to the Constitution assigns to the states all powers not granted the national government by the Constitution. It is instrumental in defining the relationship between the two levels of government, which is the essence of federalism.

34. **B** If you don't remember, use POE to rule out answers that couldn't have been mentioned in the Constitution. Judicial review allows the Supreme Court to overturn laws on the basis of their constitutionality, but wasn't established until 1803, with Chief Justice John Marshall's decision in the

1803 *Marbury v. Madison* case; eliminate (A). Recall elections and public education would be covered at the state level, and so are not mentioned in the U.S. Constitution; eliminate (C) and (D). This leaves (B), the census, which must be taken every ten years, according to Article I, Section 2 of the Constitution.

35. **A** Use Process of Elimination to rule out choices that you know aren't right. For instance, while the president may recommend bills to Congress and can strongly influence public sentiment on legislation, the president cannot directly introduce anything; eliminate (B). Likewise, the only point at which the president can address Congress is during the State of the Union, so eliminate (C). Don't overthink this question; the president may be able to influence congressional votes as the leader of his or her party, but the president cannot vote, so eliminate (D) as well. Only (A) is a right granted by Article II, Section 3 of the Constitution, which states that the president may, "on extraordinary occasions, convene both Houses, or either of them."

36. **C** This question is looking for powers that are *shared* with the Senate, which means that you can eliminate any answers that are exclusive to the executive or legislative branches. Choices (A) and (D) are powers that can only be exercised by the president, and (B) is under the sole discretion of Congress; all three of these choices can be eliminated. This means that (C) is the correct answer, which fits with Article II, Section 2 of the Constitution, which requires that two-thirds of the Senate concur with a treaty.

37. **D** Consider the choices. If (B) were true, no Republican could ever win the presidency, because most Democrats and moderate Republicans would vote Democratic. Such a sizable coalition would win every election, so eliminate (B). If (C) were true, then how conservative a candidate was during the primaries wouldn't matter, so eliminate (C). The two remaining choices are opposites of one another, so consider the scenario. Those most active in both the Republican and Democratic parties tend to be further from the political center than average rank-and-file party members. Because party activists control much of the nomination process and are more likely than others to vote in primary elections, successful presidential nominees tend to reflect the political agendas of these activists. This has been particularly true of the Republican Party in recent years; most candidates for the Republican presidential nomination focus great effort on winning support from the party's small but powerful ultraconservative wing. Choice (A) says the opposite of this, which means that (D) is the correct answer.

38. **A** Confirmation powers are not relevant to committees, so eliminate (B). In both the Senate and the House, members of committees are assigned by the majority party, so eliminate (C). Choice (D) is wrong, since committees in both the Senate and the House consist of members from both parties, although the majority party generally has more members. The correct answer is (A), as the large size of the House of Representatives means that more work can be done in committees than when all representatives are assembled on the floor.

39. **D** As chief of state, the president receives and negotiates with foreign leaders. This means that as America's role in world affairs increases, so too does the president's power. Since 1932, America has

in fact enjoyed increased prominence in foreign affairs, so you can rule out (A). Choices (B) and (C) are false statements; public confidence in the federal government has generally decreased since the 1950s, while entitlement spending has increased. This means that (D) is the correct answer. Constant media exposure has given the American public greater awareness of each president since Franklin Roosevelt. The president is now better known and more widely heard than at any time in the past. This allows the president to influence voters in a way that no president before 1932 possibly could.

40. **D** The House and the Senate must pass the same version of a bill before the president may consider it, which means that (A) can be eliminated. Be careful regarding (B) and (C)—while a bill may ultimately end up going back to the House and Senate or might get sent to the president in its original form, this is not the first thing that would happen. Choice (D) is the correct answer; the legislative bodies would meet and first try to draft a compromise bill.

41. **B** Use Process of Elimination. Choice (A) is incorrect because people are actually less likely to vote if they believe one candidate is too far ahead of the others. Choice (C) is wrong, because a strong party affiliation makes one more likely to vote. Choice (D) can also be eliminated, given that there is actually a strong correlation between higher education and a tendency to vote. Only (B) is true, given that—setting aside unions—white-collar workers vote more often than blue-collar workers.

42. **A** While the overall voting habits of white females can vary, unmarried white females have historically favored the Democratic candidate; eliminate (B). Since Franklin Roosevelt's presidency, African Americans (C) have overwhelmingly identified as Democrats in a trend that continues to the present. Barack Obama won a whopping 96% and 93% of the African American vote in 2008 and 2012, respectively. Likewise, in the 2016 presidential election, Hillary Clinton received 88% of the African American vote. The majority of youths (D) voted for candidates Jimmy Carter (1976), Bill Clinton (1996), Barack Obama (2008 and 2012), and Hillary Clinton (2016). Married, white males have preferred the Republican candidate for president in every election since 1972, which makes the answer (A).

43. **A** For a comparison question, remember that if one part of the choice is inaccurate, you can eliminate the entire choice. With that in mind, look to eliminate (B) and (C), because *McDonald v. Chicago* actually curtailed local control in favor of the Second Amendment. You can also eliminate (D), because the two choices have been swapped—it was *United States v. Lopez* that declared the Gun-Free School Zones Act unconstitutional. Choice (A) is the correct answer. *United States v. Lopez* held that Congress does not have the power to regulate guns near state-operated schools by invoking the commerce clause and *McDonald v. Chicago* found that the right of an individual to "keep and bear arms" as protected under the Second Amendment was incorporated by the due process clause of the Fourteenth Amendment.

44. **C** Use POE. The two parts of (A) contradict each other; if a state judiciary is higher than a federal one, then how is a federal one able to overturn state decisions? That's because federal courts are higher than state courts and while they *may* overturn state court decisions, it is only on the

grounds that a defendant's constitutional rights were violated. Eliminate (A). Additionally, you can eliminate (D), because federal courts are not solely appeals courts. Between the remaining choices, (B) is more extreme than (C), suggesting that state judiciaries are *entirely* autonomous, when in fact there are some exceptions, such as when state cases are appealed to federal courts on constitutional grounds, or when there is a jurisdictional concern. Choice (C) is the correct answer; eliminate (B).

45.   **C**   Use POE to rule out unlikely choices. A reprieve is a postponement of legal punishment, whereas a pardon is an immediate forgiving of a crime. Neither one has a specific number of years associated with it, so (A) can be eliminated. Pay close attention to how extreme the choices in (D) are; would it make sense for a president to be able to pardon someone but not grant that person a reprieve? Eliminate (D). The final two choices are opposites of each other. Here, knowing the definitions of the words outside of the context of your AP U.S. Government class might help you to eliminate (B), which reverses the meanings, and to choose (C), the correct answer.

46.   **D**   Democratic Party platforms generally align more closely to liberal ideological positions, whereas the Republican Party generally favors conservative ideological positions, so rule out (A). Democrats, not Republicans, tend to favor more governmental regulation of the marketplace, so cross out (B). Neither party tends to favor a national religion and Democrats are typically champions of public education, which means you can also eliminate (C). This leaves (D) as the correct answer.

47.   **C**   Start by eliminating anything that does not match with the First Amendment. Choice (B) mentions the right to an attorney, which was a judicial interpretation of the Sixth Amendment, not the First. Now turn to the Fourth Amendment; the ruling in *Wisconsin v. Yoder* pertains to the free exercise of religion, which is the First, not the Fourth, so eliminate (A). For the final two choices, you can eliminate (D) because *Roe v. Wade* was based on the Due Process of the Fourteenth Amendment, not the Fourth. Choice (C) is the correct answer, and accurately describes aspects of both amendments.

48.   **D**   Consider the ramifications of the Civil Rights Act and use Process of Elimination. This act did not involve a presidential veto or have anything to do with one branch of government checking another, so eliminate (A) and (B). If anything, the passing of this law did the opposite of (C), in that it allowed the federal government to restrict a state's power, whether that was by cutting off federal funding to discriminatory programs or allowing the Justice Department to file desegregation suits. Choice (D) is correct, as the "privileges or immunities of citizens of the United States" were being restricted, and racial discrimination and segregation still existed.

49.   **B**   *The Federalist Papers* took a negative view of political factions and would not have approved of any political system that encouraged their growth, so eliminate (A). Likewise, Republican federalism was designed to limit the influence of political factions on all levels, so (C) can be cut as well. That said, James Madison acknowledged in "Federalist No. 10" that political factions would form whenever people disagreed or put their personal welfare above the best interests of the state, so the extreme answer of (D), "any opportunity," can also be eliminated. Choice (B) is the correct answer, as federalism diluted a faction's power by separating the powers and making it hard for any one faction to control the entire governing process.

50. **B** Under the Articles of Confederation the national government was entirely dependent on the states to enforce national law, as it had no executive powers of its own, so eliminate (A). The Constitution rectified this problem by establishing the executive branch of government. Under the Articles of Confederation the national government had no authority to regulate interstate trade. The Constitution grants this power to Congress, so eliminate (C). Neither the Articles nor the original Constitution had a universal suffrage clause, so (D) is also incorrect. Choice (B) is correct, since the Articles did not allow for any federal taxation, while the Constitution enabled Washington, D.C., to levy taxes in order to fund such efforts as the military.

51. **A** National policy can be set either by Congress or the president, so use POE on those choices that would have no effect on Congress's power. Choice (B) can be immediately eliminated, as there are situations in which Congress has power, such as in the year preceding Truman's re-election. The "elastic clause" actually *expands* congressional power, so eliminate (C) as well. As for (D), Congress is often reluctant to challenge the president during wartime, as many believe that it is most important for the country to remain unified, so Congress would actually *lose* power in this situation; eliminate (D). Ultimately, what most impacts the dynamic relationship between Congress and the presidency deals with the political popularity of the two institutions.

52. **B** Cabinet leaders are appointed by the president, and the departments are established by Congress, so eliminate (A). There are no restrictions regarding whom the president can appoint, so (C) is incorrect. There are numerous federal sub-agencies and independent agencies within the bureaucracy, so (D) can also be eliminated. This leaves (B) as the correct answer: despite being appointed by the president, cabinet department leaders sometimes have goals that differ from those of the president.

53. **D** When using Process of Elimination here, remember to keep an eye out for any overly extreme examples. For instance, (A) says that *each* state needs to split its electoral votes, so if there's even one that allocates them by the winner-take-all method—there are in fact 48 that do just this—then you can eliminate (A). There are also answers that are too vague, like (B). Each state is represented by a delegation equal in number to that state's total representation in Congress (senators and members of the House). However, the number of House members for a given state is determined by proportional representation based on population, so a large state like California winds up with 54 votes whereas some states have only the minimum of 3. This is a questionable form of representation, and no correct answer will be questionable on the test, so eliminate (B). Finally, of the remaining choices, (C) can be eliminated on the grounds that the Electoral College was part of the Constitution as originally ratified, not as a later amendment. Choice (D) is therefore correct, which you may recall given that it is possible for a candidate to win the Electoral College (and the presidency) while still losing the popular vote.

54. **D** Of the members of the 111th Congress, 225 (42%) earned a law degree prior to serving in office. This fact should come as no surprise, given that the business of Congress is to pass laws. And as prominent members of the community, lawyers often have the standing to run for and win elected

office. Choice (A) may seem close, but there is very little overlap between the executive and legislative career tracks (with the exception of congresspersons who run for president). Professors, (B), and journalists, (C), are not common occupations for members of Congress.

55.   **B**   By and large, most conservatives believe in small government and individual responsibility, so rule out (A) and (D). Choice (C) describes a racial affirmative action program, which would either be opposed—or simply not promoted—by most conservatives, so rule that out. Choice (B) is the correct answer, as most conservatives are staunch defenders of the Second Amendment right to bear arms.

FREE-RESPONSE SECTION: ANSWERS AND EXPLANATIONS

Remember that you need to answer all four free-response questions in 1 hour and 40 minutes, so you do not have time to waste, nor can you skip any questions. Nevertheless, you should take time to brainstorm some ideas and to organize what you come up with before you start to write each response. Otherwise, your responses will probably be incomplete, disorganized, or both.

You should average about 25 minutes per question. Make sure you read each question carefully and respond directly to each of its components in your response. The questions are about broad issues, but they ask for specific information. A general free response that fails to address specific concerns raised by the question will not earn a high score.

Question 1

(a)   Identify ONE way that candidates for public office are using social media in their campaigns.

Here are some possible topics:
- Direct "crowdfunding" that allows a candidate to raise a little money from a lot of individuals as opposed to a lot of money from a few large corporate donors. Social media in general provides more opportunities for candidates to fund-raise.
- Targeted messaging through sites like Facebook allows candidates to more accurately (and cheaply) rally their bases, or to contact them directly. Weekly and/or daily "blasts" can be sent through email or websites.
- Grassroots activism allows a candidate to amplify his or her message by echoing it through supporters, mobilizing a more active electorate.
- Sophisticated websites help to fight off misinformation and to clearly state simple positions on complicated issues; integrated polls from third-party sites help voters figure out which candidate they most align with.
- Candidates often post videos of speeches to social media sites such as Facebook, YouTube, or Twitter.
- Candidates can purchase ads on social media sites that are frequented by potential supporters.
- Candidates use social media such as Facebook, Twitter, Instagram, Snapchat, and the like to make policy statements and respond instantly to daily news and attacks from opponents.

(b)   For the method identified in Part A, explain the advantages to the candidates of using social media in this way.

- Crowdfunding can help a candidate to avoid seeming as if they are beholden to corporate interests, and as if they are more accessible and involved with their electorate.
- Targeted messaging helps a candidate both to make sure his or her money is being spent as effectively as possible and tightly control his or her message.
- Grassroots activism helps to increase contact with supporters, spread the message, bypass the media, and excite the base.
- Cost-effectiveness—Buying advertisements on social media platforms is cheaper, and also more targeted, than going through traditional mediums.
- Increased contact with supporters—Candidates can reach people who normally don't seek out political content.
- Help to get candidate's message out—Unlimited information can be posted to websites or blogs, thus the candidate is not limited to short sound-bites.
- Speed—Updated information can be disseminated instantly.
- Bypassing the media—Social media content comes directly from the candidate, not filtered by journalists. The campaign retains control of the content and message.
- Environmental responsibility—Mailings clutter up mailboxes and create waste. The Internet is environmentally friendly.
- Fund-raising—Social media is an additional way for candidates to reach donors.

(c)   Identify and explain one way that social media can harm a candidate's campaign.

Of course, while social media campaigning has its advantages, there are also some negative aspects. Part C asks you to address this issue. Be sure to not only *identify* how social media can harm a candidate's campaign, but also explain the *effects* of this harm in as much detail as you can. Be sure that you don't go off on a tangent with your discussion of potential drawbacks. Real examples are always superior to hypotheticals. Possible examples may include:

- One-sided blogs written by representatives of the opponents' campaigns—*Anyone* can post *anything* about the candidate to social media. In many cases, the opposing side may overwhelm voters with negative attacks and drown out the positive message the candidate is trying to spread.
- Attack videos and ads by 501(c)(3) organizations—YouTube and other video sites provide an easy platform for attack ads by opposing organizations.
- Video evidence of a candidate's mistakes posted online and in real-time—Candidate gaffes can spread virally on social media sites.
- Viral emails that spread unsubstantiated rumors—Email is free and can easily be used by the opposition to promote critical or false ideas.

Now you have a plethora of items to support your claims in the essay. All you have to do is flesh out each point to include everything you know about the effects of the Internet on politics.

Question 2

(a)   Which two presidents were responsible for the greatest increases of defense spending since 1953?

First, identify the type of data that you're looking for. In this case, you're looking for increases, so you want to find steep rises on the graph. You can ignore the first, and steepest, increase, because it occurred before 1953. After that point, the two greatest increases occurred under the watch of President Reagan and President George W. Bush.

(b)   Describe a trend in the data and draw a conclusion about the defense spending habits of Republican and Democratic presidents.

- Defense spending spiked at the beginning of the Korean and Vietnam Wars, and again during the War on Terror (fought in Iraq and Afghanistan). As both Democratic and Republican presidents led the nation during these times, it appears as if presidents' political affiliation has little effect on defense spending during a time of war.
- You might also have written about the peacetime trend, in which the nation's defense budget falls to approximately four hundred billion dollars. Again, as both Republican and Democratic presidents led during these eras, one can again conclude that factors besides politics influence defense spending decisions.

(c)   Explain how the defense spending as shown in the graph relates to iron triangles within the federal government.

Iron triangles represent the symbiotic relationship between Congress, the bureaucracy, and interest groups. In the case of defense spending, congressional committees related to defense, interest groups promoting military spending, and bureaucratic agencies overseeing defense spending, such as the DoD, make up an iron triangle. At the beginning of an armed conflict, Congress would increase funding to the DoD and accept ideas from interest groups. In return, interest groups would raise money for congressional elections and lobby for the DoD. The DoD would execute Congress's wishes while granting special favors to lobbyists. This unique relationship also helps explain why defense spending returns to the $400 billion mark during peacetime. Although the nation may not need to spend this much on defense, the nature of iron triangles ensures a level of spending, political support, and granting of favors wherein all parties are satisfied.

Question 3

(a)   Identify a constitutional amendment or clause that was used to justify the decisions in both *Powell v. Alabama* (1932) and *Gideon v. Wainwright* (1963).

- *Powell* and *Gideon* were both in violation of the due process clause of the Fourteenth amendment. For *Powell*, convictions had been made under unfair conditions—only one-day trials—and were thus invalid.
- Both were also in violation of the Sixth Amendment. There can be no fair trial if a defense attorney is not provided.

(b)   Based on the constitutional amendment identified in Part A, explain how *Gideon v. Wainwright* expanded upon the decision in *Powell v. Alabama*.

- *Powell* provided the right to representation to only those accused of capital crimes.
- *Gideon* provided the right to representation for all defendants. Between *Powell* and *Gideon*, cases like *Betts v. Brady* (1942) asserted that publically appointed counsel was not required.
- Before *Gideon*, judges used their own discretion to determine whether defendants might receive court-appointed counsel, thus leading to unfair and uneven outcomes in criminal trials.

(c)   Describe historical changes that have been made to the prosecution of defendants since the *Gideon v. Wainwright* decision.

- Thousands of individuals around the country who had not received adequate representation in court were freed as a result of the *Gideon* decision.
- State and municipal courts adopted universal rules and established the offer of appointed counsel as a matter of right, without a defendant's need to petition the judge for a special appointment of counsel.
- States established Public Defender offices throughout their jurisdictions to accommodate the needs of defendants who do not have the desire or resources to acquire their own private attorneys.
- A defendant can waive his right to counsel by pleading guilty or by choosing to represent himself in court. In lieu of these choices, however, a Public Defender will be assigned to his case automatically.

Question 4

Develop an argument that explains whether increased power vested to the federal government or increased power vested to the States best achieves the founders' intent for American democracy in terms of ensuring a stable government run by the people.

- This essay is focusing on the principle of federalism, the power that the federal government has in relation to state governments. Over time, more and more power has tended to gravitate away from the states and toward Washington, D.C.

Articulate a defensible claim or thesis that responds to the prompt and establishes a line of reasoning.

- The two possible theses here are that more power entrusted to the federal government is beneficial for the smooth operation of society, or, alternatively, that the states are the rightful guardians of power and should not be usurped by Washington, D.C.

Support your claim with at least TWO pieces of accurate and relevant information.

- **Articles of Confederation:** Under these articles, which deprived the federal government of things like the power to levy taxes, the country ran into many social issues. Being unable to pay off the debts from the Revolutionary War, for example, weakened the economic progress of the new Republic. On the other hand, had states kept this autonomy, the federal government may not have later been able to abuse its power, as it did when enforcing new taxes (in the 1791's Whiskey Rebellion) or when suppressing voters in 1798's Alien and Sedition Acts.
- **Brutus No. 1** was one in a series of anonymous essays designed to raise skepticism regarding the early Constitution. The Anti-Federalist who wrote this paper objected to the overreach of federal power mainly on the grounds that it would detract from personal freedom. He demanded a Bill of Rights, warned of the power of Congress, and believed that a national standing army would be a threat to the liberty of both other nations and Americans themselves. Brutus favored a confederation of independent states with maximum autonomy. Most notably, Brutus warned that the **U.S. Supreme Court** would garner too much unchecked power.
- **Shays' Rebellion (1786)**, a Massachusetts farmers' rebellion that pointed out the weakness of the Articles and bolstered the **Federalist** cause to create a stronger federal government.
- **Bill of Rights (1787).** The first ten Amendments to the Constitution were demanded by Anti-Federalists to serve as a bulwark against excessive federal power. The **Tenth Amendment** specifically grants all powers not delegated to the federal government to revert back to the sovereignty of individual states.
- **Sixteenth Amendment (1913).** This amendment arguably expanded federal power more than any other law had done up to this point, since it allowed Congress to levy a broad-based tax on personal and business income. For the first time, all Americans with income could be required to participate in the financial maintenance of government bureaucracy. The federal budget has expanded rapidly since the passage of a national income tax.
- **Seventeenth Amendment (1913).** This amendment ended the practice of the election of senators by state legislatures and provided for the direct election of senators by citizens at the ballot box. Although the amendment certainly gave more power to the populace, it took power away from state legislatures, thus radically altering the balance of federalism up to that point. Those who favored the amendment argued that it diminished the influence of corruption and cronyism at the state level. Opponents argued that direct election of senators would allow senators to disregard the concerns of their home states.

- **Loose Constructionism**. Putting more power in the hands of the federal government requires a flexible interpretation of the Constitution, since the Constitution does not explicitly grant many powers to Washington, D.C., (though it does not forbid them, either). The creation of the **First National Bank** by **Alexander Hamilton**, for instance, was opposed by Anti-Federalists who tended toward **strict constructionism** (limitation of federal power to only powers enumerated in Article I).
- **James Madison.** Fourth president and "Father of the Constitution," he co-authored the **Federalist Papers** (along with **Alexander Hamilton** and **John Jay**). Interestingly, Madison started out as a Federalist, favoring a strong central government, then converted to Anti-Federalism in 1791, joining **Thomas Jefferson** in the newly formed (**Anti-Federalist**) **Democratic-Republican** Party. **Federalist #10** is particularly relevant to this topic, since Madison talks extensively about the dangers of factionalism and how a representative democracy is the proper antidote to imbalance of power. Madison specifically touts the virtues of a large republic over a small one, since it flattens out group differences. Thus, this document is a good choice if you are arguing in favor of federal power.

In addition to the documents above, you also have the freedom to reference the following issues. Many of them can be used to bolster either a pro-federal or pro-states argument:

- **Louisiana Purchase (1803)** and other historical **acquisitions of territory**. No doubt a positive manifestation of federal power, the Louisiana Purchase doubled the size of the United States. Such a vast tract of land could not have been acquired without federal money and influence. Napoleon ceded the Louisiana Territory in exchange for cash and debt forgiveness. Likewise, most of the modern land on which the United States stands was acquired through actions of the U.S. government, not the states. This is a powerful argument in favor of federal power.
- **Taxation/Debt**. Increased federal power inevitably leads to national taxation and debt. Republicans might argue that it is oppressive to tax working people to pay for expensive federal programs. Democrats might argue that a strong central government benefits everyone, including the working poor.
- *McCulloch v. Maryland* (1819). Under Supreme Court Chief Justice John Marshall, this case allowed the Federal government to pass laws not explicitly mentioned in the Constitution. It grants Congress **implied powers** in order to create a functioning national government. The case stopped the state of Maryland's tax on the Second Bank of the United States. The court ruled that this was a form of nullification that impeded the functioning of the federal government.
- **National Banking Acts of 1863–1866 and the Federal Reserve Act of 1913**. After the expiration of the Second Bank of the United States, this series of acts permanently established a nationally regulated banking system and a national currency.
- **New Deal (1993–1938)**. A tremendous assertion of federal power, the New Deal enacted various federally funded programs to help rebuild the American economy after the Great Depression. President Franklin D. Roosevelt's national government needed state and local government cooperation in order to implement its policies. The New Deal was highly controversial both because it required a significant outlay of federal dollars in order to succeed and because it bypassed state legislatures. President Lyndon Johnson's **Great Society** welfare programs of the 1960s were controversial for the same reasons.
- **Block grants (1980s)**. President Ronald Reagan attempted to turn some power back to the states by distributing federal money in the form of block grants. Unlike previous grants which greatly restricted the way federal money could be spent, block grants allowed states to spend money as they saw fit.

- **Decriminalization/Legalization of marijuana (1990s to present).** Various states' attempts to legalize marijuana for either medicinal or recreational use have tested the boundaries of federalism in a power struggle that is not yet resolved. Several states currently have laws which allow for the medicinal cultivation, possession, and use of marijuana. As of the elections in 2016, eight states plus the District of Columbia have passed measures legalizing marijuana for recreational use. They are Alaska, Washington, Oregon, California, Nevada, Colorado, Maine, and Massachusetts. As more states continue to follow their lead, this issue will no doubt continue to be an important test of the balance of state and federal power.
- **Gun control.** Gun control is an interesting example of the see-saw of federalism. The Second Amendment of the Constitution guarantees the individual right to keep and bear arms, while states and cities have broad latitude to limit ownership in certain locales, set requirements for ownership of guns, and need not recognize the gun laws of other states. The federal government, on the other hand, asserts its authority upon states by requiring background checks, forbidding the ownership of guns by felons, and banning the possession of guns on school property.

Respond to an opposing or alternative perspective using refutation, concession, or rebuttal.

A good rebuttal to an opposing point of view requires knowing the pros and cons of each side of the debate.

Federal Power

Pros:

- Abundant financial resources
- National reach and scope
- Uniform laws and standards nationwide
- Extensive national infrastructure for implementation of laws and enforcement of policies

Cons:
- More potential for waste and inefficiency at a large scale of implementation
- A "one size fits all" approach may not meet the needs of all states
- Takes power and decision-making away from the people
- Allows one political party to gather power (factionalism)

State Power

Pros:

- Allows for a diversity of approaches to tough problems.
- Allows solutions targeted to the regional and demographic needs of each locale.
- Smaller programs tend to run more efficiently.
- Funding can come in a variety of ways, not always tied to an income tax.
- Through the election of state representatives and governors, the people have more direct participation in the process.

Cons:
- Too much variation from state to state can create confusion and irregular enforcement across state lines.
- States may struggle to fund initiatives that the federal government could fund more easily.
- Enforcement is limited by the resources in each state, county, and municipality.
- Some states may neglect to address issues altogether.

Glossary

adversarial system A system of law in which the court is seen as a neutral area where disputants can argue the merits of their cases.

affirmative action Government-mandated programs that seek to create special employment opportunities for minorities, women, and other victims of past discrimination.

amendment Addition to the Constitution. Amendments require approval by two-thirds of both houses of Congress and three-quarters of the states. The first ten amendments make up the Bill of Rights.

amicus curiae **briefs** "Friend of the court" briefs that qualified individuals or organizations file in lawsuits to which they are not a party, so the judge may consider their advice in respect to matters of law that directly affect the cases in question.

appellate jurisdiction Term used to describe courts whose role is to hear appeals from lower courts.

Articles of Confederation The United States' first constitution. The government formed by the Articles of Confederation lasted from 1781 (the year before the end of the Revolutionary War) to 1789. The government under the Articles proved inadequate because it did not have the power to collect taxes from the states, nor could it regulate foreign trade to generate revenue from import and export tariffs.

bicameral legislature Consisting of two legislative houses. The United States has a bicameral legislature; its two houses are the House of Representatives and the Senate.

Bill of Rights First ten amendments to the U.S. Constitution. The Bill of Rights guarantees personal liberties and limits the powers of the government.

blanket primary Primary election in which voters may select a candidate from any party for each office. Blanket primaries use the same procedure as general elections. (Note: This type of primary has been struck down in states where it once existed by the Supreme Court. A variation of the primary, the nonpartisan blanket primary, currently exists in Louisiana and Washington.)

block grants Federal money given to states with only general guidelines for its use. The states have the authority to decide how the money will be spent.

bread-and-butter issues Those political issues that are specifically directed at the daily concerns of most working-class Americans, such as job security, tax rates, wages, and employee benefits.

broad constructionism Belief that the Constitution should be interpreted loosely when concerning the restrictions it places on federal power. Broad constructionists emphasize the importance of the elastic clause, which allows Congress to pass laws "necessary and proper" to the performance of its duties.

Brown v. Board of Education The 1954 case in which the Supreme Court overturned the "separate but equal" standard as it applied to education. In a 9-to-0 decision, the court ruled that "separate educational facilities are inherently unequal." "Separate but equal" had been the law of the land since the court had approved it in *Plessy v. Ferguson* (1896).

budget deficit Condition that arises when federal expenditures exceed revenues; in other words, when the government spends more money than it takes in.

budget resolution Set of budget guidelines that must pass both houses of Congress in identical form by April 15. The budget resolution guides government spending for the following fiscal year.

categorical grants Federal aid given to states with strings attached. To receive the money, the states must agree to adhere to federally mandated guidelines for spending it.

caucus Meeting of local party members for the purpose of choosing delegates to a national party convention. The term also refers to a meeting of the Democratic members of the House of Representatives.

census The process, mandated by the Constitution, by which the population of the United States is officially counted every ten years. Census data is then used to help distribute federal money and to reapportion congressional districts.

checks and balances The system that prevents any branch of government from becoming too powerful by requiring the approval of more than one branch for all important acts.

civil court Court in which lawsuits are heard. In contrast, criminal cases are heard in criminal court.

civil disobedience Nonviolent civil disobedience requires activists to protest peacefully against laws they believe unjust and to be willing to accept arrest as a means of demonstrating the justice of their cause. The notion was popularized by 19th-century American writer Henry David Thoreau and was practiced by Martin Luther King, Jr.

civil liberties Those protections against government power embodied in the Bill of Rights and similar legislation. Civil liberties include the right to free speech, free exercise of religion, and right to a fair trial.

civil rights Those protections against discrimination by the government and individuals. Civil rights are intended to prevent discrimination based on race, religion, gender, ethnicity, physical handicap, or sexual orientation.

Civil Rights Act of 1964 Federal law that made segregation illegal in most public places, increased penalties and sentences for those convicted of discrimination in employment, and withheld federal aid from schools that discriminated on the basis of race or gender.

civil service system Method of hiring federal employees based on merit rather than on political beliefs or allegiances. This system replaced the spoils system in the United States.

class action suit A lawsuit filed on behalf of a group of people, and whose result affects that group of people as a whole. Interest groups such as the NAACP often use these as a means of asserting their influence over policy decisions.

clear and present danger test Interpretation by Justice Oliver Wendell Holmes regarding limits on free speech if it presents clear and present danger to the public or leads to illegal actions; for example, one cannot shout "Fire!" in a crowded theater.

closed primary Primary election in which voting is restricted to registered members of a political party.

cloture A motion in the Senate to end debate, often used in the event of a filibuster. A cloture vote requires a three-fifths majority of the Senate.

coalition A combination of groups of people who work together to achieve a political goal. For example, the coalition of the Democratic Party is largely made up of urban dwellers on the coasts, minority groups, and young people. Coalitions also form among legislators who work together to advance or defeat a particular bill.

commander in chief The president's role as leader of all United States military forces. This is one of the executive powers authorized in the Constitution.

concurrent powers Constitutional powers shared by the federal and state governments.

conference committee Congressional committee that includes representatives of both houses of Congress. Their purpose is to settle differences between the House and Senate versions of bills that have been passed by their respective legislatures.

Congressional Budget Office Congressional agency of budget experts who assess the feasibility of the president's plan and who help create Congress's version of the federal budget.

congressional district The geographically defined group of people on whose behalf a representative acts in the House of Representatives. Each state is divided into congressional districts of equal population, with larger states having more districts and representatives than small states. Congressional districts are reapportioned every ten years according to new census data.

conservative A political ideology that tends to favor defense spending and school prayer and to disapprove of social programs, abortion, affirmative action, and a large, active government. Conservatives are generally affiliated with the Republican party.

constitutional convention An as-of-yet untried method by which the Constitution may be amended. To call a constitutional convention, two-thirds of all state legislatures must petition the federal government; not to be confused with the Constitutional Convention when the Constitution was written.

cooperative federalism Preeminent form of U.S. federalism since the passage of the Fourteenth Amendment. The Fourteenth Amendment initiated the long demise of dual federalism by providing the national government the means to enforce the rights of citizens against state infringement. The Progressive Era, the New Deal, and the Great Society all increased federal involvement in state government. The result is a system called cooperative federalism in which the national and state governments share many powers.

criminal court Court in which criminal trials are heard. In contrast, lawsuits are heard in **civil court**.

dealignment A recent trend in which voters act increasingly independent of a party affiliation. This is partially the result of television because candidates can appeal directly to the electorate without relying on their party. One consequence is split-ticket voting, which leads to a divided government in which neither party controls both the executive and the legislative branch.

delegated powers Constitutional powers granted solely to the federal government.

direct democracy Form of government in which all enfranchised citizens vote on all matters of government. In contrast, in a representative democracy, voters choose representatives to vote for them on most government issues.

divided government A government in which the presidency is controlled by one party and Congress is controlled by the other. This has become a common occurrence in recent decades as voters have begun to act more independently of parties and increasingly vote split tickets.

double jeopardy The act of trying an individual a second time after he has been acquitted on the same charges. Double jeopardy is prohibited by the Constitution.

dual federalism Form of U.S. federalism during the nation's early history. During this period, the federal and state governments remained separate and independent. What little contact most Americans had with government occurred on the state level, as the national government concerned itself primarily with international trade, construction of roads, harbors, and railways, and the distribution of public land in the West.

due process Established legal procedures for the arrest and trial of an accused criminal.

earmark A provision within legislation that appropriates money to a specific project, usually to benefit a small number of individuals or a region.

elastic clause The section of the Constitution that allows Congress to pass laws "necessary and proper" to the performance of its duties. It is called the elastic clause because it allows Congress to stretch its powers beyond those that are specifically granted to it (enumerated) by the Constitution.

Electoral College Constitutionally established body created for the sole purpose of choosing the president and vice president. During general elections, voters choose a presidential ticket. The winner in each state usually receives all of that state's electoral votes in the Electoral College. A majority of electoral votes is required for victory in the Electoral College; if such a majority cannot be reached, the election result is determined by the House of Representatives.

eminent domain   The power of the government to take away property for public use as long as there is just compensation for property taken.

entitlement programs   Social insurance programs that allocate federal funds to all people who meet the conditions of the program. Social Security is the largest and most expensive entitlement program. Because they are a form of mandatory spending, it is incredibly difficult to cut funds to entitlement programs during the budgetary process.

Equal Rights Amendment   Failed constitutional amendment that would have guaranteed equal protection under the law for women (1970s).

establishment clause   Section of the Constitution that prohibits the government from designating one faith as the official religion of the United States.

***ex post facto* laws**   If allowed, these laws would punish people for actions that occurred before such actions were made criminal.

exclusionary rule   Rule that prohibits the use of illegally obtained evidence at trial. The Supreme Court has created several exceptions to the exclusionary rule, notably the objective good faith rule and the inevitable discovery rule.

executive agreements   Presidential agreements made with foreign nations. Executive agreements have the same legal force as treaties but do not require the approval of the Senate.

executive privilege   The right of the president to withhold information when doing so would compromise national security (for example, in the case of diplomatic files and military secrets). Executive privilege is not mentioned in the Constitution. It is, rather, part of the unwritten Constitution.

extradition   Process by which governments return fugitives to the jurisdiction from which they have fled.

Federal Reserve Board   Executive agency that is largely responsible for the formulation and implementation of monetary policy. By controlling the monetary supply, the Fed helps maintain a stable economy.

federalism   Term describing a system under which the national government and local governments (state governments, in the case of the United States) share powers. Other federal governments include Canada, Switzerland, and Australia.

The Federalist Papers   A series of essays written by James Madison, Alexander Hamilton, and John Jay to defend the Constitution and persuade Americans that it should be ratified. These documents presented the concerns and issues the framers faced as they created a blueprint for the new government.

Fifteenth Amendment (1870)   Prohibited states from denying voting rights to African Americans. Southern states circumvented the Fifteenth Amendment through literacy tests and poll taxes.

filibuster   A lengthy speech that halts all legislative action in the Senate. Filibusters are not possible in the House of Representatives because strict time limits govern all debates there.

First Amendment   Protects the rights of individuals against the government by guaranteeing the freedom of speech, the press, religion, and assembly.

fiscal year   Twelve-month period starting on October 1. Government budgets go into effect at the beginning of the fiscal year. Congress and the president agree on a budget resolution in April to guide government spending for the coming fiscal year.

Fourteenth Amendment (1868)   Prevented the states from denying "due process of law" and "equal protection under the law" to citizens. The amendment was specifically aimed at protecting the rights of newly freed slaves. In the 20th century, the Supreme Court used the amendment to strike down state laws that violate the Bill of Rights.

Freedom of Information Act (1974) Act that declassified government documents for public use.

front-loading Because early primaries have grown increasingly important in recent years, many states have pushed forward the date of their primary elections. Political analysts refer to this strategy as front-loading.

full faith and credit clause Section of the Constitution that requires states to honor one another's licenses, marriages, and other acts of state courts.

general election Election held on the Tuesday after the first Monday of November, during which voters elect officials.

gerrymandering The practice of drawing congressional district lines to benefit one party over the other.

Gideon v. Wainwright **(1963)** Supreme Court case in which the court ruled that a defendant in a felony trial must be provided a lawyer free of charge if the defendant cannot afford one.

Gramm-Rudman-Hollings Bill (1985) Set budget reduction targets to balance budget but failed to eliminate loopholes.

Great Compromise Settlement reached at the Constitutional Convention between large states and small states. The Great Compromise called for two legislative houses: one in which states were represented by their populations (favoring the large states) and one in which states received equal representation (favoring the small states).

Great Society President Lyndon B. Johnson's social/economic program, aimed at raising the standard of living for America's poorest residents. Among the Great Society programs are Medicare, Medicaid, Project Head Start, Job Corps, and Volunteers in Service to America (VISTA).

Griswold v. Connecticut **(1965)** Supreme Court decision in which the court ruled that the Constitution implicitly guarantees citizens' right to privacy.

Hatch Act (1939) A congressional law that forbade government officials from participating in partisan politics and protected government employees from being fired on partisan grounds; it was revised in 1993 to be less restrictive.

House of Representatives Lower house of U.S. Congress, in which representation is allocated to states in direct proportion to their population. The House of Representatives has sole power to initiate appropriations legislation.

House Rules Committee Determines the rules for debate of each bill, including whether the bill may be amended. This is the most powerful committee in the House. The Senate, which is smaller, has no rules for debate.

impeachment Process by which a president, judge, or other government official can be tried for high crimes and misdemeanors. Andrew Johnson was impeached but was found not guilty and was not removed from office.

indictment A written statement of criminal charges brought against a defendant. Indictments guarantee that defendants know the charges against them so they can plan a defense.

inevitable discovery Exception to the exclusionary rule that allows the use of illegally obtained evidence at trial if the court determines that the evidence would eventually have been found by legal means.

initiative Process through which voters may propose new laws. One of several Progressive Era reforms that increased voters' power over government.

interest group Political group organized around a particular political goal or philosophy. Interest groups attempt to influence public policy through political action and donations to sympathetic candidates.

iron triangle Also called subgovernment. Iron triangles are formed by the close working relationship among various interest groups, congressional committees, and executive agencies that enforce federal regulations. Working together, these groups can collectively exert a powerful influence over legislation and law enforcement.

Jim Crow laws State and local laws passed in the post–Reconstruction Era South to enforce racial segregation and otherwise restrict the rights of African Americans.

joint committee Congressional committee composed of members of both houses of Congress, usually to investigate and research specific subjects.

judicial activism Term referring to the actions of a court that frequently strikes down or alters the acts of the executive and/or legislative branches.

judicial restraint Term referring to the actions of a court that demonstrates an unwillingness to break with precedent or to overturn legislative and executive acts.

judicial review The power of the Supreme Court to declare laws and executive actions unconstitutional.

Ku Klux Klan Nativist hate group founded during the Reconstruction Era. The Klan terrorized black people throughout the south, especially those who attempted to assert their civil rights. The Klan also preaches hatred of Catholics and Jews.

legislative oversight One of Congress's most important tasks. In order to check the power of the executive branch, congressional committees investigate and evaluate the performance of corresponding executive agencies and departments.

liberal Descriptive of an ideology that tends to favor government spending on social programs, affirmative action, a woman's right to an abortion, and an active government, and to disfavor defense spending and school prayer. Liberals are generally affiliated with the Democratic Party.

Lilly Ledbetter Fair Pay Act (2009) Law that closed the loophole that limited suits on discriminatory pay.

limited government Principle of government that states that government powers must be confined to those allowed it by the nation's Constitution.

line-item veto Power held by some chief executives (such as governors) to excise some portions of a spending bill without rejecting the entire bill. The purpose of this power is to allow executives to eliminate frivolous appropriations. The president's claim to the line-item veto was denied by the Supreme Court.

mandate Level of support for an elected official as perceived through election results.

***Marbury v. Madison* (1803)** Supreme Court decision that established the principle of **judicial review**.

Marshall, John Third Chief Justice of the Supreme Court (he served from 1800 to 1835). A Federalist who worked to increase the powers of the federal government over the states. Marshall established the principle of judicial review.

***Miranda v. Arizona* (1966)** Supreme Court case in which the court ruled that, upon arrest, a suspect must be advised of the right to remain silent and the right to consult with a lawyer.

national convention Occasion at which a political party officially announces its presidential nominee and reveals its party platform for the next four years. Today's national conventions are merely media events; nominees have already been determined by primary election results.

National Organization for Women (NOW) Feminist political group formed in 1967 to promote legislative change. NOW lobbied for the failed Equal Rights Amendment to the Constitution.

National Security Council Presidential advisory board established in 1947. The NSC consults with the president on matters of defense and foreign policy.

Nineteenth Amendment (1920) Granted voting rights to women.

nomination Endorsement to run for office by a political party.

objective good faith Exception to the exclusionary rule that allows the use of illegally obtained evidence at trial if the court determines that police believed they were acting within the limits of their search warrant when they seized the evidence.

Office of Management and Budget Executive branch office responsible for drawing up the president's proposals for the federal budget.

open primary Primary election in which voters may vote in whichever party primary they choose, though they must select that party before entering the voting booth.

original jurisdiction Term used to describe a court's power to initially try a case. Courts in which cases are first heard are those with original jurisdiction in the case. By contrast, appellate courts hear challenges to earlier court decisions.

override The Constitutional power of Congress to supersede a president's veto by a two-thirds majority in both houses. Such a vote is difficult to achieve, however, so overrides are fairly rare.

pardon Cancellation of criminal punishment. Presidents and governors have the power to grant pardons to those awaiting trial and to those convicted of crimes.

Patriot Act (2001) Act passed in response to the terrorist attacks of September 11, 2001, granting broad police authority to the federal, state, and local governments to interdict, prosecute, and convict suspected terrorists.

platform Statement of purpose and policy objectives drafted and approved by political parties at their national conventions. Party platforms rarely exert much influence on day-to-day politics.

***Plessy v. Ferguson* (1896)** Supreme Court ruling that "separate but equal" facilities for different races are not unconstitutional. This ruling opened the door to 75 years of state-sanctioned segregation in the South.

pocket veto If the president fails to approve a bill passed during the last ten days of a congressional session, the bill does not become law. This process is called a pocket veto.

poison-pill amendment Amendment to a bill proposed by its opponents for the specific purpose of decreasing the bill's chance of passage. Also known as a killer amendment.

policy implementation The process by which executive departments and agencies put legislation into practice. Agencies are often allowed a degree of freedom to interpret legislation as they write guidelines to enact and enforce the law.

political action committee (PAC) The fundraising apparatus of interest groups. Donations to and contributions from PACs are regulated by federal law. PACs contribute heavily to the reelection campaigns of representatives and senators sympathetic to the PAC's political agenda.

political party Group of people with common political goals, which hopes to influence policy through the election process. Parties run candidates for office who represent the political agenda of party members. They therefore serve as an institutional link between the electorate and politicians.

Populists Political party of the late 1800s. The Populists primarily represented farmers and working-class Americans. They sought inflationary economic policies to increase farm income. They also lobbied for a number of Democratic reforms that would later be adopted by the Progressives, such as direct election of senators.

pork barrel Budget items proposed by legislators to benefit constituents in their home state or district. Such expenditures are sometimes unnecessary but are passed anyway because they are politically beneficial.

president *pro tempore* Individual chosen to preside over the Senate whenever the vice president is unavailable to do so. The president *pro tempore* is chosen by the Senate from among its members.

primary elections Form of election held by the majority of states, during which voters select the nominees for political parties. Winners of primary elections appear on the ballot during the general election.

prior restraint Censorship of news material before it is made public.

privileges and immunities clause Section of the Constitution stating that a state may not refuse police protection or access to its courts to U.S. citizens because they live in a different state.

progressive income tax A progressive tax increases tax rates for people with higher incomes. Those citizens at the poverty level, for example, may pay few or no taxes. Middle-class citizens may be taxed at a 15% rate, while the wealthy are taxed at two or three times that rate. The goal of a progressive tax is to allow those with greater need to keep more of what they earn while taking more from those who can best afford it.

quorum The minimum number of people required for the legislature to act.

realignment Occurs when a party undergoes a major shift in its electoral base and political agenda. The groups of people composing the party coalition may split up, resulting in a vastly different party. Realignments are rare and tend to be signaled by a critical election. The last realignment occurred during the New Deal, when many working-class and ethnic groups joined together under the Democratic party.

recall election Process through which voters can shorten an office holder's term. One of several Progressive Era reforms that increased voters' power over government.

redistricting Process by which congressional districts are redrawn to reflect population changes reported by census data. Each district must have an equal number of residents. Redistricting typically occurs with reapportionment, a process in which seats are redistributed among states in the House. States may lose or gain seats during reapportionment, but the total House membership remains 435.

referendum Process through which voters may vote on new laws. One of several Progressive Era reforms that increased voters' power over government.

regulatory agency Executive agency responsible for enforcing laws pertaining to a certain industry. The agency writes guidelines for the industry, such as safety codes, and enforces them through methods such as inspection.

representative democracy Form of government under which citizens vote for delegates who in turn represent citizens' interests within the government. In contrast, a direct democracy requires all citizens to vote on all government issues. The United States is a representative democracy.

reserved powers Constitutional powers that belong solely to the states. According to the Tenth Amendment, these powers include any that the Constitution does not either specifically grant the national government or deny the state governments.

***Roe v. Wade* (1973)** Supreme Court case that decriminalized abortion.

runoff primary Election held between top two vote-getters in a primary election, when neither received a legally required minimum percentage of the vote. Many states require a runoff when no candidate receives at least 40% of the primary vote for his or her party.

sampling error Margin of error in public opinion poll. Most polls are accurate within a margin of ±4%.

saving amendment Amendment to a bill proposed in hopes of softening opposition by weakening objectionable elements of the bill.

Schenck v. United States Supreme Court case involving limits on free speech rights. The *Schenck* case established the "clear and present danger" principle in determining what type of speech could be restricted.

search warrant   Document issued by the courts to allow the police to search private property. To obtain a warrant, the police must go before a judge and explain (1) where they want to search and (2) what they are looking for. A search warrant also limits where the police may search and what they may take as evidence (Fourth Amendment).

select committee   Temporary committee of Congress, usually created to investigate specific issues.

selective incorporation   Process by which the Supreme Court has selectively applied the Fourteenth Amendment to state law.

Senate   Upper house of Congress, in which each state has two representatives. The Senate has the sole power to approve cabinet, ambassadorial, and federal judicial appointments. International treaties must receive two-thirds approval from the Senate.

senatorial courtesy   A tradition whereby candidates for the federal bureaucracy are appointed by the president and selected from a list of nominees submitted by senators.

separation of powers   The system that prevents any branch of government from becoming too powerful by dividing important tasks among the three branches. Also called the system of checks and balances.

shield law   Law guaranteeing news reporters the right to protect the anonymity of their sources. Many states have passed shield laws, but there is no federal shield law.

Sixteenth Amendment (1913)   Authorized Congress to impose and collect federal income taxes.

soft money   Political donations made to parties for the purpose of general party maintenance and support, such as get-out-the-vote campaigns, issue advocacy, and advertisements that promote the party (but not individual candidates). Soft money contributions to political parties were banned in 2002 by the Bipartisan Campaign Reform Act (BCRA) (also known as the McCain-Feingold Bill).

Speaker of the House   Individual chosen by members of the House of Representatives to preside over its sessions.

split-ticket voting   Choosing candidates from different parties for offices listed on the same ballot. Voters have been more inclined to vote a split ticket in recent decades. This trend has led to divided government.

spoils system   The political practice of trading government jobs and preferences for political and financial support. President Andrew Jackson was the first to be widely accused of using the spoils system to reward political friends and supporters.

standing committee   A permanent congressional committee.

strict constructionism   Belief that the Constitution should be read in such a way as to limit the powers of the federal government as much as possible. Strict constructionists emphasize the importance of the Tenth Amendment, which reserves to the states all powers not explicitly granted to the federal government.

Super PAC   A type of political action committee that does not have donation limits, but cannot donate directly to a specific candidate.

supremacy clause   Section of the Constitution that requires conflicts between federal and state law to be resolved in favor of federal law. State constitutions and laws that violate the U.S. Constitution, federal laws, or international treaties can be invalidated through the supremacy clause.

Supreme Court   Highest court in the United States. The only federal court specifically mentioned in the U.S. Constitution.

Thirteenth Amendment (1865)   Abolished slavery.

Three-Fifths Compromise Agreement reached at the Constitutional Convention between Southern and Northern states. The South wanted slaves counted among the population for voting purposes but not for tax purposes; the North wanted the exact opposite. Both sides agreed that three-fifths of a state's slave population would be counted toward both congressional apportionment and taxation.

Twenty-fourth Amendment (1964) Outlawed poll taxes, which had been used to prevent the poor from voting.

Twenty-second Amendment (1951) Limited the number of years an individual may serve as president. According to the Twenty-second Amendment, a president may be elected no more than twice.

Twenty-sixth Amendment (1971) Lowered the voting age from 21 to 18.

unanimous consent decree Agreement passed by the Senate that establishes the rules under which a bill will be debated, amended, and voted upon.

United Nations International organization established following World War II. The United Nations aims to preserve international peace and foster international cooperation.

unwritten Constitution Certain deeply ingrained aspects of our government that are not mentioned in the Constitution, such as political parties, political conventions, and cabinet meetings.

veto The power held by chief executives (such as the president or governors) to reject acts of the legislature. A presidential veto can be overridden by a two-thirds majority vote of both houses of Congress.

Voting Rights Act of 1965 Federal law that increased government supervision of local election practices, suspended the use of literacy tests to prevent people (usually black people) from voting, and expanded government efforts to register voters. The Voting Rights Act of 1970 permanently banned literacy tests.

War on Poverty Those programs of President Lyndon Johnson's Great Society that were specifically aimed at assisting the poor. Among these programs was Volunteers in Service to America (VISTA), Medicaid, and the creation of the Office of Economic Opportunity.

War Powers Act Law requiring the president to seek periodic approval from Congress for any substantial troop commitment. Passed in 1973 in response to national dissatisfaction over the Vietnam War.

Warren Court (1953–1969) The Supreme Court during the era in which Earl Warren served as Chief Justice. The Warren Court is best remembered for expanding the rights of minorities and the rights of the accused.

Watergate The name of the hotel in which spies working for President Richard Nixon's 1972 reelection campaign were caught breaking into Democratic National Headquarters. The name Watergate soon became synonymous with a number of illegal activities undertaken by the Nixon White House. The resulting scandal forced Nixon to resign the presidency in 1974.

writ of *certiorari* A legal document issued by the Supreme Court to request the court transcripts of a case. A writ of *certiorari* indicates that the court will review a lower court's decision.

writ of *habeas corpus* A court order requiring an explanation as to why a prisoner is being held in custody.

The Constitution
of the United
States of America

Note: Text in *italics* indicates that a section of the Constitution is no longer in effect.

Preamble

We the people of the United States, in order to form a more perfect union, establish justice, insure domestic tranquillity, provide for the common defense, promote the general welfare, and secure the blessings of liberty to ourselves and our posterity, do ordain and establish this Constitution for the United States of America.

Article I

Section 1. All legislative powers herein granted shall be vested in a Congress of the United States, which shall consist of a Senate and House of Representatives.

Section 2. The House of Representatives shall be composed of members chosen every second year by the people of the several states, and the electors in each state shall have the qualifications requisite for electors of the most numerous branch of the state legislature.

No person shall be a Representative who shall not have attained to the age of twenty-five years, and been seven years a citizen of the United States, and who shall not, when elected, be an inhabitant of that state in which he shall be chosen.

Representatives *and direct taxes*[1] shall be apportioned among the several states which may be included within this union, according to their respective numbers, *which shall be determined by adding to the whole number of free persons, including those bound to service for a term of years, and excluding Indians not taxed, three-fifths of all other Persons.*[2] The actual Enumeration shall be made within three years after the first meeting of the Congress of the United States, and within every subsequent term of ten years[3], in such manner as they shall by law direct. The number of Representatives shall not exceed one for every thirty thousand, but each state shall have at least one Representative; and until such enumeration shall be made, the state of New Hampshire shall be entitled to choose three, Massachusetts eight, Rhode Island and Providence Plantations one, Connecticut five, New York six, New Jersey four, Pennsylvania eight, Delaware one, Maryland six, Virginia ten, North Carolina five, South Carolina five, and Georgia three.

When vacancies happen in the Representation from any state, the executive authority[4] thereof shall issue writs of election to fill such vacancies. The House of Representatives shall choose their speaker and other officers; and shall have the sole power of impeachment.

Section 3. The Senate of the United States shall be composed of two Senators from each state, *chosen by the legislature thereof*[5], for six years; and each Senator shall have one vote.

Immediately after they shall be assembled in consequence of the first election, they shall be divided as equally as may be into three classes. The seats of the Senators of the first class shall be vacated at the expiration of the second year, of the second class at the expiration of the fourth year, and the third class at the expiration of the sixth year,[6] so that one third may be chosen every second year; *and if vacancies happen by resignation, or otherwise, during the recess of the legislature of any state, the executive thereof may make temporary appointments until the next meeting of the legislature, which shall then fill such vacancies.*[7]

No person shall be a Senator who shall not have attained to the age of thirty years, and been nine years a citizen of the United States and who shall not, when elected, be an inhabitant of that state for which he shall be chosen. The vice president of the United States shall be President of the Senate, but shall have no vote, unless they be equally divided. The Senate shall choose their other officers, and also a President *pro tempore*[8], in the absence of the vice president, or when he shall exercise the office of President of the United States. The Senate shall have the sole power to try all impeachments. When sitting for that purpose, they shall be on oath or affirmation. When the President of the United States is tried, the Chief Justice shall preside: And no person shall be convicted without the concurrence of two thirds of the members present.

Judgment in cases of impeachment shall not extend further than to removal from office, and disqualification to hold and enjoy any office of honor, trust or profit under the United States: but the party convicted shall nevertheless be liable and subject to indictment, trial, judgment and punishment, according to law.

Section 4. The times, places and manner of holding elections for Senators and Representatives, shall be prescribed in each state by the legislature thereof; but the Congress may at any time by law make or alter such regulations, except as to the places of choosing Senators.

The Congress shall assemble at least once in every year, *and such meeting shall be on the first Monday in December*[9], unless they shall by law appoint a different day.

Section 5. Each House shall be the judge of the elections, returns and qualifications of its own members, and a majority of each shall constitute a quorum[10] to do business; but a smaller number may adjourn from day to day, and may be authorized to compel the attendance of absent members, in such manner, and under such penalties as each House may provide.

Each House may determine the rules of its proceedings, punish its members for disorderly behavior, and, with the concurrence of two thirds, expel a member.

Each House shall keep a journal of its proceedings, and from time to time publish the same, excepting such parts as may in their judgment require secrecy; and the yeas and nays of the members of either House on any question shall, at the desire of one fifth of those present, be entered on the journal.

Neither House, during the session of Congress, shall, without the consent of the other, adjourn for more than three days, nor to any other place than that in which the two Houses shall be sitting.

Section 6. The Senators and Representatives shall receive a compensation for their services, to be ascertained by law, and paid out of the treasury of the United States. They shall in all cases, except treason, felony and breach of the peace, be privileged from arrest during their attendance at the session of their respective Houses, and in going to and returning from the same; and for any speech or debate in either House, they shall not be questioned in any other place.

No Senator or Representative shall, during the time for which he was elected, be appointed to any civil office under the authority of the United States, which shall have been created, or the emoluments[11] whereof shall have been increased during such time: and no person holding any office under the United States, shall be a member of either House during his continuance in office.[12]

Section 7. All bills for raising revenue shall originate in the House of Representatives; but the Senate may propose or concur with amendments as on other Bills.

Every bill which shall have passed the House of Representatives and the Senate, shall, before it become a law, be presented to the President of the United States; if he approve he shall sign it, but if not he shall return it[13], with his objections to that House in which it shall have originated, who shall enter the objections at large on their journal, and proceed to reconsider it. If after such reconsideration two thirds of that House shall agree to pass the bill, it shall be sent, together with the objections, to the other House, by which it shall likewise be reconsidered, and if approved by two thirds of that House, it shall become a law[14]. But in all such cases the votes of both Houses shall be determined by yeas and nays, and the names of the persons voting for and against the bill shall be entered on the journal of each House respectively. If any bill shall not be returned by the President within ten days (Sundays excepted) after it shall have been presented to him, the same shall be a law, in like manner as if he had signed it, unless the Congress by their adjournment prevent its return[15], in which case it shall not be a law.

Every order, resolution, or vote to which the concurrence of the Senate and House of Representatives may be necessary (except on a question of adjournment) shall be presented to the President of the United States; and before the same shall take effect, shall be approved by him, or being disapproved by him, shall be repassed by two thirds of the Senate and House of Representatives, according to the rules and limitations prescribed in the case of a bill.

Section 8. The Congress shall have power to lay and collect taxes, duties, imposts and excises, to pay the debts and provide for the common defense and general welfare of the United States; but all duties, imposts and excises shall be uniform throughout the United States;

- To borrow money on the credit of the United States;
- To regulate commerce with foreign nations, and among the several states, and with the Indian tribes;
- To establish a uniform rule of naturalization, and uniform laws on the subject of bankruptcies throughout the United States;
- To coin money, regulate the value thereof, and of foreign coin, and fix the standard of weights and measures;
- To provide for the punishment of counterfeiting the securities and current coin of the United States;
- To establish post offices and post roads;
- To promote the progress of science and useful arts, by securing for limited times to authors and inventors the exclusive right to their respective writings and discoveries;
- To constitute tribunals inferior to the Supreme Court;
- To define and punish piracies and felonies committed on the high seas, and offenses against the law of nations;
- To declare war, grant letters of marque and reprisal[16], and make rules concerning captures on land and water;
- To raise and support armies, but no appropriation of money to that use shall be for a longer term than two years;
- To provide and maintain a navy;
- To make rules for the government and regulation of the land and naval forces;
- To provide for calling forth the militia to execute the laws of the union, suppress insurrections and repel invasions;

- To provide for organizing, arming, and disciplining the militia, and for governing such part of them as may be employed in the service of the United States, reserving to the states respectively, the appointment of the officers, and the authority of training the militia according to the discipline prescribed by Congress;
- To exercise exclusive legislation in all cases whatsoever, over such District (not exceeding ten miles square) as may, by cession of particular states, and the acceptance of Congress, become the seat of the government of the United States[17], and to exercise like authority over all places purchased by the consent of the legislature of the state in which the same shall be, for the erection of forts, magazines, arsenals, dockyards, and other needful buildings; and
- To make all laws which shall be necessary and proper for carrying into execution the foregoing powers, and all other powers vested by this Constitution in the government of the United States, or in any department or officer thereof.[18]

Section 9. *The migration or importation of such persons as any of the states now existing shall think proper to admit, shall not be prohibited by the Congress prior to the year one thousand eight hundred and eight, but a tax or duty may be imposed on such importation, not exceeding ten dollars for each person.*[19]

The privilege of the writ of habeas corpus[20] *shall not be suspended, unless when in cases of rebellion or invasion the public safety may require it.*

- No bill of attainder[21] or *ex post facto* law[22] shall be passed.
- *No capitation, or other direct, tax shall be laid, unless in proportion to the census or enumeration herein before directed to be taken.*[23]
- No tax or duty shall be laid on articles exported from any state.
- No preference shall be given by any regulation of commerce or revenue to the ports of one state over those of another: nor shall vessels bound to, or from, one state, be obliged to enter, clear or pay duties in another.
- No money shall be drawn from the treasury, but in consequence of appropriations made by law; and a regular statement and account of receipts and expenditures of all public money shall be published from time to time.
- No title of nobility shall be granted by the United States: and no person holding any office of profit or trust under them, shall, without the consent of the Congress, accept of any present, emolument, office, or title, of any kind whatever, from any king, prince, or foreign state.

Section 10. No state shall enter into any treaty, alliance, or confederation; grant letters of marque and reprisal; coin money; emit bills of credit; make anything but gold and silver coin a tender in payment of debts; pass any bill of attainder, *ex post facto* law, or law impairing the obligation of contracts, or grant any title of nobility.

No state shall, without the consent of the Congress, lay any imposts or duties on imports or exports, except what may be absolutely necessary for executing its inspection laws; and the net produce of all duties and imposts, laid by any state on imports or exports, shall be for the use of the treasury of the United States; and all such laws shall be subject to the revision and control of the Congress.

No state shall, without the consent of Congress, lay any duty of tonnage, keep troops, or ships of war in time of peace, enter into any agreement or compact with another state, or with a foreign power, or engage in war, unless actually invaded, or in such imminent danger as will not admit of delay.

Article II

Section 1. The executive power shall be vested in a President of the United States of America. He shall hold his office during the term of four years, and, together with the vice president, chosen for the same term, be elected, as follows:

Each state shall appoint, in such manner as the Legislature thereof may direct, a number of electors, equal to the whole number of Senators and Representatives to which the State may be entitled in the Congress: but no Senator or Representative, or person holding an office of trust or profit under the United States, shall be appointed an elector.

The electors shall meet in their respective states, and vote by ballot for two persons, of whom one at least shall not be an inhabitant of the same state with themselves. And they shall make a list of all the persons voted for, and of the number of votes for each; which list they shall sign and certify, and transmit sealed to the seat of the government of the United States, directed to the President of the Senate. The President of the Senate shall, in the presence of the Senate and House of Representatives, open all the certificates, and the votes shall then be counted. The person having the greatest number of votes shall be the President, if such number be a majority of the whole number of electors appointed; and if there be more than one who have such majority, and have an equal number of votes, then the House of Representatives shall immediately choose by ballot one of them for President; and if no person have a majority, then from the five highest on the list the said House shall in like manner choose the President. But in choosing the President, the votes shall be taken by States, the representation from each state having one vote; a quorum for this purpose shall consist of a member or members from two thirds of the states, and a majority of all the states shall be necessary to a choice. In every case, after the choice of the President, the person having the greatest number of votes of the electors shall be the vice president. But if there should remain two or more who have equal votes, the Senate shall choose from them by ballot the vice president.[24]

The Congress may determine the time of choosing the electors, and the day on which they shall give their votes; which day shall be the same throughout the United States.

No person except a natural born citizen, or a citizen of the United States at the time of the adoption of this Constitution[25], shall be eligible to the office of President; neither shall any person be eligible to that office who shall not have attained to the age of thirty five years, and been fourteen years a resident within the United States.

In case of the removal of the President from office, or of his death, resignation, or inability to discharge the powers and duties of the said office, the same shall devolve on the vice president, and the Congress may by law provide for the case of removal, death, resignation or inability, both of the President and vice president, declaring what officer shall then act as President, and such officer shall act accordingly, until the disability be removed, or a President shall be elected.[26]

The President shall, at stated times, receive for his services, a compensation, which shall neither be increased nor diminished during the period for which he shall have been elected, and he shall not receive within that period any other emolument[27] from the United States, or any of them.

Before he enter on the execution of his office, he shall take the following oath or affirmation: "I do solemnly swear (or affirm) that I will faithfully execute the office of President of the United States, and will to the best of my ability, preserve, protect and defend the Constitution of the United States."

Section 2. The President shall be commander in chief of the Army and Navy of the United States, and of the militia of the several states, when called into the actual service of the United States; he may require the opinion, in writing, of the principal officer in each of the executive departments, upon any subject relating to the duties of their respective offices, and he shall have power to grant reprieves and pardons for offenses against the United States, except in cases of impeachment.

He shall have power, by and with the advice and consent of the Senate[28], to make treaties, provided two thirds of the Senators present concur; and he shall nominate, and by and with the advice and consent of the Senate, shall appoint ambassadors, other public ministers and consuls, judges of the Supreme Court, and all other officers of the United States, whose appointments are not herein otherwise provided for, and which shall be established by law: but the Congress may by law vest the appointment of such inferior officers, as they think proper, in the President alone, in the courts of law, or in the heads of departments.

The President shall have power to fill up all vacancies that may happen during the recess of the Senate, by granting commissions which shall expire at the end of their next session.

Section 3. He shall from time to time give to the Congress information of the state of the union, and recommend to their consideration such measures as he shall judge necessary and expedient; he may, on extraordinary occasions, convene both Houses, or either of them, and in case of disagreement between them, with respect to the time of adjournment, he may adjourn them to such time as he shall think proper; he shall receive ambassadors and other public ministers; he shall take care that the laws be faithfully executed, and shall commission all the officers of the United States.

Section 4. The President, vice president and all civil officers of the United States, shall be removed from office on impeachment for, and conviction of, treason, bribery, or other high crimes and misdemeanors.

Article III
Section 1. The judicial power of the United States, shall be vested in one Supreme Court, and in such inferior courts as the Congress may from time to time ordain and establish. The judges, both of the supreme and inferior courts, shall hold their offices during good behavior, and shall, at stated times, receive for their services, a compensation, which shall not be diminished during their continuance in office.

Section 2. The judicial power shall extend to all cases, in law and equity, arising under this Constitution, the laws of the United States, and treaties made, or which shall be made, under their authority; to all cases affecting ambassadors, other public ministers and consuls; to all cases of admiralty and maritime jurisdiction; to controversies to which the United States shall be a party; to controversies between two or more states; between a state and citizens of another state[29]; between citizens of different states; between citizens of the same state claiming lands under grants of different states, and between a state, or the citizens thereof, and foreign states, citizens or subjects.

In all cases affecting ambassadors, other public ministers and consuls, and those in which a state shall be party, the Supreme Court shall have original jurisdiction. In all the other cases before mentioned, the Supreme Court shall have appellate jurisdiction, both as to law and fact, with such exceptions, and under such regulations as the Congress shall make.

The trial of all crimes, except in cases of impeachment, shall be by jury; and such trial shall be held in the state where the said crimes shall have been committed; but when not committed within any state, the trial shall be at such place or places as the Congress may by law have directed.

Section 3. Treason against the United States, shall consist only in levying war against them, or in adhering to their enemies, giving them aid and comfort. No person shall be convicted of treason unless on the testimony of two witnesses to the same overt act, or on confession in open court.

The Congress shall have power to declare the punishment of treason, but no attainder of treason shall work corruption of blood, or forfeiture except during the life of the person attainted.[30]

Article IV

Section 1. Full faith and credit shall be given in each state to the public acts, records, and judicial proceedings of every other state.[31] And the Congress may by general laws prescribe the manner in which such acts, records, and proceedings shall be proved, and the effect thereof.

Section 2. The citizens of each state shall be entitled to all privileges and immunities of citizens in the several states.

A person charged in any state with treason, felony, or other crime, who shall flee from justice, and be found in another state, shall on demand of the executive authority of the state from which he fled, be delivered up, to be removed to the state having jurisdiction of the crime.[32]

No person held to service or labor in one state, under the laws thereof, escaping into another, shall, in consequence of any law or regulation therein, be discharged from such service or labor, but shall be delivered up on claim of the party to whom such service or labor may be due.[33]

Section 3. New states may be admitted by the Congress into this union; but no new states shall be formed or erected within the jurisdiction of any other state; nor any state be formed by the junction of two or more states, or parts of states, without the consent of the legislatures of the states concerned as well as of the Congress.

The Congress shall have power to dispose of and make all needful rules and regulations respecting the territory or other property belonging to the United States; and nothing in this Constitution shall be so construed as to prejudice any claims of the United States, or of any particular state.

Section 4. The United States shall guarantee to every state in this union a Republican form of government, and shall protect each of them against invasion; and on application of the legislature, or of the executive (when the legislature cannot be convened) against domestic violence.

Article V

The Congress, whenever two thirds of both houses shall deem it necessary, shall propose amendments to this Constitution, or, on the application of the legislatures of two thirds of the several states, shall call a convention for proposing amendments, which, in either case, shall be valid to all intents and purposes, as part of this Constitution, when ratified by the legislatures of three fourths of the several states, or by conventions in three-fourths thereof, as the one or the other mode of ratification may be proposed by the Congress; provided that no amendment which may be made prior to the year one thousand eight hundred and eight shall in any manner affect the first and fourth clauses in the ninth section of the first article; and that no state, without its consent, shall be deprived of its equal suffrage in the Senate.

Article VI
All debts contracted and engagements entered into, before the adoption of this Constitution, shall be as valid against the United States under this Constitution, as under the Confederation.

This Constitution, and the laws of the United States which shall be made in pursuance thereof; and all treaties made, or which shall be made, under the authority of the United States, shall be the supreme law of the land[34]; and the judges in every state shall be bound thereby, anything in the Constitution or laws of any State to the contrary notwithstanding.

The Senators and Representatives before mentioned, and the members of the several state legislatures, and all executive and judicial officers, both of the United States and of the several states, shall be bound by oath or affirmation, to support this Constitution; but no religious test shall ever be required as a qualification to any office or public trust under the United States.

Article VII
The ratification of the conventions of nine states, shall be sufficient for the establishment of this Constitution between the states so ratifying the same.

Done in convention by the unanimous consent of the states present the seventeenth day of September in the year of our Lord one thousand seven hundred and eighty seven and of the independence of the United States of America the twelfth. In witness whereof We have hereunto subscribed our Names,

Signed:

G. Washington—President, and 38 representatives of the states

Amendments to the Constitution
[Note: Amendments I through X are collectively known as the "Bill of Rights."]

Amendment I (1791)
Congress shall make no law respecting an establishment of religion, or prohibiting the free exercise thereof[35]; or abridging the freedom of speech, or of the press; or the right of the people peaceably to assemble, and to petition the government for a redress of grievances.

Amendment II (1791)

A well regulated militia, being necessary to the security of a free state, the right of the people to keep and bear arms, shall not be infringed.

Amendment III (1791)

No soldier shall, in time of peace be quartered in any house, without the consent of the owner, nor in time of war, but in a manner to be prescribed by law.

Amendment IV (1791)

The right of the people to be secure in their persons, houses, papers, and effects, against unreasonable searches and seizures, shall not be violated, and no warrants shall issue, but upon probable cause, supported by oath or affirmation, and particularly describing the place to be searched, and the persons or things to be seized.

Amendment V (1791)

No person shall be held to answer for a capital[36], or otherwise infamous crime[37], unless on a presentment or indictment of a grand jury, except in cases arising in the land or naval forces, or in the militia, when in actual service in time of war or public danger; nor shall any person be subject for the same offense to be twice put in jeopardy of life or limb[38]; nor shall be compelled in any criminal case to be a witness against himself, nor be deprived of life, liberty, or property, without due process of law; nor shall private property be taken for public use, without just compensation.

Amendment VI (1791)

In all criminal prosecutions, the accused shall enjoy the right to a speedy and public trial, by an impartial jury of the state and district wherein the crime shall have been committed, which district shall have been previously ascertained by law, and to be informed of the nature and cause of the accusation; to be confronted with the witnesses against him; to have compulsory process for obtaining witnesses in his favor, and to have the assistance of counsel for his defense.

Amendment VII (1791)

In suits at common law, where the value in controversy shall exceed twenty dollars, the right of trial by jury shall be preserved, and no fact tried by a jury, shall be otherwise reexamined in any court of the United States, than according to the rules of the common law.

Amendment VIII (1791)

Excessive bail shall not be required, nor excessive fines imposed, nor cruel and unusual punishments inflicted.

Amendment IX (1791)

The enumeration in the Constitution, of certain rights, shall not be construed to deny or disparage others retained by the people.

Amendment X (1791)

The powers not delegated to the United States by the Constitution, nor prohibited by it to the states, are reserved to the states respectively, or to the people.

Amendment XI (1795)

The judicial power of the United States shall not be construed to extend to any suit in law or equity, commenced or prosecuted against one of the United States by citizens of another state, or by citizens or subjects of any foreign state.

Amendment XII (1804)

The electors shall meet in their respective states and vote by ballot for President and vice president, one of whom, at least, shall not be an inhabitant of the same state with themselves; they shall name in their ballots the person voted for as President, and in distinct ballots the person voted for as vice president, and they shall make distinct lists of all persons voted for as President, and of all persons voted for as vice president, and of the number of votes for each, which lists they shall sign and certify, and transmit sealed to the seat of the government of the United States, directed to the President of the Senate.

The President of the Senate shall, in the presence of the Senate and House of Representatives, open all the certificates and the votes shall then be counted; the person having the greatest number of votes for President, shall be the President, if such number be a majority of the whole number of electors appointed; and if no person have such majority, then from the persons having the highest numbers not exceeding three on the list of those voted for as President, the House of Representatives shall choose immediately, by ballot, the President. But in choosing the President, the votes shall be taken by states, the representation from each state having one vote; a quorum for this purpose shall consist of a member or members from two-thirds of the states, and a majority of all the states shall be necessary to a choice. And if the House of Representatives shall not choose a President whenever the right of choice shall devolve upon them, *before the fourth day of March next following*[39], then the vice president shall act as President, as in the case of the death or other constitutional disability of the President.

The person having the greatest number of votes as vice president, shall be the vice president, if such number be a majority of the whole number of electors appointed, and if no person have a majority, then from the two highest numbers on the list, the Senate shall choose the vice president; a quorum for the purpose shall consist of two-thirds of the whole number of Senators, and a majority of the whole number shall be necessary to a choice. But no person constitutionally ineligible to the office of President shall be eligible to that of vice president of the United States.

Amendment XIII (1865)

Section 1. Neither slavery nor involuntary servitude, except as a punishment for crime whereof the party shall have been duly convicted, shall exist within the United States, or any place subject to their jurisdiction.

Section 2. Congress shall have power to enforce this article by appropriate legislation.

Amendment XIV (1868)

Section 1. All persons born or naturalized in the United States, and subject to the jurisdiction thereof, are citizens of the United States and of the state wherein they reside.[40] No state shall make or enforce any law which shall abridge the privileges or immunities of citizens of the United States; nor shall any state deprive any person of life, liberty, or property, without due process of law; nor deny to any person within its jurisdiction the equal protection of the laws.

Section 2. Representatives shall be apportioned among the several states according to their respective numbers, counting the whole number of persons in each state[41], excluding Indians not taxed. But when the right to vote at any election for the choice of electors for President and vice president of the United States, Representatives in Congress, the executive and judicial officers of a state, or the members of the legislature thereof, is denied to any of the *male* inhabitants of such state, being *twenty-one* years of age, and citizens of the United States, or in any way abridged, except for participation in rebellion, or other crime, the basis of representation therein shall be reduced in the proportion which the number of such *male* citizens shall bear to the whole number of male citizens *twenty-one* years of age in such state.[42]

Section 3. No person shall be a Senator or Representative in Congress, or elector of President and vice president, or hold any office, civil or military, under the United States, or under any state, who, having previously taken an oath, as a member of Congress, or as an officer of the United States, or as a member of any state legislature, or as an executive or judicial officer of any state, to support the Constitution of the United States, shall have engaged in insurrection or rebellion against the same, or given aid or comfort to the enemies thereof. But Congress may by a vote of two-thirds of each House, remove such disability.

Section 4. The validity of the public debt of the United States, authorized by law, including debts incurred for payment of pensions and bounties for services in suppressing insurrection or rebellion, shall not be questioned. But neither the United States nor any state shall assume or pay any debt or obligation incurred in aid of insurrection or rebellion against the United States, or any claim for the loss or emancipation of any slave; but all such debts, obligations and claims shall be held illegal and void.

Section 5. The Congress shall have power to enforce, by appropriate legislation, the provisions of this article.

Amendment XV (1870)

Section 1. The right of citizens of the United States to vote shall not be denied or abridged by the United States or by any state on account of race, color, or previous condition of servitude.

Section 2. The Congress shall have power to enforce this article by appropriate legislation.

Amendment XVI (1913)

The Congress shall have power to lay and collect taxes on incomes, from whatever source derived, without apportionment among the several states, and without regard to any census of enumeration.

Amendment XVII (1913)

The Senate of the United States shall be composed of two Senators from each state, elected by the people thereof, for six years; and each Senator shall have one vote. The electors in each state shall have the qualifications requisite for electors of the most numerous branch of the state legislatures.

When vacancies happen in the representation of any state in the Senate, the executive authority of such state shall issue writs of election to fill such vacancies: Provided, that the legislature of any state may empower the executive thereof to make temporary appointments until the people fill the vacancies by election as the legislature may direct.

This amendment shall not be so construed as to affect the election or term of any Senator chosen before it becomes valid as part of the Constitution.

Amendment XVIII (1919)

Section 1. After one year from the ratification of this article the manufacture, sale, or transportation of intoxicating liquors within, the importation thereof into, or the exportation thereof from the United States and all territory subject to the jurisdiction thereof for beverage purposes is hereby prohibited.

Section 2. The Congress and the several states shall have concurrent power to enforce this article by appropriate legislation.

Section 3. This article shall be inoperative unless it shall have been ratified as an amendment to the Constitution by the legislatures of the several states, as provided in the Constitution, within seven years from the date of the submission hereof to the states by the Congress.[43]

Amendment XIX (1920)

Section 1. The right of citizens of the United States to vote shall not be denied or abridged by the United States or by any state on account of sex.

Section 2. The Congress shall have power to enforce this article by appropriate legislation.

Amendment XX (1933)

Section 1. The terms of the President and vice president shall end at noon on the twentieth day of January, and the terms of Senators and Representatives at noon on the third day of January, of the years in which such terms would have ended if this article had not been ratified; and the terms of their successors shall then begin.[44]

Section 2. The Congress shall assemble at least once in every year, and such meeting shall begin at noon on the third day of January, unless they shall by law appoint a different day.

Section 3. If, at the time fixed for the beginning of the term of the President, the President elect[45] shall have died, the vice president elect shall become President. If a President shall not have been chosen before the time fixed for the beginning of his term, or if the President elect shall have failed to qualify, then the vice president elect shall act as President until a President shall have qualified; and the Congress may by law provide for the case wherein neither a President elect nor a vice president elect shall have qualified, declaring who shall then act as President, or the manner in which one who is to act shall be selected, and such person shall act accordingly until a President or vice president shall have qualified.

Section 4. The Congress may by law provide for the case of the death of any of the persons from whom the House of Representatives may choose a President whenever the right of choice shall have devolved upon them, and for the case of the death of any of the persons from whom the Senate may choose a vice president whenever the right of choice shall have devolved upon them.

Section 5. Sections 1 and 2 shall take effect on the fifteenth day of October following the ratification of this article.

Section 6. This article shall be inoperative unless it shall have been ratified as an amendment to the Constitution by the legislatures of three-fourths of the several states within seven years from the date of its submission.

Amendment XXI (1933)
Section 1. The eighteenth article of amendment to the Constitution of the United States is hereby repealed.

Section 2. The transportation or importation into any state, territory, or possession of the United States for delivery or use therein of intoxicating liquors, in violation of the laws thereof, is hereby prohibited.[46]

Section 3. This article shall be inoperative unless it shall have been ratified as an amendment to the Constitution by conventions in the several states, as provided in the Constitution, within seven years from the date of the submission hereof to the states by the Congress.

Amendment XXII (1951)
Section 1. No person shall be elected to the office of the President more than twice, and no person who has held the office of President, or acted as President, for more than two years of a term to which some other person was elected President shall be elected to the office of the President more than once. But this article shall not apply to any person holding the office of President when this article was proposed by the Congress, and shall not prevent any person who may be holding the office of President, or acting as President, during the term within which this article becomes operative from holding the office of President or acting as President during the remainder of such term.

Section 2. This article shall be inoperative unless it shall have been ratified as an amendment to the Constitution by the legislatures of three-fourths of the several states within seven years from the date of its submission to the states by the Congress.

Amendment XXIII (1961)[47]

Section 1. The District constituting the seat of government of the United States shall appoint in such manner as the Congress may direct:

A number of electors of President and vice president equal to the whole number of Senators and Representatives in Congress to which the District would be entitled if it were a state, but in no event more than the least populous state; they shall be in addition to those appointed by the states, but they shall be considered, for the purposes of the election of President and vice president, to be electors appointed by a state; and they shall meet in the District and perform such duties as provided by the twelfth article of amendment.

Section 2. The Congress shall have power to enforce this article by appropriate legislation.

Amendment XXIV (1964)

Section 1. The right of citizens of the United States to vote in any primary or other election for President or vice president, for electors for President or vice president, or for Senator or Representative in Congress, shall not be denied or abridged by the United States or any state by reason of failure to pay any poll tax or other tax.

Section 2. The Congress shall have power to enforce this article by appropriate legislation.

Amendment XXV (1967)

Section 1. In case of the removal of the President from office or of his death or resignation, the vice president shall become President.

Section 2. Whenever there is a vacancy in the office of the vice president, the President shall nominate a vice president who shall take office upon confirmation by a majority vote of both Houses of Congress.

Section 3. Whenever the President transmits to the President pro tempore of the Senate and the Speaker of the House of Representatives his written declaration that he is unable to discharge the powers and duties of his office, and until he transmits to them a written declaration to the contrary, such powers and duties shall be discharged by the vice president as Acting President.

Section 4. Whenever the vice president and a majority of either the principal officers of the executive departments or of such other body as Congress may by law provide, transmit to the President pro tempore of the Senate and the Speaker of the House of Representatives their written declaration that the President is unable to discharge the powers and duties of his office, the vice president shall immediately assume the powers and duties of the office as Acting President.

Thereafter, when the President transmits to the President pro tempore of the Senate and the Speaker of the House of Representatives his written declaration that no inability exists, he shall resume the powers and duties of his office unless the vice president and a majority of either the principal officers of the executive department or of such other body as Congress may by law provide, transmit within four days to the President pro tempore of the Senate and the Speaker of the House of Representatives their written declaration that the President is unable to discharge the powers and duties of his office. Thereupon Congress shall decide the issue, assembling within forty-eight hours for that purpose if not in session. If the Congress, within twenty-one days after receipt of the latter written declaration, or, if Congress is not in session, within twenty-one days after Congress is required to assemble, determines by two-thirds vote of both Houses that the President is unable to discharge the powers and duties of his office, the vice president shall continue to discharge the same as Acting President; otherwise, the President shall resume the powers and duties of his office.

Amendment XXVI (1971)

Section 1. The right of citizens of the United States, who are 18 years of age or older, to vote, shall not be denied or abridged by the United States or any state on account of age.

Section 2. The Congress shall have the power to enforce this article by appropriate legislation.

Amendment XXVII (1992)

No law, varying the compensation for the services of the Senators and Representatives, shall take effect, until an election of Representatives shall have intervened.

Notes

[1] This clause says that the government may assess taxes on the states only on the basis of population. Amendment XVI changed this by allowing the government to tax individuals' incomes.

[2] *Other persons* meant slaves. Amendment XIII abolished slavery, and Amendment XIV nullified the *three-fifths* clause.

[3] This is the clause that requires a national census every 10 years. The census is taken to apportion congressional representation; it is also used by Congress to decide how to distribute federal funding.

[4] The *executive authority* of a state is the governor.

[5] Amendment XVII changed this; senators are now elected by state voters, not by the state legislature.

[6] This section applied only to the first two Senates to guarantee senatorial elections every two years from the beginning of the Republic.

[7] Amendment XVII changed this by allowing the governor to make such temporary appointments.

[8] The president *pro tempore* presides over Senate when the vice president is not present.

[9] Amendment XX changed this date to January 3.

[10] *Quorum* means the minimum number of people required for the legislature to act. In other words, the Senate cannot begin a session unless at least 51 members are in attendance. Once a session has begun, however, the senators may leave the floor.

[11] *Emoluments* means payments.

[12] A congressperson cannot hold a second government job. This is a central component of the *separation of powers* within the U.S. government.

[13] The president's veto power.

[14] Congress can override a presidential veto with a two-thirds vote in both houses.

[15] This is called a *pocket veto* by the president. He does not return the bill to Congress, but because Congress has adjourned, the bill does not become law. Congress must then re-pass the law in its next session to force the president to consider it again.

[16] *Letters of marque and reprisal* allow private citizens to arm their boats so that they can attack enemy ships. In other words, Congress has the power to license private navies (called *privateers*). Given the circumstances of modern warfare, the chances that Congress will ever again exercise this power are pretty small.

[17] This section refers to the District of Columbia (Washington, D.C.).

[18] This is the elastic clause.

[19] This section prohibited Congress from outlawing the importation of slaves until the year 1808. In 1808, Congress did in fact outlaw the import of slaves.

[20] A *writ of habeas corpus* is used by a defendant to appear before a judge, who determines whether the government has the right to hold the defendant as a prisoner. A defendant's right to a writ of habeas corpus is what prevents the government from arresting and imprisoning people without just cause.

[21] A *bill of attainder* is a law that finds an individual guilty of a capital offense (usually treason). Because it denies an individual's right to a fair trial, it is prohibited by the Constitution.

[22] An *ex post facto* law is one that declares an action a crime retroactively.

[23] Amendment XVI negated this section by altering Congress' power to impose taxes.

[24] Amendment XII overrides this section of the Constitution.

[25] This clause was inserted to provide for the first presidents, who as colonists had been born British subjects.

[26] This entire paragraph was modified by Amendments XX and XXV.

[27] *Emolument* means payment.

[28] This paragraph enumerates several key features of the system of *checks and balances*.

[29] Amendment XI prohibits an individual from using the federal courts to sue a state other than her state of residence.

[30] This paragraph says that if Congress finds a person guilty of treason, it may punish that person but not his heirs.

[31] States must accept the actions of one anothers' governments. Every state must accept every other state's driver's licenses, marriage licenses, legal decisions, and so on.

[32] The process described in this section is called *extradition*.

[33] This section refers to escaped slaves. It was nullified by Amendment XIII.

[34] This means that federal law takes priority when federal law and state law conflict. In *McCulloch v. Maryland*, Chief Justice Marshall interpreted this to mean that the federal government could nullify laws that contradicted federal law.

[35] *Free exercise* means the freedom to practice whatever religion you choose.

[36] A *capital* crime is one punishable by death.

[37] An *otherwise infamous crime* is one that is considered serious enough to be punishable by imprisonment.

[38] This is the *double jeopardy* clause. A person cannot be tried again if a court finds him not guilty in a prior trial.

[39] Amendment XX changed this date to January 20th.

[40] This sentence grants citizenship to the former slaves.

[41] This sentence overrides the *three-fifths* clause in the body of the Constitution.

[42] This section grants voting rights only to males over the age of 21. Amendment XIX extended voting rights to women; Amendment XXVI lowered the voting age to 18.

[43] Amendment XVIII was repealed by Amendment XXI.

[44] This amendment shortened the amount of time that a president serves after he has been voted out of office.

[45] *President elect* refers to someone who has been elected president but has not yet taken the oath of office. Whenever the presidency changes hands by election, there is a president elect between Election Day and Inaugural Day.

[46] Amendment XXI repealed prohibition but it did not prohibit state and local governments from imposing prohibition. This section makes it a federal crime to transport liquor to a dry county (area in which alcoholic beverages are prohibited).

[47] This amendment gave residents of the District of Columbia the right to vote for president.